MY
UNFINISHED
BUSINESS

MY UNFINISHED BUSINESS

Autobiographical essays by

DAN S. KENNEDY

Advantage.

Published by Advantage, Charleston, South Carolina.
Member of Advantage Media Group.

ADVANTAGE is a registered trademark, and the Advantage colophon is a trademark of Advantage Media Group, Inc.

Printed in the United States of America.

10 9 8 7 6 5 4 3

ISBN: 978-1-59932-109-7
LCCN: 2009924241

Cover design and layout design by George Stevens.

This publication is designed to provide accurate and authoritative information in regard to the subject matter covered. It is sold with the understanding that the publisher is not engaged in rendering legal, accounting, or other professional services. If legal advice or other expert assistance is required, the services of a competent professional person should be sought.

Advantage Media Group is proud to be a part of the Tree Neutral® program. Tree Neutral offsets the number of trees consumed in the production and printing of this book by taking proactive steps such as planting trees in direct proportion to the number of trees used to print books. To learn more about Tree Neutral, please visit www.treeneutral.com.

Advantage Media Group is a publisher of business, self-improvement, and professional development books and online learning. We help entrepreneurs, business leaders, and professionals share their Stories, Passion, and Knowledge to help others Learn & Grow. Do you have a manuscript or book idea that you would like us to consider for publishing? Please visit advantagefamily.com or call 1.866.775.1696.

UPDATE INFORMATION
(2019)

This book was originally written in 2008-2009, and has had one round of up-dates since. This 3rd Edition has had up-dates added throughout the book in 2019, and its Chapters 80 and 81 have been replaced.

I believe Britney Spears had written 3 or 4 autobiographies by age 30. Something like that. There are quite a few celebrities who wind up doing at least a couple of them. Some live longer than they thought they would. This was never a complete and chronological bio anyway, so I've settled for these little up-date notes.

I keep in touch with a lot of people through monthly newsletters, like the *No B.S. Marketing Letter* (about much more than marketing), published by NoBSInnerCircle.com. People keep up-to-date with what's going on with me this way.

In any case, I second the poet Robert Frost's observation: "In three words I can sum up everything I've learned about life.

It. Goes. On."

CONTENTS

SECTION ONE
Early Years   **16**

CHAPTER 1   17

CHAPTER 2
Cleveland, Ohio   21

CHAPTER 3
What Did You Hear At The Top Of The Stairs?   25

CHAPTER 4
What Today's Kids Miss   27

CHAPTER 5
Childhood Memories   32

CHAPTER 6
Rich Dad, Poor Dad, One Dad   45

CHAPTER 7
There Must Be A Pony In Here Somewhere   51

CHAPTER 8
My Father   56

CHAPTER 9
My Mother   60

CHAPTER 10
Thanks To My Parents   63

CHAPTER 11

My Buddy, My Car 65

CHAPTER 12

Other Peoples' Car Stories 69

CHAPTER 13

My Worst Day With My Father 72

CHAPTER 14

Two Hot Dogs For A Buck 75

CHAPTER 15

Houses I Have Lived In 77

CHAPTER 16

High School 84

CHAPTER 17

What Life Was Like When I Graduated High School 89

CHAPTER 18

Viet Nam 91

CHAPTER 19

Bartending At The Bowery 94

SECTION TWO
Adventures in Business **97**

CHAPTER 20

My One And Only Job 98

CHAPTER 21

And He Huffed And He Puffed 104

CHAPTER 22

Water, Water Everywhere. Let's Go Have A Drink   112

CHAPTER 23

Millionaire Entrepreneur Needs Writer Who
Has Read And Believes In The Principles Of
'Think And Grow Rich', 'Magic Of Thinking Big'
And 'Magic Of Believing'   115

CHAPTER 24

The Comeback, The End   128

CHAPTER 25

Unjustly Accused   136

CHAPTER 26

Shakespeare And I Agree   143

CHAPTER 27

The Greatest Sale I Ever Made   148

CHAPTER 28

Congratulations Captain,
Here Are The Keys To The Titanic   152

CHAPTER 29

Hey Dude, Where's My Car?   156

CHAPTER 30

Chapter 11 And Chapter 7   158

CHAPTER 31

He Doesn't Play Well With Others   162

CHAPTER 32

The Case Of The Disappearing
Real Estate Speculator   166

CHAPTER 33

Inside The Infomercial Business   171

CHAPTER 34

On The Road Again, I Just Can't Wait To Get

On The Road Again   177

CHAPTER 35

Being A Published Author   182

CHAPTER 36

Thoughts About Books   189

CHAPTER 37

Intellectual Equity   192

CHAPTER 38

You Can Either Agree With Me Or Be Wrong   196

CHAPTER 39

If You're Going To Screw Me,

At Least Wear A Condom   200

SECTION THREE
Inside Dan Kennedy   **205**

CHAPTER 40

Therapy's Expensive. Jumping Up And Down

On Bubblewrap, Cheap. You Decide.   206

CHAPTER 41

It's 5:00 P.M. Somewhere   211

CHAPTER 42

Birthdays   214

CHAPTER 43

Arrested Development   217

CHAPTER 44

Me and Psycho-Cybernetics   221

CHAPTER 45

Why It's Really All About Self-Improvement   227

CHAPTER 46

Your Dreams Should Die Hard   233

CHAPTER 47

Turning Points   243

CHAPTER 48

My Most Difficult Decisions   248

CHAPTER 49

Who Do I Envy?   254

CHAPTER 50

Six Handles On A Casket   260

CHAPTER 51

Days In The Life   263

CHAPTER 52

I Have A Lot Of Trouble With Ordinary Life   270

CHAPTER 53

They Laughed When I Sat Down At The Piano,
Until I Started to Play   272

CHAPTER 54

Nostalgia   277

CHAPTER 55

Use Of Influence   280

SECTION FOUR
Marriage, Divorce   **284**

CHAPTER 56

Men Are From Mars,

Relationship Experts Are Full Of Shit   285

CHAPTER 57

First Wife, Second Wife   290

CHAPTER 58

Married To A Pisces   293

SECTION FIVE
Renegade Millionaire Strategies   **295**

CHAPTER 59

How Far We Have Come   296

CHAPTER 60

Evolution And Revolution   298

CHAPTER 61

Business Secrets I Wish I'd Discovered

Twenty Years Sooner   301

CHAPTER 62

Me & Employees   305

CHAPTER 63

Why I Admire And Have Closely Studied

Donald Trump   312

CHAPTER 64

What's Your Schtick?   319

CHAPTER 65

Lessons From Sinatra   322

CHAPTER 66

Whose Opinion Matters?   327

CHAPTER 67

A Defiant Contrarian,

An Equal Opportunity Annoyer   332

CHAPTER 68

Sooner or Later, You Sleep In Your Own Bed.

Might As Well Please Yourself.   335

CHAPTER 69

"I Planned To Change The World

But I Couldn't Get A Babysitter"   341

CHAPTER 70

It's Still Early And You Can't Judge

How The Day Was   345

SECTION SIX
Political Commentary   347

CHAPTER 71
If I Ran For President   348

CHAPTER 72
Darwinism - And The Secret To My Success   355

CHAPTER 73
Who Should Vote?   360

CHAPTER 74
The Book Chapter That Wasn't   362

CHAPTER 75
Michael Moore Is A Big, Fat Anti-American   365

CHAPTER 76
America, The Amazing   376

SECTION SEVEN
A Few Favorite Stories   379

SECTION EIGHT
And Now the End is Near   394

CHAPTER 77
Why I Have Nearly Quit Speaking   395

CHAPTER 78
Why I'm Quitting Business Altogether   398

OTHER BOOKS BY THE AUTHOR   409

EPILOGUE & PROLOGUE CIRCA 2019   411

SECTION ONE

Early Years

CHAPTER 1

So Far

So far I have lived through:

1 job
29 years in business (not counting 3 years while still in high school)
11 different businesses
3 careers
2 cars repossessed, same year
1 corporate bankruptcy, one personal bankruptcy
2 lawsuits
4 clients (1 of which, very close friend and mentor) sent to prison
3 businesses sold
As many as 47 employees
4 major business/life reinventions
2 relocations
2 divorces
22 years of marriage #2, 3 years of marriage #1
1 step-daughter's teenage years
14 years of alcohol abuse (appx., depending on definition)
2 parents' deaths
12 years of torturous, incessant travel
1800 speeches
12 books writtten for publishers
1 novel, unfinished, in progress for 15 years
1,000's of ads, sales letters written
43 television infomercial projects
18 ghost-writing jobs
8 U.S. Presidents, including the Carter Depression, Reagan Revival
2 friends' political campaigns
1 return to horseracing
14 wins (to-date)
Ample number, last place finishes
1 Disease (Diabetes)
2 modest fortunes made, 1 kept

I have done business <u>before</u> FAX, Internet, cellphones, PC's. These days I work with a whole generation of entrepreneurs who can't remember or fathom not being able to e-mail the world. Let alone waiting for the television to warm up!

Here are a few facts about life in these United States the year I was born:

Average price of a new house: $10,250.00. New car: $1,700.00. Tuition to Harvard University: $800.00 a year. Movie ticket: .70. Gas: .22 a gallon. Postage stamp: .03. Loaf of bread from a bakery: .17. Package of Kool-Aid: .05.

Big doin's : the Rose Bowl parade was telecast in color for the first time. Dr. Salk's new polio vaccine was given to children for the first time. Construction began on Disneyland. Disney airs the first episode of 'Davy Crockett' on TV. (I had a Davy Crockett hat when I was a kid. Did you?) President Dwight Eisenhower advanced the exciting idea of creating an interstate highway system. L. Ron Hubbard founded Scientology. The Cleveland Browns were pro football champions - which hasn't happened since. Kraft introduced individually wrapped cheese slices.

Average life expectancy was 68 years. Average annual household income was $3,960.00.

Nutrilite, one of the earliest network marketing companies, ran full-page magazine ads featuring celebrity spokesperson, famous actor Alan Ladd, with his wife and children. As trivia for you, Rich DeVos and Jay Van Andel were Nutrilite distributors. They left in a dispute over the compensation plan, took a handful of top distributors with them, and started their own multi-level marketing company, originally called The American Way Association, later abbreviated to Amway. Years later, Amway acquired Nutrilite.

Born in '54: Howard Stern, John Travolta, Ron Howard and Kathleen Turner. Fitting. Just as Howard is 'king of all media', I'm 'king of info-marketing'. I share Travolta's good looks, Howard's genius and Turner's sex appeal.

UPDATE!

Some of the numbers on my "So Far, I Have Lived Through' list have changed. For example, I'm now at 40+ years in business. Four overlapping careers instead of three. Yet, what I do and how I do it really hasn't changed much. The constancy of it all surprises even me, and I'm the one striving to engineer it.

The marriage years number has lengthened, although it can be counted several different ways. My 3rd wife is my 2nd wife. Gap in between.

I'm over 2,500 compensated speeches and seminars. Over 25 books written for publishers. The unfinished novel is still unfinished, but I have had two mystery novels published, co-authored with Les Roberts. You can get them at amazon. One is in the racing world: WIN, PLACE OR DIE. The second is in the speaking and seminar world: SPEAKING OF MURDER.

There have been a couple more U.S. Presidents. Hardly anybody saw President Trump coming back in 08, or even when he began officially running. I am on record, predicting his victory very early, days after he descended the gold escalator to announce.

I've now been driving in harness horse races for 11 years, and have a lot more than the stated 14 wins under my belt. I drive in about 100 races a year. I compete, incidentally, as a professional, not an amateur.

The fortune made has, I'm happy to report, hung around and grown year by year.

CHAPTER 2

Cleveland, Ohio

One of Bob Hope's several autobiographies, I believe the earliest began "...so old Ski Nose began his vaudevillle career in Cleveland." Bob was born here and began performing here. One of the city's favorite sons. Drew Carey lived here too. Maybe it's a good city for funny-men. I try.

I think being born here and growing up here had some real impact. Cleveland is an underdog city. A city looked down on and made fun of. One of our mayors tried labeling this "The Northcoast." It is more widely known as "The Mistake On The Lake." Cleveland has such a bad rap that Clevelanders take on a pugnacious, assertive personality in self-defense.

Cleveland winters can be - and often are - brutal. We drive through mountains of snow, skid on ice, freeze, go months without seeing the sun. This, too, makes us tough and, in an odd way, we feel superior to the wimps who live in more favorable climates, who are terrorized if so much as a snow flake falls in their geography. We sneer when schools and businesses close because a freak weather system dumped a few inches in places like Virginia or Texas. A few inches. Anything less daunting than three feet and zero degrees isn't even worth thinking about.

I have in my clipping files a Dilbert cartoon that represents Clevelander-entrepreneurs' approach to weather. It was mine, when I was in the ad business here and had employees. Unfortunately I can't show you the cartoon, because of its creator's and publisher's nasty habit of suing anybody who reprints them. So I'll tell it to you, just like I used to annoy my grandfather by telling him the comic strips. In the first panel, Dilbert faces his pointy-headed boss and says "The weather is getting worse. Maybe we should close the office." The boss says 'No.' Next panel, Dilbert says: "The forecast is for blizzards, freezing rain, tsunamis, deadly lava flows, and precision guided ball lightning. " Third panel, Dilbert continues: "And radiation and enlarged swarms of killer bees." Boss says:

"Get some snow tires, you big baby."

Due to our sports teams' performance, Clevelanders are expert at handling disappointment. (Last time the Indians won the pennant was the year I was born. Our beloved Cleveland Browns were stolen and trucked out of town in the dead of night to become the Baltimore Ravens. Later, we got the team identity back. But the new team - well, as I was writing this, 3-7, just beaten in an ugly, low score game by the lowly Jets. To find a way to lose that game, the extremely reliable field goal kicker had to shank not one, but two. It has been 41 years since the city has had a championship in any professional sport. I was 10 years old, the microwave was barely finding its way into kitchens and lots of homes still had black and white TV's.)

Cleveland politics provides us with a healthy sense of humor. We have had a mayor whose hair caught on fire during a press conference - the same month the Cuyahoga River also caught fire, so clogged with pollutants that spontaneous combustion was possible. We've had the Boy Mayor, who, after virtually bankrupting the city, somehow got elected to Congress, then ran for President in 2004, proposing we replace the Department of Defense with a Department of Peace. Once, a relative of his was busy robbing a bank across the street from one of his press conferences.

Personally, I like Cleveland, but I wouldn't want to live there. I live a half hour outside the city, midway between Cleveland and Akron, and claim neither city. But Cleveland does have a number of really outstanding restaurants and Playhouse Square, a very lively eclectic cluster of theaters, offering off-Broadway productions, one man shows, top stand-up performers. Public Square once was a fabulous downtown center but unfortunately that exists only in memory. There is Lake Erie, an incredibly expansive public parks system, and, hey, did I mention good restaurants? No, it is not even close to being a world-class, cosmopolitan city like San Francisco or Vancouver B.C. or, of course, New York, But it is a lot better than Pittsburgh. Here's how our radio folks announce the time: "It's 2;00 and Pittsburgh still sucks." And the weather is better than Buffalo.

People seriously ask why I moved back here, why I choose to live here when I could, in fact, live anywhere. And believe me, there are times I ask that of myself. There are a number of places I'd like to live for a year or two but probably won't, including Maui, San Diego, San Francisco, Las Vegas, Manhattan, Nantucket, Nassau. The answer, on its face, is simple. I am here because of harness racing. There is no harness racing to speak of west of the Mississippi, so most choices share bad weather in common, in the midwest. Northfield Park, here, is about the only harness track with year-round racing. It is the track I grew up at, and it is where the trainer I hooked up with and now wouldn't want to part ways with under any circumstances. So here I am. It is possible the closing of this track, in face of competition from Indian casinos, and tracks with slots in neighboring states, will force me to move in the future. I hope not.

There may be a more complex explanation as well. I'm told elephants travel great distances to return to their birthplaces in their old age, going "home" to die. Maybe that's what's going on. The inexorable, subconscious pull of nostalgia.

Anyway, here I am. Everybody's gotta be somewhere.

I am, incidentally, bemused by people desperate to travel great distances, especially out of this country. I lived in Phoenix from 1978 to 2004, and never got to the Grand Canyon. Never drove all the back roads. Never got to the places I like enough. In Cleveland, I didn't get to the zoo at all last year, there are at least a dozen terrific restaurants I didn't get to all year, I missed shows at Playhouse Square, events at Stan Hywet. Didn't set foot in the Art Museum. There are five Disney resorts in Orlando that I haven't yet vacationed at. I'm clearly not going to live long enough to get everywhere I like and everywhere I want to go in this country, probably not even in my home state. What do I need to fly 14 hours and put up with monstrous inconvenience for?

People often ask me - genuinely puzzled - what I'll do when I retire. They can't seem to conceive of anything I might do with my time, not working. I've got a very long list. Starting with the zoo.

CHAPTER 3

What Did You Hear At The Top Of The Stairs?

I talk about this in my *'Wealth Attraction Seminar'*, available on audio CD's, and have written about it in connection with the attraction of wealth.

I'm not sure kids today have this actual experience; I'm sure they still somehow get the end result. My friends had exactly the same experience. We got put to bed at 8 or 9, then we snuck back out to the top of the stairs and eavesdropped on the adults' conversations below.

I was actually pretty fortunate, especially compared to most people I compare notes with about this. When I was in these formative years and the first grooves were going into my internal recordings, most of what I heard was positive, optimistic, happy, prosperous, celebrative of iniative, work, accomplishment. My Dad and Mom worked together in their thriving commercial art business. They were just discovering 'success education' -- in fact, I recall them buying used Earl Nightingale recordings from the family attorney. What I heard them talking about themselves and with other adults was translated into my brain as 'success programming.' It was a great country, business was great, people were great, life was great. What I recall hearing about me was positive too.

We've discussed this at considerable length in my Wealth Coaching Group, and most of the very successful entrepreneurs in that group recall hearing a lot of much less positive things, more mixed messages from the top of their stairs - and acknowledge they've had to work hard at un-doing and replacing that "unprosperous" programming, some acknowledging they still catch it inhibiting them even today. By unprosperous programming, I mean ideas like: money's hard to come by (money doesn't grow on trees); rich people are evil, get rich by taking unfair advantage, or are just lucky; life in unfair; etc. It's much more complex than this, but you get the idea.

My two younger brothers are dramatically less successful than I am, and have very, very different attitudes about money than I do. People who know us all question whether it's even possible we came from the same parents and same upbringing. And we didn't. By the time my brothers were listening at the top of the stairs, my family's financial status had changed completely, my parents were under immense and unrelenting financial pressure, and almost all the conversation screamed: *lack*. What success talk did occur, involved with the Amway business, was forced and false, something akin to the scared person whistling desperately in the dark while walking past a graveyard. I wonder how much of my brothers' absence of career, business or financial success is traceable to how different what they heard at the top of the stairs was to what I heard. I suspect a lot. To his credit, my middle brother has exhibited some entrepreneurial iniative, currently has his own small business, is talking about becoming a real estate 'flipper', and I have guarded optimism.

RESOURCES!

My book, *No B.S. Guide to Wealth Attraction for Entrepreneurs, 3rd Edition* is available at amazon and other booksellers. Recordings from several of my wealth-related trainings, seminars and mastermind meetings are available via NoBSInnerCircle.com.

CHAPTER 4

What Today's Kids Miss

olin Powell and I discussed this backstage, when we were both speakers on the 'Success' events ---- the differences in lessons we learned by the way families and households worked when we were growing up and the way they work now.

Today, for example, the majority of people do grocery shopping daily, every other day, at random. Supermarkets are open 24 hours, 7 days a week. People stop at convenience stores on the way home just to get tonight's food. Contrast this to how things worked in the 1960's. I've compared notes, and find my experience fairly representative. We went to the grocery store once a week and only once a week, on Saturday morning. And we went to the Hough Bakery next door to Krogers, to get one treat. So here was the lesson: you work Monday through Friday to earn the money, then you get to go to the store and get your food as a reward. As soon as I was old enough to earn money, my allowance tied to doing certain chores, and extra money for helping in the business, I got to go to Gray's Drugstore and a discount store, Uncle Bill's, in that same shopping center, that same Saturday morning and buy things for myself. Comic books, for example. *Work first, reward second, in order.*

Today's kids neither see or experience this lesson.

It is my opinion that there are many life lessons people of my age learned through observation and experience within our family and neighborhood environments that today's kids miss.

Our television was very different, too. Our sitcoms and family dramas taught life lessons. Our westerns and cop-bad guy shows drew very clear, simple black/white lines of right and wrong. I was a big Roy Rogers fan, and influenced by it. In fact, I went to Sunday School not because my parents and grandmother wanted me to. I'd have fought them tooth 'n nail if Roy hadn't said to go.

Growing up in the remainder of the 1950's through early 60's, my views about family life were firmly rooted in Leave It To Beaver, Donna Reed, etc. For example, we all sat down and ate dinner together at the same time every evening, and God forbid coming late to dinner or asking to be excused before everyone was done. Homework came before television. There was a limit of one phone call a night, in or out. One TV, in the living room, and my parents determined what was watched. Traditions, family rituals, and grandparents were respected. Sunday dinner was nearly always at my grandmother's, even when we had a much larger, more comfortable home and she a cramped apartment - the proper thing to do was to go to grandmother's. At Thanksgiving, it literally was "over the river and through the woods to grandmother's house we go", the other grandparents, my mother's parents. Christmas was held at our home, and even after moving out as an adult, it would never have occurred to me to suggest my parents schlep to me for the holidays; the correct show of respect, the family hierarchy and traditions mandated going there, to them.

I realize I sound old and fuddyduddyish, but it is my firm conviction that none of the changes in American family life have been progressive or beneficial. What passes for family life today is much more like Ozzy Osbourne's house than Ozzie and Harriet's house, and the results are not good.

Many parents have completely ceded authority, unfortunately to no one, and their kids operate in a "Lord Of The Flies' environment. When the Columbine killings occurred, and it was revealed that these kids had been stockpiling weapons and ammo in one of their garages for months, I shook my head in amazement. I couldn't keep one measly Playboy stashed for a week without getting caught. I can't imagine trying to build up a secret armory.

Anyway, I actually resent the disintegration of family tradition, of respect for position. It was a bone of contention in the family when Carla and I were married. I am very hard-headed about this.

During my childhood years, my parents were happily married, their relationship healthy and good, to my recollection. They worked together in business , and I can only presume that directed my later choices, as I've been in business and worked with both of my wives.

It is very evident to me, from my own experiences, and from discussions with many clients and coaching members, that our adult lives, our attitudes, beliefs, are all strongly influenced by what we see, hear and experience in childhood. No one ever completely outruns this early input. Can very negative childhood experience be overcome? Of course. Study enough autobiographies and biographies of successful achievers and you will find ample evidence of that. But here's something any parent ought to think long and hard about, and think often about: what lessons are being taught, day to day, by what your sons or daughters observe, hear and overhear? They are listening at the top of the stairs.

I became Jennifer's step-father when she was 8 or 9, and Carla and I raised her, with her visiting her biological father, while Marty, my stepson lived with their biological father and visited us. I'd give myself only a B-, maybe even a C+ as Jen's step-father. For some of those years I was under intense financial pressure and I was drinking very heavily. I'm sorry about that. On the other hand, Jennifer has, herself, told me she's aware of strengths she has that she feels I contributed to, ways in which I positively and permanently influenced her, and that means a great deal to me. Anyway, getting her as a pre-fab daughter without going through the sleepless night, diapers years was just fine by me. She was a really great kid, she's grown into a terrific woman and good mother. Carla deserves most of the credit. I'll take a little. And I'm grateful to have had Jen in my life.

I can't be involved in her life much now, nor can I be involved much with her sons, and that's unfortunate. While I wouldn't go so far to say I regret not having kids of my own, if I were ten years younger and had my current knowledge and perspective, I'd welcome the opportunity of being a parent again and doing a better job of it. But I am not ten years younger, and I have no interest in attending a son or daughter's high school graduation on a day pass from the old folks' home.

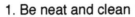

Roy Rogers' Riders Rules

1. Be neat and clean
2. Be courteous and polite
3. Always obey your parents
4. Protect the weak and help them
5. Be brave but never take chances
6. Study hard and learn all you can
7. Be kind to animals and take care of them
8. Eat all your food and never waste any
9. Love God and go to Sunday School regularly
10. Always respect our flag and our country

Happy Trails, from Roy, Dale and Trigger

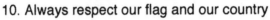

CHAPTER 5

Childhood Memories

Here's a dozen or so things stuck in my mind....

My newspaper making kit

I got this for Christmas one year. It had rubber stamps to make headlines and a primitive typesetting device, ink,. pre-designed newspaper page layouts, so you could write, set type and make onesy-twosy copies of a front page of a newspaper. Even as a child I had the tendency of turning everything into a major endeavor. I say I've refused to take up golf not out of disinterest, but out of fear; I imagine in short order, I'd have a full-time instructor, be trying out for the senior tour, and own a country club. In this case, the little newspaper making toy turned into a full-blown newspaper operation. I commandeered the storage closet under the back porch, hired other kids as reporters, badgered neighbors to subscribe, and until we all lost interest, ground out a weekly newspaper filled with fascinating neighborhood news.

My James Bond 007 briefcase

This was a cool toy. I was a big spy fan - Bond, Man From U.N.C.L.E., Woman From U.N.C.L.E. This plastic briefcase contained a toy gun that shot plastic darts or pellets. The gun was positioned inside the case with its muzzle against a little, concealed hole, and there was a little button by the handle, so you could use the briefcase itself as a gun. It also came with a camera and it, too, was positioned inside so you could surreptiously take photographs with one side of the attache case, by squeezing the attache case handle. It also contained a silencer for the gun, I think a tape recorder, and secret compartments. I still like spy stuff, by the way. Last year I bought and watched the DVD's of all The Avengers episodes - the ones with Diana Rigg, not that other woman. This year I got the British series The Protectors with Robert Vaughan. I wonder why somebody's not re-running The Man From U.N.C.L.E. Oh, and a really, really, really good spy movie, recent, is The Tailor Of Panama, with Pierce Brosnan as sort of a washed up, out to pasture, hard drinking, scheming, sleazy version of Bond.

My dogs.

I miss my dogs. I had a black and brown dog named Trixie when I was a little kid. I have no idea what mixed breed she was. After Trixie passed away, I had a big, golden colored, long haired, clumsier dog, again breed unknown or forgotten, even name now forgotten. Both dogs were loyal best friends, waiting eagerly for me to come home, accompanying me anywhere I went. Every boy should have a dog.

Our pet menagerie.

You name it, we had it. Thousands of gallons of water in 30 different aquariums, stocked with different kinds of guppies and tropical fish. One year, one of our guppies, Dad's and mine, won Best Of Show, in Cleveland. Its tail disintegrated the day following the Show. We kept photograph, trophy and newspaper clipping, but flushed fish. There's a life lesson. I had two hamsters, we had about 80 long-hair Angora guinea pigs, which we bred, selling offspring to pet shops. We had two African parrots, both spoke, one, Oscar, sang along with Dad and Dean Martin and rang like a phone so convincingly you answered it. The other one, Billy, bit. I had a rabbit. Litter-box trained, so he could be loose. Dogs and cats. Briefly, a three-legged, toothless alligator. And a coatimundi named Tinkerbelle.

A *coatimundi* is a very cool animal. It has a raccoon striped tail, but it's tensile like a monkey's. It has little raccoon paws, and can open cupboards, unscrew jar lids. And it has a long ant-eater nose. Tinkerbelle could stick its nose well into Dad's mouth and take little biscuits off his tongue, an act my mother thought disgusting. Tinkerbelle would walk on a leash like a dog, and Dad liked taking her on a leash to a shopping center and watching people do triple takes.

I have a permanent scar in my right hand from Tinkerbelle, but it was my fault.

On Cleveland television, there was a hugely popular kids' program called 'Barnbaby', a character with pointy ears pre-Spock, straw hat, I think supposed to be some kind of leprechaun. He had a sidekick, Woodrow The Woodsman, and an invisible parrot. For one glorious week, the plot line made Barnaby invisible and the parrot visible, and somehow our parrot got the starring role, and I got to skip school and go to the TV studio everyday. I sat and talked with Barnaby in his dressing room, as he put on his ears and make-up. He advised me: stay out of show business.

Dad and the animals also appeared on The Mike Douglas Show. That was big time TV. Produced here in Cleveland but nationally syndicated. The day Dad was on, with parrot and coatimundi, the actress Betty White was on. Tinkerbelle sat in her lap. Tinkerbelle bit Mike Douglas.

Occasionally, we did store grand openings with the menagerie, for a client Dad did advertising for, Baileys Discount Department Stores. On two such occasions, we all dressed up in circus costumes. I was a clown, with a top hat with a clear plastic front, and my hamster inside. By the end of the day the little rat had shit all over my head and chewed up hunks of my hair.

Oh, my mother had a finch for a while too. Until my cat, Mickey, ate it.

If I ever totally stop traveling, I'd like to have a parrot.

My utter lack of athletic ability

I was always the last kid chosen to be on any team, until I got smart enough to be the kid who owned and brought the ball. I bear no ill will - I should have been picked last. I couldn't catch, throw, hit, run fast, and it never got better. My most vivid gym class memory is being stuck at the bottom of the rope, standing on the knot, unable to pull myself up even a foot. Getting hollered at for the requisite five minutes each time before being allowed to step aside. I actually got a 'D' in Phys Ed. In junior high school, I was a tall, skinny kid. Tall enough everybody thought I should be playing basketball, including coaches. A couple times I got pushed and cajoled and nagged into trying out for teams, but even though I did develop a decent outside, long-distance shot, that wasn't yet in vogue, and I couldn't play defense to save my life -- my legs and feet got all tangled up and I knocked myself or others down a lot -- so I never wound up playing. I haven't changed much as an adult either. The last time I tried golf, I drove the ball about a foot off the ground at 90 miles an hour sideways, into one of the little metal "Cart Crossing" signs - which boomeranged it back into my forehead, knocking me out cold. I'd still be the last guy chosen.

The sandhill and the pine forest

I cannot understand the kids today content to spend all their time indoors, playing video games, having virtual war, cops 'n robbers, sports experiences instead of real ones. I couldn't wait to get out of the house. About half the time, there were a dozen or so neighborhood kids, and we played war games at the cliffs in the giant sandhill behind the greenhouses, played Robin Hood in the enormous pine forest, raced bikes down the huge hill from the houses to the sandhill, played baseball or football in the big field between two of the houses. When nobody was available, I was perfectly content to roam through the pine forest myself, bicycle great distances around the greenhouses. Pretend to be a spy and sneak around behind the greenhouses, through the greenhouses, up into the loft. In the summer, it was out the door in the morning, usually with my dog, and not back until dusk and dinner time. Sure, some days I stayed in, and I was a bookworm, and not all that fond of cold, wet winter, so I would sit on the heated window seat in the library or in the sunroom and read. But more often than not, out into the world. I just can't imagine sitting on my butt and fiddling with X-Box and Playstation worlds in lieu of heading out to explore, to adventure, to fight, to spy, to ride. I think parents would do their kids a big favor if they locked up the electronics and kicked their kids out of the house and told them to go do something.

My room

I had a very good room of my own as a kid, in our big English Tudor house. Up the street, one family had five boys, about one year apart in age, in a too small house. As I recall, there were three sharing one room, two sharing another. They envied my room, an apartment by comparison. I had a bunk bed for no reason other than I liked having the option of sleeping up or down, or letting the dog have the bottom, or laying out projects on the top bunk. I had a desk, a row of bookcases, a large walk-in closet with a built in wall of drawers, a window seat by the window over-looking the pool and side yard. I imagine the room was not as big as my memory says it was, but it was big.

This upstairs also had a clothes chute - very cool. You shoved your dirty laundry in the chute and it zoomed past the first floor into a big wood laundry hamper in the basement laundry room. This chute was also a nifty thrill ride for my cat, Mickey. I would pop him in and send him zooming down the chute. I know, I know, you are shocked at my cruel animal abuse. Well, I gotta tell you, he'd go down the chute, run all the way upstairs and dare me to send him down again. Maybe I was a perverted little monster, but the cat was whacked to.

What I never had in my room is, I think significant. I had a stereo, but I did not have a television nor a telephone. I watched TV in the living room, supervised. I made or received telephone calls without privacy.

Going on deliveries with my grandmother

My grandmother often did deliveries and pick-ups for Dad's commercial art business. That meant driving into downtown Cleveland, going to about a dozen different ad agencies, printing companies and a few non-trade clients' offices, to drop off completed typesetting, layouts and artwork, and pick up new work. For several summers, I tagged along whenever I could. I went from the big job for a really little guy of pushing the elevator buttons and carrying packages, to planning the route, running in and out while she double-parked, to jotting down job instructions.

My grandmother was a difficult woman, and she and my mother had a strained relationship of mutual tolerance. She was fiercely defensive of Dad. And she worked hard her entire life and viewed it as virtue. I can never remember her not being old. But as she got really old, her driving deteriorated dangerously. I found myself actually holding my breath as she wove through downtown Cleveland traffic like a New York cabbie on crack. Our returning home from these missions in one piece a constant miracle. Many years later, she was still driving - how I have no idea.

Next door neighbor, Richard P.

Our neighbor on Schaaf Road was endlessly fascinating to me. With 20-20 hindsight, I believe my fascination was fueled by his incredible, outrageous autonomy. He absolutely cared not one whit what anybody thought of him, hated all social convention, rebelled at his wife's social climbing, lived life entirely on his terms. The polite label would be "eccentric." Their huge English tudor home was a near twin of ours, both built by Richard's father or grandfather. Richard owned greenhouses and grew lettuce and tomatoes, had a pig farm. He was a farmer. And his preferred dress was the matching dark green work shirt and pants you buy at Sears. Drank beer, smoked cigars, and fed cigar butts and beer to his fat, unsociable bulldog that waddled around with him.

I recall getting all dressed up and going with my dressed-up parents next door to one of Richard's wife, Lavonne's big cocktail parties. She was dressed up, the giant living room filled with dressed up people. A couple women in uniforms walking around with silver trays of little cocktail weenies in pastry and fancier little food items. And in the midst of it, ignoring it all, Richard sat in his beat-up recliner chair, in his green work clothes, drinking beer from a bottle, refusing to let her party interfere with him watching his favorite TV show, 'The Flintstones.' Oh, and his pet white mouse - that lived in his shirt pocket - crawling around on him. His bulldog lying on one side of the chair. Me immediately parking myself next to the dog. Perfect!

Once the Flintstones ended, Richard decided the fancy food was unfit for man nor beast, and convinced my father to go to Kentucky Fried Chicken and bring back a bucket of chicken. While the high falutin' party went on around him, we sat on his little island, ate chicken and watched TV. Perfect!

Dad's Playboy magazines

If most guys my age are honest, they remember the Playmates from their fathers' Playboy Magazines. I do. Jo Collins pops immediately to mind. We all owe an enormous debt to Hugh Hefner.

The Brooklyn Heights Playboy Club

Playboys were also involved in one of the only two instances when I got in serious trouble as a kid. At, I think 13 or 14 years old, I organized our own Playboy Club in a garage loft, and convinced several of the neighborhood girls to be the bunnies, in bathing suits. Got one to go topless. We got caught, and everybody else pinned the blame on me as the mastermind who led them all astray. My father let the neighbors and my mother think he punished me much more severely than he did, including a strapping behind my closed bedroom door -- the belt hitting a pair of pants draped over a chair, me howling in an Oscar winning performance.

The freedom of the bicycle

My bicycle was the first taste of real liberation and independence I got, and for a while I was gone on it constantly. With the bike, I could go much greater distances, much farther away than on foot. And I did. Later, Dad dug out a really old Briggs & Stratton motor scooter that he had once ridden back and forth to his first job, after he came home from the Army. He got that thing cleaned up, fixed up and running again, and I had limited use of that on the back roads that ran around the commercial greenhouses that lined Schaaf Road behind everybody's houses.

The swingset and the squirrels

My swingset was situated adjacent to two huge trees, home to a half dozen of squirrels. The squirrels eventually came to consensus that I was harmless, and they developed the habit of sitting almost in a semi-circle, just beyond the furthest point I reached swinging, and curiously watched me for surprisingly long periods of time. The entire time I lived in Arizona, I never saw a squirrel. That thought never occurred to me until I was sitting on my deck in my new Ohio home and saw squirrels playing and chasing each other. I like watching them running around out there. Envy them their energy.

Summers and Saturdays at the track

My father took a serious swing at harness racing as a career and business, from 1964 to 1970. He later wrote about these years in a scrapbook, with a note giving credit for support to a "long-suffering Ida (my Mom) for her foolish husband." If he actually considered himself foolish for pursuing his dreams, that's unfortunate and sad.

Anyway, I loved the racetrack. In the backstretch I found the most incredible collection of characters, heroes and rascals; I learned to respect and love the horses ; I liked the work ; I liked making money ; and I liked gambling. I was there almost every day during the summers when school was out, most Saturdays, but in those years the track closed from November until April, and I really hated the month of October. As the racing season drew to a close, it meant people packed up and moved to other tracks or to fairgrounds, and I faced a long winter without this 'community.' I started out making coffee runs from barn to track kitchen, walking horses, then cleaning harnesses, then cleaning stalls, by the second year, able to work as a groom, fully taking care of a horse. One summer I worked part-time helping out a couple in their late 60's with a few racehorses, the Roush's. One summer I worked full-time as a groom for Bernie Shepherd. Other times I worked for Dad. I remember several of the horses I took care of. Max Commander. Widowers Schotchman, a horse Bill Brinkerhoff let me pick out at a sale and he bought. A really good 3year old Bernie had, Storky M. Knight. The best horse my Dad had was a tough, gutsy, undersized mare, Miss Jan K. Another one Dad had, Mark's Jerry, had a weird growth in the center of his spine, right where the harness rests, and Dad created a giant foam pad with a hole cut in it to encase and cover the lump. Another horse whose name I can't recall had his nose break out all the time in really bad, oozing pimples and I spent hours every week rubbing Noxema into it. Racehorses, by the way, take a lot of time and patience and loving care if they're going to do well. Some have to stand in big rubber boots full of ice or ice water and some won't unless you sit there with them for the hour or so. They need liniments rubbed in, feet packed with special mud, walked, taken to the blacksmith shop. Each horse not only has its own personality, it has its own changing collection of aches, pains, injuries that must be cared for. I took pride in being able to do the work, do it well, earn the respect of the adults, and help the horses I cared for perform well.

If either my father or I had figured out a way to extract a good living from training these horses, I'd never have gone into any other line of work. Ironically, you may owe a word of thanks to my father giving up his passion.

One memory vivid from these years is incredible physical fatigue. Even a kid could be driven to utter exhaustion by this work, the hard physical labor, long hours and, in summer, humidity and heat.

Adult conversations

I was privy to - and keenly interested in - adult conversations very early, at 7 and 8 years old. Because the business was in our home, there were employees and clients, the family lawyer, the accountant all coming and going. A lot of meetings took place in the living room. I was never shooed out of the room, and if I asked a question or said something, I was included. Once a week, my godparents, an old Army buddy of Dad's and his wife, and occasionally another couple came to play cards. They used the dining room, I watched TV in the adjacent living room, but listened to them, and wandered in and out, watching and listening. I also went to good restaurants with my parents often, and behaved as miniature adult, not child. What sticks in my mind most about all this is feeling superior to other kids my age, that I knew things they didn't know, and that I was welcomed into an adult world when they weren't; at their houses, they were exiled to the basement or rec room when the adults gathered in kitchen or living room.

How the neighborhood worked

In his speeches, Colin Powell talks about how his neighborhood worked everybody had dozens of "aunts", all leaning out their second floor apartment windows, spying on everything, ratting every kid out to his parents. An entire neighborhood of adults raising the neighborhood kids. Ours was very similar. No aunts in second floor windows and no kick ball in the street. But a row of houses, and all the parents in all the houses engaged in a conspiracy to raise all the neighborhood kids, to watch out for us, to keep us out of serious trouble, to chase us home at dinner time. If one disciplined us, our parents backed him or her up.

The stables up the street

A long, long hike, or long bike ride up the street was a public riding stable. As soon as I could get there, before I was allowed to go that far from home, I got there and convinced the owner to let me clean stalls and groom horses after school for some ridiculously small wage I can no longer recall. Then I went home with my good news, bad news story. Bad news: I'd violated an edict and gone a half mile or so further away from home than authorized. Good news: I had my first job.

And Dad falls off the roof again.

A lot of guys recall having to help their fathers fix things around the house or work on the family jalopy. Having to hold the light - never in the right place. Fetch the tools. Bear the brunt of their fathers' frustration with projects not going well. I had that experience too, but it was trivial compared to the yearly horror show we called: putting up the Christmas lights.

According to the Centers for Disease Control and Prevention, about 5,800 people were treated in emergency rooms during the 2003 holiday season, from injuries sustained while putting up outdoor Christmas lights, as well as decorating trees indoors. If the annual average is only 5,000, that'd total 250,000 people in my lifetime. Popular accidents include falling off backs of couches while trying to balance on them to put the star or angel on top of the tree, slicing arteries with broken ornaments and falling off roofs. Ho, ho, ho.

Our grand tradition was, the Saturday after Thanksgiving, to decorate the giant English Tudor house, bushes across the front of the house, and trees in the front yard. There was a huge lit star that got strapped to the chimney. Strings of lights that stretched from the chimney out to all the trees. A million lights, around every window, under every eave. Every year,

Dad planned to do this job from 3:00 to 6:00 PM. That Saturday night, 'The Wizard Of Oz' was always aired at 7:00 PM. I did not see the first half of that movie until I was 20 years old. Usually, right around 6:30 or 7:00, we were on our way to Gray's drug store, to use its TV tube tester, to find which tube was burnt out in one of the giant Santa Claus decorations we had. Or to buy more fuses for the strings of lights. Or some other damned thing. Unless, of course, we were on our way to the E.R. after Dad slid from chimney down the slanted slate roof, gathering speed until launch at gutter, out into the yard. Because God has such a terrific sense of humor, this was usually the day of the worst snow and ice storm of the year, too. I cannot begin to tell you how much I looked forward to this happy day each year. Ho, ho, ho and ho.

CHAPTER 6

Rich Dad, Poor Dad, One Dad

With a quick apology to Robert Kiosaki, for swiping his 'Rich Dad, Poor Dad' title, I had both in *one* Dad.

It is an experience of immense value: 'rich' as a kid but then 'poor' as a teen. I wouldn't wish it on anybody, but it was a useful experience.

When I was a child, until my earliest teens, we were a very well-to-do-family. I believe the yearly income from the home-based business was over $50,000.00 a year in the 1960's, and that was some serious dough then. We lived in a very large home, bought a new car every year, had a full-time housekeeper, ate in fine restaurants --- in fact, I remember going to a very fancy, very expensive Italian restaurant where I insisted on getting three grilled cheese sandwiches for dinner.

I guess we weren't really rich, but I can't recall ever hearing the words "we can't afford it."

Things changed dramatically right around 1967 or 1968, I think. The business ceased to exist, the house was sold one step ahead of foreclosure, and we moved out into the country - a decision I never understood.

A number of things really stick in my mind about our worst financial years as a family.

One, constantly being cold. The house was heated with heating oil, which was delivered by tanker truck. Our thermostat was never set higher than

58. The worst winters, the heating oil company cut off credit and had us on 'cash', but wouldn't deliver anything less than a fill-up, so Dad dangerously bought ordinary gasoline day to day, a few gallons at a time, and dumped that in. The whole house and our clothes smelled like an oil spill. They both smoked and I wondered when the house would explode. I can recall ripping boards off the interior walls of the decrepit barn to cut up and use in the fireplace.

Two, embarrassment. The high school I went to handled two communities, Richfield and Bath. Oddly, given its name, Richfield was the poorer of the two, populated by a lot of blue collar people, truck drivers and farmers. But even by Richfield standards, we were way, way, way down the economic totem pole. My clothes, our cars and Dad's second jobs were all humiliating. At one of the worst times, with no car running, Dad walked and hitch-hiked to his 11 to 7 shift at a gas station some 15 miles from our house, and it didn't take long for every kid in the neighborhood to know about it.

Then there was Charlie Molino's winter coat. I looked in my closet the other day, and I have five different winter coats. A big, super-warm parka good in sub zero temperatures. A less bulky but very warm coat lined with Thinsulate. A long, dress coat. Two medium weight jackets. When I was 13 or 14, I had none. I had outgrown mine to an impossible extent.

Dad's coat was a hopelessly worn out blue number with flannel lining showing through holes and tears. Seeing it, one of the owners he trained horses for, Charlie Molino, gave Dad one of his old ones. A big, bulky, heavy gray herringbone car coat. Dad gave it to me. I was a lot taller than Charlie, shooting up, and skinny. 26 inch waist. The coat made me look like that Jabba The Hut creature from Star Wars. The coat weighed about 1,000 pounds until it got wet from snow or rain, then its weight tripled.

Worse, of course, it had handme-down written all over it. I hated the damned thing and hated winter because of it.

The girl I had the hots for in 6th and 7th grade lived in Bath, was in with the 'cool crowd', and way, way out of reach.

Three, food. With the exception of the two months we were getting food stamps, there was never enough food, and what there was, was of the fill you up cheap variety. Like macaroni and cheese. For years, I would not touch the stuff. Once I had a car and was making some money, I avoided eating at home, or, if there, ate only tiny amounts, to leave more for Dad. In one year, he lost so much weight, he had several of his single breasted sports coats converted to double-breasted.

Four, tension. My mother managed the money, the bills - and the bill collectors. While Dad would get despondent, he would bring himself out of it, and even at the worst of times, he was generally an optimistic, good-humored man. My mother was frustrated, angry, resentful and unhappy constantly, incessantly. I don't fault her. But it was brutal. There was occasionally voiced but always evident disappointment and disrespect for Dad, palpable tension between them all the time. He would frequently bemoan the fact that he could-n't seem to do anything right, in her eyes. I was the buffer between them, and it was not a welcome responsibility.

Fifth, negative anticipation. The prevailing family attitude we all shared was a sense of foreboding, waiting for the next disaster. Right now, one of the guys who works at the racetrack in our barn is a very good guy but an avowed pessimist. One night, after his horse won, I cheerfully congratulated him and he glumly said, "Yeah, now I'll get cancer." That's how it was in our house everyday. Even when there was victory, there was no celebration. It was overshadowed by the massive financial pressures and the expectation of the next disaster certain to be racing toward us.

Sixth, not keeping my money. I started making money of my own very early, and I did all sorts of things to make it. In high school, I made as much as a thousand dollars a month from my Amway business and selling other stuff at different times, advertising specialties, Stuart McGuire shoes, office supplies. I made money betting horses and running a penny and nickel blackjack game in the school cafeteria. But I was always getting tapped, always chipping in for family disasters. The blown transmission in the station wagon, the flooded basement, the heating oil, the flare-up of my parents' dental problems.

I started my first job broke. And at separate times, as an adult, I have also been very, very broke. I have had many nights where what's for dinner was determined by how much change I found fallen inside the car seat. I've also run up monstrous debt, living off credit cards, paying one with the other.

I know what real despair over lack of money feels like.

I have enormous empathy for what the politicians call "the working poor", and I've always made a practice of over-tipping waitresses, bellhops, cabbies, delivery people, and sometimes tipping people who do not ordinarily get tipped. I have snuck money to people. Paid for groceries when the person in front of me in line came up short and was going to put something back. I know what a huge thing it was for Dad to come home from a shift at the Holiday Inn, where he set up for meetings but also delivered room service orders, with five or ten or twenty bucks. Once Alice Cooper stayed there, to perform at the Coliseum, and Dad came home with his autograph and a $50.00 tip, at a time when that $50.00 was of greater consequence than $500,000.00 would be to me today. He delivered two room service orders and Alice Cooper went out of his way to thank him and be cordial to him. They had a fairly lengthy conversation. Remember this, please, as you go about your daily activities. You can absolutely make some working stiff's day with a kind word, a few minutes of conversation, a decent tip.

I saw firsthand how easy it is to get so mired in problems, so overwhelmed with an onslaught of adversity, you lose all ability to think creatively and clearly, lose all optimism and energy, become mentally, emotionally and physically impotent. I saw how this consumed them and resolved not to permit the same impotence to occur. Throughout my adult life, I've made a diligent effort to devote some time every day toward working on positive steps toward goals, never just survival. When I was running General Cassette Corporation, where there was a crisis a minute, I made them line up and wait for at least one uninterrupted hour each day, while I ignored them and focused on marketing, sales, new opportunities.

I'm a very good mental compartmentalizer. In Psycho-Cybernetics language, I can 'clear the calculator' almost anytime, anywhere, lock whatever was getting my attention away, focus on whatever I need or choose to focus on. I have little storage boxes in my head, and I can put even the most dire thing away in a box, close the lid, and then not think about it until I deliberately take that lid back off that box.

Having a 'rich Dad, poor Dad' gave me a lot of things to observe, to form my beliefs about money and success. Even when the family was dead broke, I always believed I would get rich. The evidence of abundant opportunity was, and is, too great to ignore. I have come to certainty that there are many, many reasons to be poor in America, but there are really no good reasons to stay poor. Anyone can have a wipe-out, just as we did. A lot of people, including business owners, are only one or two bad decisions away from financial disaster. Anyone can draw the bad lottery ticket and be born into poverty. But no financial condition is permanent unless the individual accepts it as such.

My parents never recovered financially through their own devices. Ultimately, I moved them to Phoenix, they worked for me, and in their later years, I supported them.

I went through my own business and financial wipe-out every bit as severe as theirs, but I was more resilient, I had better information, I had seen what not to do in reaction, and I rebounded, and have gone on to become wealthy. Whenever I write or talk about this, I knock on wood, and say a little prayer that I will never have to mount another such comeback. It's no fun. But I can tell you from personal experience that financial problems cannot be permanent without permission.

CHAPTER 7

There Must Be A Pony In Here Somewhere

You undoubtedly know the ancient, tread-worn-off joke with the positive thinking punch line. That's not for this chapter.

The first night we lived in the new house in Richfield, I heard unfamiliar animal noises. The next morning Dad said he heard the same. The second night the same noises woke both of us up, and we headed toward the barn and the woods immediately behind it to investigate. And we found a very hungry Shetland pony.

The people we bought the house from had left him behind, and not bothered to mention his existence. Somehow, we had previously looked at the barn and not seen him - that day he must have been down the hill behind the barn, in the furthest back part of the pasture. It quickly became clear they had neglected him for some time. His hooves were so overgrown he could barely walk. He was half starved.

And that's how I got a pony.

He was blind in one eye. Had a huge bloated belly that never went down much, even though we got grain into his daily diet. And he had little tolerance for being ridden, none for being saddled. I sometimes rode him bareback down the steep hill to the creek, and then along the creek through the valley that ran behind everybody's properties on the road, but he tired easily, so mostly, we walked, with him tagging along like a big dog.

He came to enjoy the companionship, and for a year or so, if I went several days without spending any time with him, he'd knock down one of the rotted, barely standing fence sections, come up to the house and hang around eating grass right outside the front windows to get some attention. My mother was scared of horses, and one day, when Dad and I were both at the track, the pony, Smoky, let himself in the back door of the house and was standing in the kitchen when my mother came down the hall. She stayed locked in the back bedroom until we got home to find Smoky laying on the dining room floor in front of the fireplace, asleep.

We gave him a much better life than he'd had. But I carry some guilt around with me to this day about his last years. If I ever went into therapy, this is undoubtedly a childhood memory that would be analyzed. I'm not prone to guilty feelings and hardly ever moved or manipulated by guilt. I never once cleaned up my plate because there were starving children in some distant land; the connection always escaped me. I never send a donation when the Indian tribe or orphans send me pre-printed address labels. It just doesn't work with me. But I have never shaken the ghosts of guilt about this pony.

The last two winters I was there, and a kid, the barn was simply overrun with rats. Not mice. Rats. Large rats. And I am terrified of them. There were days I simply couldn't bring myself to go out there at all, and a lot of days I barely dropped a can of grain, refilled the water trough, and skedaddled. I rarely cleaned the stall. Those winters he was by himself, and had the run of the place, coming in and out of the barn as he pleased, and he spent a lot of time outside snuffling through snow to still graze. But he was badly neglected by me those winters, out of my fear and weakness, and I've never gotten it out of my psyche.

Beyond that, I'd outgrown him. He and I went from being frequent companions, to me the occasional visitor. It is the experience in the song 'Puff The Magic Dragon', which I can't listen to without feeling badly about the loneliness of his final years. If there's a horse heaven, I hope he's got a kid who never ages, horse buddies, a big pasture with a creek and an endless supply of carrots. Be okay with me if my eternity was being the kid.

I did extract a lesson from all this. Over time, not instantly. I've come to believe that the things I am most likely to wind up regretting, feeling badly about, occur anytime I let weakness and fear control my behavior. That doesn't stop it from ever happening, of course. No one ever acts in perfect accordance with the knowledge they possess. But I'm conscious of it and call myself on it when I can. There have been a number of business situations, especially during the turbulent years keeping General Cassette afloat, that I would have preferred avoiding people the company owed money to, avoiding certain confrontations, one way or another "not going out to the rat infested barn", when I reminded myself of the result: give into momentary fear, get a lifetime of regrets.

There are lots of times in one's life when the choice of simply avoiding the rats ie. giving into negative emotions like fear or weakness - or even ego - confront us, and essentially we make the fight or flee decision. It is such a universal experience there is even a Kenny Rogers song about it, once a hit, titled 'The Coward Of' some county, I forget the rest of the title. I recall only one line verbatim: "promise me son, you won't do the things I've done." I may mess up the details too, but as I recall, it is about a father who was a brawler, killed a man, suffered as result, and counseled his son against violence; the kid was picked on and known as a coward; ultimately, toughs assault his girlfriend or wife and he shoots men who deserved to be shot. I don't mention it as precise parable or suggestion we return to gun-on-hip justice, but the reason it sticks in my mind, linked loosely to my experience with my pony, and a couple other significant life events, is as reminder that cowardice carries a heavy and lasting emotional price tag.

There are lots and lots of ways entrepreneurs exhibit cowardice. They procrastinate and avoid confrontation with badly behaving or under-performing employees, ultimately firing them months or even years after they felt they should have. They suffer silently but resentfully in a partnership with growing inequity. They let a long-time vendor get away with murder. They let a big client abuse them, cut their margins to the bone, out of their own fear of losing that piece of business and being unable to replace it.

A client I can't name here, about ten years ago, let a famous speaker bully him into bringing that speaker in as a partner. Essentially, the bully said: do this deal with me or I will go in competition with you and crush you. I, and every other advisor to my client, urged him to tell the bully to head on down the road. But my client let the bully scare him. The result was an ugly, ugly mess. The bully was impossible to deal with and incompetent. He skyrocketed costs but added nothing to profits. He alienated people important to the client. And he was in breach of contract in the first week. Soon, my client sued him and was sued by him. Chalked up lawyer bills of $50,000.00 a month and ultimately wound up paying the bully to go away, and the bully then went into competition with him, armed with lots of insider information. My client went bankrupt.

Anytime you find yourself making a business decision based on fear, fear that decision more than you fear whatever's scaring you into making it.

A REQUEST:

If you are looking for a good, worthwhile charity to support, consider New Vocations. This organization takes racehorses with career ending injuries or that have aged and slowed, rehabilitates them, re-trains them to be riding horses, and gets them adopted into good homes, under supervision to insure proper care. A lot of the work done with the horses is done with troubled young people, for whom working with horses seems to be therapeutic. You can get information at www.newvocations.com, or call Dot Morgan at 937947-4020. Please let them know I sent you.

CHAPTER 8

My Father

My father was a man of varied and eclectic interests and talents. A renaissance man. He was a good cook and baker. For several years, his commercial art business sponsored local bowling teams, and I recall tagging along one night a week when he bowled in the men's league, the next night, while Mom went bowling, he baked a cake or pastries. Dad had a minor in Shakespearean literature, a business major. He was a good pianist, and also played the sax and trombone, in the Army, and while going to school, in the orchestra at the local burlesque house. He wrote music, and had two songs published. He had a good singing voice, and there was almost always Dean Martin or Frank Sinatra music playing in the home office or car, and he sang along quite capably. He wrote poetry. Painted landscapes and seascapes.

He was a true romantic - something one apparently does not inherit.

His romantic nature must have been a big contributing factor to his extramarital affair.

This was a mess. Although my parents did not divorce, I'd guess that had more to do with economics and co-dependency, my mother's tendency toward martyrdom, and the fact that divorce just wasn't something people did. But it made their marriage hell for many years afterward. It made things very difficult for me too. I was the "cover" while it was going on, viewed as much a betrayer as my father by my mother once it was discovered, and on his side, sharing his pain in the aftermath. It was a full-blown love affair, not a sexual dalliance, and my father was heart-broken by its end. The woman was the wife in a couple of close friends, who I called Aunt and Uncle, who owned two pet stores.

As a result of all this, I developed a rock-solid determination never to become embroiled in such an extra-marital affair and, although frankly tempted and invited on several occasions, never did, during either marriage. It is my firm belief that the only ethical thing to do if you're really dissatisfied in a marriage is either fix or flee; honestly exit. But not carry on an affair.

I understand some of the pressures and frustrations that motivated my father's choices. I think both he and Mom had blame. Ultimately, though, his behavior betrayed a marital vow and is the only blemish on my father's entire life, otherwise an admirable life in every respect.

I have certainly done a number of things I'm not proud of, that I wouldn't want to see in the newspaper, even that others might judge harshly. But the extra-marital affair is one mistake I've avoided.

Dad was a man with a huge, generous heart. Loyal to a fault to friends, with a tendency to project more friendship into a relationship than actually existed. Casual acquaintances rarely stayed that way. Some of the pain, unpleasantness and expense in my life has been caused by the same sort of loyalty to a fault. I guess Dad's unwavering loyalty to his friends had a big impact on me. I have, on several occasions, and one very notable occasion, stuck with friends or associates who were clearly engaged in self-destructive behavior and thus toxic, long after good sense dictated ending the relationships. Even with 20/20 hindsight, I've concluded I'd rather be the person who is disappointed than the one who disappoints, rather loyal to fault that not to be relied on. On the other hand, I am much more cautious and intolerant of being taken advantage of than Dad ever was.

My father had a gift at getting strangers to tell him their life stories within five minutes of meeting him. In Phoenix, Dad and Mom ate at an El Toritos once a week. This is a chain restaurant. But the one waiter soon had my parents invited to their daughter's wedding, and years later, when Dad was in the nursing home briefly before returning home, the waiter visited and brought food. The bartender also came to visit.

Dad was also someone with real, marketable talents and skills that could have made him rich and successful, possibly famous. He had incredible tenacity, and took commitments very seriously. I recall, in his first business, when I was a kid, seeing him stay up all night and work fifteen, sixteen hours straight to get ads ready, to meet a deadline. Had he known what I know now about marketing, he'd have easily turned any of several things he did well into wealth. He missed out on a lot because of this missing link in his knowledge, as do many, many people.

I got my 'work ethic' from Dad. It is blessing and curse. I have to be careful not to do hard work when smart work would be better. I fight guilt over not working at all. That's the curse. But the blessing is a real blessing. When I observe and compare myself to others, I am shocked at how little work others do, how little they get done, how undisciplined they are.

One of the things I've learned, and counsel my clients and coaching members about, is avoid the trap of applying attitude, know-how, skills, work ethic, etc. that, on a 1 to 10, are an 8, to an opportunity that, in size and importance, on a 1 to 10, is a 2.

Dad was fiercely loyal to and supportive of me from childhood on. I recall getting suspended in junior high school for refusing to cut my very long hair. The two week suspension lasted only one day, as my father marched into the principal's office at 9;00 AM the morning after I was sent home. Although bald, my father sported a circle of hair, very long in the back. I could only hear snippets of the yelling behind the principal's door, but several things stick in my memory. One, my father's expressed theory that the totally bald principal was jealous of healthy, long hair, probably indicative of being cursed with a tiny penis. Second, the suggestion that stifling an 'A' student's creative self-expression was stupid. Third, threatening to sue the pants off the school system - long before such litigation was in vogue. And four, threatening to kick the principal's bony ass.

I miss Dad. I also wish I could have done more, that I did more to make his life better in his last years. I did a lot. But I could have done more.

I always admired his mental toughness. And I admire his decisions at the end, his determination to die with dignity, on his terms. In hospice, he methodically had final conversations with relatives and friends, had a lengthy conversation with me, then made a deliberate decision it was time. Refused any attempts to artificially extend his life. And went to sleep.

CHAPTER 9

My Mother

My relationship with my mother was never as close as with Dad, and at times, was strained.

After the affair, we were pretty much estranged, as she knew I'd facilitated Dad's deceptions, and as sides had to be chosen, I chose his.

Years later, when I was working as a sales rep, and in my advertising business, for reasons I no longer recall, I started dropping by the house during the day, late in the morning, for coffee with Mom, and these 1/2 hour conversations provided a new relationship. Our relationship in later years, after I moved them to Phoenix, was good, although I once had to fire her, and that made for a tense and awkward couple of weeks, with Dad coming to work everyday, leaving her at home, going home every night.

Mom was extremely smart and extremely well read. I doubt she ever read less than a book a week, and some years, a book a day. I was introduced to positive thinking literature like Norman Vincent Peale's and Dorthea Brande and Claude Bristol, great mystery writers like Rex Stout and Earle Stanley Gardner, and literary authors like Hemingway by Mom. As a kid, I "stole" books she'd read, and I vaguely remember something of a ruckus when I got caught with the novel 'Peyton Place', considered racy at the time but, of course, quaintly tame by today's standards.

She was an organized, efficient, disciplined worker. She'd worked as a bank teller after graduating college but soon switched to full-time in the first family business, the commercial art studio, as typist, office manager and bookkeeper. It was always interesting to me, incidentally, that she took care of both business and family finances, and gave Dad an allowance. That never felt right to me, and I cannot conceive of turning over control of the money to anybody.

Dad worked for me in my first advertising business in Ohio, then again at General Cassette Corporation in Phoenix. The first time Mom worked for me was in Phoenix at General, from about 1980 to 1983 or so. When we started and spun off the SuccessTrak business, with hundreds of seminars for chiropractors and dentists, she virtually ran that -- up to 15,000 customers, multistep mailings, order processing and a newsletter, all manually, the "database" notebooks full of 33-up Avery label master pages.

Although they didn't get along all that well, Mom and my wife Carla shared a business liability: both fiercely territorial and unwilling or unable to delegate or share power, instead continually accepting a growing workload.

Mom's health was poor and deteriorating for a number of years, and I now suspect she was an undiagnosed diabetic. She had a severe stroke and, unfortunately, my clearest memories are of the two years she spent afterwards, confined to a hospital bed, dependent on tube feeding, and unable to speak. Visiting her was very painful. I could and should have visited more, maybe read aloud from books or something, I don't know. I have a profound "flee" reaction to hospitals. If I am ever in such a state, I hope there's someone who is a good enough friend to unplug me. I imagine being clear-headed, if she was, and unable to communicate, only making intelligible sounds, to be worse than physical incarceration, a truly horrible torture. My father believed he could understand some of her sounds and that they communicated via hand squeezes, and I hope he was right. He spent hours with her every single day and never missed a day, although the toll that took on him was obvious.

My mother suffered in her life emotionally, late in life physically. I saw her fundamentally unhappy a lot of the time, and wish that hadn't been the case. Personally, I have been unwilling to stay in any situation or circumstances making me consistently unhappy for very long. It seems likely my unwillingness to do so has its roots in my observation of her very visible dissatisfaction.

CHAPTER 10

Thanks To My Parents

The other day, for a tape program, I interviewed a very successful salesman, abandoned by his father at age one, raised by an alcoholic mother who frequently told him he would never amount to much in life, telling him what a lousy man his father was, telling him that "the apple never falls far from the tree." He has become successful in his career inspite of this, and in my opinion, inspite of an extremely pugnacious personality undoubtedly born out of his anger and resentment over his upbringing. He is the sort of miracle that is actually, surprisingly quite common, proof that we can conquer any demons, overcome any obstacles.

I feel fortunate that I never had any such adversity. In the birth lottery, I came out okay.

My parents gave me many things for which I am very grateful.

I had a good childhood. I had very tough junior high and high school years. But at the same time, I was ingrained with the virtues of determination, of getting up after you get knocked down, of fighting through adversity, of being tough-minded. Robert Schuller's book title *'Tough Times Don't Last But Tough People Do'* is a favorite of mine.

Most importantly, both my parents were great encouragers. They went along with every project, every hare-brained scheme, every business venture, from my earliest memories to their deaths. They were enormously proud of me and my achievements. They were never critics. They never once stated or displayed any doubts that I would do whatever I said I was setting out to do. They took my side in battles. They sacrificed for my benefit.

I learned to work, and to value a job well done for its own sake, whether recognized or celebrated by others or not, whether producing any significant, immediate tangible rewards or not.

Thanks to them, I was introduced to the existence of opportunity and the concept of developing personal ability at an early age. The greatest tragedy of our failed public education system is neither of these things being taught. I have met many people with abilities that could be developed, that could carry them to prosperity, security, and success who simply have no idea how to develop those abilities. I have met many people who literally have no awareness of the vast, wonderful opportunities open to them. The 'opportunity concept' is foreign to them. Their view of their own possibilities is extremely small, extremely limited. It is a huge advantage to have been born to these parents, to have been given an understanding of 'opportunity' and of 'ability.'

CHAPTER 11

My Buddy, My Car

"Where are you going?" "Out." "When will you be back?" "Later."

A man may not remember the day or month or even the year he met his wife, may not remember old girlfriends' names. Forget all sorts of things about people. But he can recall every car and every detail about every car, and the distance of time breeds nostalgic fondness for the cars of the past, the cars of our youth. Especially the first car. I even remember the little white plastic doohickey on the keyring, imprinted in faded gold lettering, advertising a tavern that was out of business.

My first car was a 1960 Chevrolet Impala, and it was not 1960. I bought it for $50.00. $25.00 down, $5.00 a month. It was turquoise, blue and white, white roof, huge fins. It had over 100,000 miles on it and had not aged well. The floor was patched with license plates. In wet or winter weather, water and slush squirted up through holes in the floor. The roof leaked. One window sagged and wouldn't stay all the way up. There was a lot of rust. But by far its biggest flaw was the rear frame, rusted through and cracked on both sides, past the rear wheels. So the long trunk and fins were held up by frames wrapped in wood blocks (from a set of blocks I'd had as a kid, that had been my Dad's when he was a kid) and duct tape, then wired and turnbuckled forward to a more solid part of the car. This meant you could not jack up the car to change a rear tire; it had to be towed to a gas station with an x-frame. And you couldn't put weight in its trunk. It had bald tires. I'll say this for her, she always started.

Parked outside in frigid weather, covered in snow, she still always started. Certainly can't say that about any woman I've ever been involved with. And, in ratio terms, I've never made as good an investment. I drove her for over a year, added nearly 50,000 miles and ultimately got $25.00 for her when she died - and I took out and kept the 8-track player.

This Chevy died in a heart wrenching way, which I describe later in this book.

It deserved a gentler demise, a gracious retirement. It didn't get one.

I have a little metal model of her in my home.

Next, my JFK Lincoln. A huge boat of a car. Battleship gray 1964 Town Car with suicide doors. Its body had seen better days, the steering was so sloppy you had to turn the wheel around twice to make a sharp turn. I only paid $300.00 for it, so no shame. It did have a big 8 cylinder engine, lots of power, lots of speed. I drove her all over my five state sales territory for four months while waiting for my company car. I also recall picking up a girl for a first date in the Lincoln. It was a long driveway. Halfway to the street, the girl made an unkind comment about the car. By the time I got to the street, I'd made my decision. I put her out there and drove off.

This car was so heavy that, once it was moving, it had so much momentum I once ran out of gas coming down the off ramp of the Ohio Turnpike at Exit #11 and coasted all the way down the ramp, onto Route 21, down that highway into the gas station.

It was so long and big and bulky, I once got it wedged in a circular exit from a parking garage in Columbus, Ohio. Right front fender, left rear fender, stuck.

The brand spankin' new company car provided by my one and only employer Price/Stern/Sloan was a 1974 Chevelle Malibu Classic, maroon, white top. My first new car. And sadly, not much of a car. In eight months working for P/S/S, it needed two transmissions replaced. Its ride never recovered from my girlfriend nearly totalling it the second week I had it, while I was out of town, in L.A., at the company sales meeting. It wasn't easy explaining how I did $6,000.00 damage to this car when I wasn't there. Ultimately, its final moment with me was a bitter, bitter cold, sub-zero morning in Grand Rapids, Michigan, when I unfroze the door lock, opened the door and had its hinges crack in half. Driving from Grand Rapids home to Cleveland with the driver's side door in the back seat and snow swirling in all over me - and being stopped three different times by the Highway Patrol - was a life-changing event. As soon as I got home, I called the office and quit.

I immediately bought my own new car, a 1974 American Motors Javelin, flame red, white racing stripes, white bucket seats, black interior, white top. I loved this car. I'd love to have one now. I smashed it up pretty good on a little trip to Murray, Kentucky described elsewhere in this book.

I traded what was left of the Jav in for a new 1975 Mercury Cougar. That model was the same as the Lincoln Mark IV. A big, long hood. Maybe the best car I ever owned.

I was still living at home, but spending a whole lot of time at the Akron apartment of the slightly older divorcee I later married. One night, driving home very late, slightly drunk, I dozed off at the wheel and the car banged its way along the side of a cliff, against a guard rail until I woke up from the thump-thump-thump and screaming, scraping. The passenger side of the car was ground meat.

That morning I traded what was left of the Cougar in on a 1976 Olds Cutlass Supreme, silver and black.

That car was repossessed.

Two days after it was repo'd, I leased a 1978 Lincoln Continental Town Car, a magnificent beast. An odd metallic rose color, maroon top, maroon interior. That's the car I drove to Phoenix in, and had there until it was repossessed.

Two cars repossessed in one 12 month span. Not good.

I briefly had a really old, bad Cadillac on weekly payments from a tote-the-note lot.

I briefly drove a friend's Pontiac TransAm, the Smokey And The Bandit car, gold with black firebird on hood, pop out glass roof. The engine idled at 40 miles an hour. I got two speeding tickets the same day. Actually, in the same hour. Two neighboring communities. All within four miles. Then a good, used Cadillac. Then a brand new Lincoln.

From there forward it doesn't matter much. Cars don't matter at all to me now. But I miss my 60 Chevy, my 64 Lincoln in spirit. I don't miss driving around on bald tires in leaking, rusty, dangerous cars. But I miss them in spirit. I miss my Javelin, my Cougar, my rose-colored Lincoln. I miss my youth, which has disappeared right along with the cars. I miss the fumbling, figuring-it-out-as-I-went sex that occurred in several of those cars. I miss the ability to be joyous and excited and superior and powerful just from getting behind the wheel of a brand new car.

Now that I think about it, maybe I'll go buy a car.

CHAPTER 12

Other Peoples' Car Stories
(Reprinted from Esquire Magazine, October 1998)

My Car Story by Brian Wilson (The Beach Boys)

My father gave me a 1957 Ford Fairlane for my 16th birthday. It was beautiful - cream and burgundy two-tone with burgundy interior. Man, I loved that car. It was so smooth and fast. That old Fairlane will always hold a special place in my heart for many reasons. For one, it was the car that I went on my first "car date" in. That's right, I took Caroline Mountain out on the town in that car. It was so cool. For another thing, I wrote "Surfer Girl" in it; ya know, when a young guy gets a cherried-out new car like that for his birthday, it can be pretty darned inspiring. I kept that car immaculate. I washed it every Saturday morning. I remember one time I wanted the interior to smell really good, so I took a bottle of my mother's perfume and was going to use just a drop to give it a nice aroma. I ended up dropping it, and the whole bottle spilled onto the floor mat. I never got the smell out. Forty years later, that car probably still smells like my mom's perfume.

My Car Story by Elmore Leonard (Great novelist. Egs. "Get Shorty")

In the mid 1950's I worked for an advertising agency writing print ads, magazine and newspaper, on the national Chevrolet account. One evening after work, the senior vice-president and account executive, Colin Campbell, stopped by my office to say his Bel Air was in for service and to ask if I could give him a lift home. We lived in adjoining suburbs north of Detroit. Together then, we left the General Motors building and walked two blocks to the lot where I parked for fifty cents a day. I should mention that Mr. Campbell was Mr. Chevrolet at the agency, perhaps the product line's most loyal champion. He would spot typos missed by proofreaders. As we approached my car, I said "Here we are."

Mr. Campbell said "Where?" looking around for a Chevy Bel Air or at least a Biscayne.

I said, "Right here."

He said "This is what you drive?"

I admitted it was.

He stared at the sporty little subcompact, light-blue, with the canvas top that rolled all the way back, and said "What is it?"

I told Mr. Campbell it was a rear-engine Fiat 600.

He said, "Oh." And that was about it for conversation on the way home.

My Car Story by Evel Knievel

My first car was a 1924 Dodge truck that I bought used for $35 - outlaw transmission, silent starter, and as good as any 4-wheel drive jeep or fancy SUV that has been made to this day. Seven or eight of my pals and I used to drive it up and down the mining slag dumps outside Butte, Montana, through the swamps where we hunted ducks, or up and over any obstacles we could find. That Dodge never stopped.

One day I decided to show a friend how good it ran. I was stopped in front of his house on Harrison Avenue with the hood up, and I was revving up the engine by holding the throttle open with my hand. I revved it up so high that the timing chain snapped inside the engine and shot straight into the air, about 90 feet high. It came down right in front of the house, splat!, and I was damned lucky I wasn't killed. The truck continued to run without the timing chain for over a year and it didn't quit until I rolled it over and totaled it. Though I've had about fifty cars in my life, from custom Caddy wagons to the world's only Stutz convertible, nothing will ever compare to that old Dodge. Now that was a car.

PS: I met Evel Knievel. Sort of. I was checking in at the Red Lion Hotel near the San Jose Airport, late at night. I stood waiting while the one desk clerk was arguing with a guest on the phone. Next thing I knew, that guest, Evel Knievel, appeared in pajamas, barefoot, elbowed me aside, reached across the counter, grabbed the desk clerk by his lapels, drug him over the counter, and beat him to a pulp. I did not ask Mr. Knieval for his autograph.

CHAPTER 13

My Worst Day With My Father

Dad and I had a lot of very bad days. Being broke, really broke, does that.

The worst is, only in very recent years, not still a totally painful memory. It has humor and pathos. Like almost all high comedy, it is based on tragedy separated from itself by time.

At the time, Dad's car had collapsed and there was no money to fix it, so we were sharing my '60 Chevy Impala, described earlier. On this particular day, a particularly nasty winter storm was dumping an inch or so of snow per hour. When we arrived home at 6:00 P.M., after already pushing the old Chevy out of customer's driveway and ditch, the long, long driveway to our house was covered over with nearly a foot of snow. Wind was piling up drifts. Every few feet, a dip. Four or five spots, even the hint of tire tracks. We could have parked on the road, walked in, got shovels and spent a good two hours doing the back-breaking labor of moving snow, freezing our hands and feet. Calling someone to plow it was out of the question. That would have cost ten bucks.

I started to get out and begin the long walk. Dad stopped me. An especially grim look took over his face. He backed the car into the not-long-ago plowed driveway of the neighbor across the street. He gunned the engine to the max while standing on the brake, then raised his foot and said "Here we go."

The old girl's bald tires spun, somehow grabbed and we shot across the street as if launched from a cannon. She hit those drifts and did her level best to plow her way to the garage. Her best was not nearly good enough. About halfway there, she sunk nose first like a sinking ship, shuddered mightily, and softly died. She listed to my side so far I could not open my door into the window high snow. We climbed out the door on the driver's side. Plodded into the house. Dad called Al, the guy who owned the gas station where Dad worked the 11-7 shift three nights a week as a third means of getting money.

Al arrived a half hour or so later, with his tow truck.

But remember, this car did not lend itself to being towed. The rear frame was cracked on both sides, wired and duct taped together. The bumper was on with wire and duct tape too. Al crawled through the freezing snow under the car to attach tow straps to the frame on either side, well toward the front of the cracks. My Dad got in and started the car and to her credit, she struggled and started. Their plan was to ever-so-gently combine the pulling of the tow truck with the car's own engine's contributions, just enough to get the Chevy out of the drift, onto the more useable surface we had now created with some shoveling, some smashing down of snow with the tow truck.

I have no idea if this could have worked. What I know is that the tow truck's tires spun a little and either out of frustration or instinctive reaction or who knows? Al hit the gas a little hard and that tow truck jerked rather than very gently pulled. I'm not sure if Dad had her in Reverse or not either.

The car cracked completely in half.

Al backed up with the trunk, rear seat and back half of the frame attached to the tow straps. Dad sat in the front half of the car, its nose still stuck down in the drift. His head on the steering wheel. His weeping audible.

"Everything is funny
as long as it is happening
to someone else."

- Will Rogers

CHAPTER 14

Two Hot Dogs For A Buck

I wrote about my worst times with my dad, so I felt I should mention good times too. There were many. Certainly, as a little kid, sitting on the corner of the huge drawing board while he worked. Going and watching him bowl, and consuming unlimited quantities of orange soda pop in big glass bottles. Mostly, though, the time period that is most treasured by me is the handful of years he was training racehorses. Ironically, the worst day, and some of the best times have something in common: neither of us having any money.

On several different occasions in my life, I have been so cash-without that getting food was linked to discovering change long lost in car seats or gathering up and returning bottles or some similar pathetic exercise.

The several years that my father was trying to make a profitable business or career out of his love for training racehorses was the first of those times. The months when there was no racing, from late October until April, were real starvation months. Income ground to a near halt. The first year, the response was to pile up credit card debt and live on that. This made the next year worse.

In these winter months, the horses moved from the racetrack to a fairgrounds some 40 miles or so away. I was in school during the week but every Saturday morning, at about 5 AM, I stumbled bleary-eyed to the ice cold car and went to the fairgrounds with Dad, to feed, water and exercise the horses.

On the way back from the Canton fairgrounds every Saturday, we would stop at Summit Mall mostly just to get warm, hang out and procrastinate about going home. And to get lunch of sorts. Most Saturdays, the lunch counter at the Woolworths store had a 2 Hot Dogs For $1 deal, and we'd have enough money to get that, a coffee for Dad and a Coke for me. Some Saturdays, though, they wouldn't have that special. Then he'd pretend not to be hungry and just get a coffee, and I'd get a hot dog and Coke. After I caught on, I'd sometimes pretend not to be hungry.

After we got honest, we'd get a dog and each eat half. Fortunately, both the entertainment and distraction of watching the people at the mall and the glorious warmth of the mall were free.

During these few years, these winters were the worst. There was basically no money in winter training; you were in a holding pattern until racing season. So Dad worked, once at a window factory, at a gas station, fit in taking care of the horses everyday, and worked on their direct sales business. All added together, though, the income was never enough to handle their accumulated debt and regular expenses.

Looking back, these terrible times were great times with my Dad. We shared something a lot of kids never get to share with their fathers: time. I can't honestly say I wouldn't trade these times for anything. I think I'd still swap 'em out if we could turn back time and he could have succeeded at what he most wanted to do. But that's not possible. So what I do have is the memory, and the eternal respect for his generosity, bravery actually, put forth in the simple act of pretending not to be hungry when he was.

The other day, I noticed McDonalds was running a two cheeseburgers-for-a-buck promotion. I wonder if they realize that, for somebody, somewhere, that's a Godsend? And dammit, where was that deal when we needed it?

CHAPTER 15

Houses I Have Lived In

The house we lived in when I was born was on West 25th Street in old Brooklyn. It had been my grandmother's house, and my parents had moved in with her when they were first married. Dad added an office onto the back of the house. It was a small row house in a nondescript neighborhood. I don't remember a lot about it.

The house we moved to when I was a little kid, that I remember thoroughly, was on Schaaf Road in Brooklyn Heights. This house was a huge English Tudor house with a sunroom, a library, huge sunken living room with fireplace, dining room and kitchen on the first floor, a fully finished basement same square footage as house, upstairs a large master suite, a second large bedroom, two smaller bedrooms, a large center room, and a walk-out second floor porch. There was also a full height attic that was could have been converted into additional rooms. Off the kitchen, a large porch. And a large covered carport you drove under. The front porch entry featured three giant stone steps with carved stone lions on either side. There was a three car garage with a big shop area with a workbench, and a big attic. The back of the house and garage was up against a large hill that you could roll down or sled on in winter. The front and side yards were huge, and we added a full size, above ground pool with redwood decks. There was a playground put in for me, with swingset, slide, and a clubhouse my grandfather built. The library had built in floor to ceiling bookshelves, built in bar. The sunroom extended forward from one end of the house, with oversize windows all the way across its front. We had the aquariums and the two parrots in the sunroom.

The basement housed the family business. Dad had a good-sized office, with huge drawing board, light table and desk. Lanci, a layout artist and pretty good cartoonist had his drawing board and work area in one corner of a big open room, then there were ten or twelve IBM typewriters in two rows, where Mom, another employee, and I worked — once I was old enough to type. There was a big file room, with a big desk. I also had a separate playroom, which had been a coal chute. In there, a train board, a car racing set up, shelves. And there was a laundry room.

The house we moved to when I was in junior high school was a much smaller ranch, from a cookie cutter builder. Much smaller kitchen but big dining room with hardwood floor and fireplace, living room, down a hallway my bedroom, a bedroom my brothers had to share, the master bedroom and only one bathroom. Full basement, two car garage. No air conditioning, only a window unit stuck in the living room window.

My first apartment was huge, in a new complex in the Cuyahoga Valley. I moved there with my first wife; when we were married I was half living at her apartment, half still living with my parents. When we moved to Phoenix, we got an apartment, which I kept post-divorce until marrying Carla.

Actually, getting to Phoenix is kind of an entertaining little story. I had never been there and only knew what I'd read, seen in literature, been told by Pete Lillo. I had seen condos on a golf course that looked great and were very affordable. What I didn't know until we got to Phoenix was that those condos and golf course were in the south Phoenix ghetto. And rental prices were not nearly as affordable in any part of the city you'd want to live in. The apartment we got was okay, but an odd collection of interior colors, and too small. Way too small for my wife and I. We each needed space. Way, way too small. My guess is the cozy confinement accelerated the demise of the marriage dramatically. Oh, yeah, the colors. Blue, yellow and white plaid wall paper in the kitchen, 1960's green shag carpet throughout, need I go on?

Anyway, post marriage number one, we can move onto wife number two, Carla.

Her house was in a blue collar neighborhood, a very small block construction ranch, with only evaporative cooling, not air conditioning. If you've never lived in the southwest, that won't mean much to you. It didn't to me either. She told me it worked just like air conditioning and I had no reason to call her a lunatic until the first 90-degree day. Let me explain. Evaporative cooling circulates cooled water through pipes inside the walls and on the roof. The cooler it makes it, the more humid it makes it. To get it to 75 inside on a 110 outside, you create water beading up on the inside walls. One step away from rain. The first 110 degree day, when she got home, I was in my underwear, lying on my back on the floor, with several blocks of ice from the store in a plastic tub at my feet, with an electric fan blowing air over the ice, up my body. That weekend we leased a bigger, nicer air-conditioned house. With rare exception, I am decisive.

It is quite possible that the joke in hell is evaporative cooling.

Shortly after arriving in Phoenix, driving around, I discovered two communities of patio homes, condos and freestanding townhomes built on the grounds of and around top resort hotels, The Pointe, and Pointe Tapetio. I loved the houses, the immaculate grounds, the proximity to hotels and great restaurants, the mountain views, the works. And I got the visualization of living there plugged into my subconscious. At the time this occurred, buying a home of any kind was so far out of reach financially it was literally inconceivable. Only a couple years later, I lease optioned a home there and we moved in. We later bought another, even better home there, and, lived in Pointe Tapetio until the divorce.

One of the things I liked best about the second Pointe home was the huge window in the living room that looked out into the secluded back yard, nature preserve area behind the yard, and mountain view beyond it. Orange trees. Lots of birds. Occasionally rabbits. Peace, quiet, privacy. I did not get to enjoy that yard nearly as much as I wish I had - I was traveling way too much, and under enormous time pressure when home. It was a great house and a great neighborhood.

My current home, which began as a second residence, is halfway between Cleveland and Akron, in a small town, about eight minutes from the race-track. Few Arizona homes have basements; most Ohio homes do. In this one, the entire basement is finished as office, with a conference room large enough to accommodate my Gold/VIP coaching group meetings. I have a large office, there's a second, smaller office used as a communications room -- FAX, computers, a large third office which doubles as file room and exercise room, with treadmill, back stretcher and Total Gym, two walk-in closets, a galley kitchen, and open center area. The house itself is a cluster home, on a quiet cul de sac with six others. My rear deck faces a woods and a common area shared by three other homes. In good weather I sometimes work out on the deck with laptop or even do my coaching calls there. The upstairs features a large, open 'great room' with fireplace, in which I've installed a hulking black Faith Popcorn desk, but tend to spread my work to kitchen table, kitchen counter and living room. Everywhere, I guess. There's a large master suite, second bedroom, and small library and reading room. I have one massage recliner in the bedroom, another in the library. I like the house a lot.

People are sometimes surprised by my, I guess, modest home. They must expect some big mansion with circular drive, fountain, chauffeur standing next to the Bentley. That's never interested me. Both Pointe homes in Phoenix and this one, zero maintenance. That's what interests me. I will not handle garden hose or snow shovel. Impressing anybody with big, fancy house or expensive cars or Rolexes, all something I outgrew years ago.

I am very big on creating what I call a 'success environment', that is conducive to my productivity and, when desired, relaxation. My office is full of 'psychological triggers', including lots of clocks (for awareness of time), lots of wealth and money symbols (for prosperity consciousness), Disney art and items (for creativity), and many other items that have meaning for me, that reinforce the kind of thinking I want. I use a lot of space, because I function best with visible piles, not hidden files. I like a lot of things within reach when I write, so I sit between a big credenza with desk and another desk, have two big bookshelves, a TV, a radio and CD player, my most used reference books, all handy as I use the computer. I work in organized clutter.

I use a lot of organizational tools, somewhat haphazardly. I have a full storyboard taking up an entire wall in my storage room, and I use a portable storyboard with little 3x5" cards. There are file boxes, file folder holders, containers of one kind or another all over the place. Lee Milteer turned me on to using gigantic clear zip-loc bags to put client or project materials in, and I like this a lot. A bag can contain a big, fat pile, you can see what's in it, you can write on it with a marker, and they can stand up in a box.

I have a very good, very comfortable leather recliner and hassock in my basement office, facing the electric fireplace. Sometimes I sit there to work or think or talk on the phone. I also occasionally choose to take a quick nap there rather than going upstairs.

I think it's important to create your own success environment, that works best for you. There's no one right or best such environment. I know very successful, productive people who operate best in a pristinely neat, organized environment with everything filed with precision. I know other equally productive people with workplaces that look as if hurricanes recently hit and departed. I have had clients who needed absolute quiet, others who can work in a bus station at rush hour. Some who swear by feng shui, others who could be hung upside down in a cave like bats and - when in their zone - not notice. It's up to you to figure out what best supports you and organize your workplace appropriately.

Well, what is a house, anyway? If you've ever seen one in the early stages of construction, you intellectually know, it's not much. It's a box. A frame, some stuffing between sheets of paper stretched between the frame, sheets of drywall, paint. A real illusion. I drove through the part of south Florida ravaged by Hurricane Andrew. The illusion exposed. But emotionally, we take our houses very, very seriously.

For me, above all else, it is sanctuary. I hate being disturbed or invaded in my home. In Phoenix, I actually had a decorative iron security gate attached to a cage around the front entry, with no doorbell on it. If I didn't know in advance someone was coming and opened the gate, an unexpected person could not get to the front door to ring the bell or knock. They were stymied. At home now, I have my main telephone with the answering device in it downstairs, in the basement office. I never check messages, never know there are messages when I come home. I am quite capable of ignoring messages for days, FAXes for days. Ignore a ringing doorbell. I do not receive mail or packages at my home. I defend my private time and place.

My home is also my workplace, and always has been. Even the times I've had business offices outside the home, I've worked more at than away from home. How people commute to and from an office everyday is utterly beyond me. I treasure the 5-minute commute. I picked the current home as much for the ideal nature of the workplace it provided as anything. And it is in the only upscale neighborhood within 10 minutes of the racetrack.

CHAPTER 16

High School

While I was going to high school, I thought it was a complete and total waste of time. With 20/20 hindsight, I think it was only about an 80% waste of time.

As soon as I determined that the teachers weren't making money and most were unhappy about their jobs and incomes, my interest in what they had to say faded.

The biggest thing for me in high school was getting out of classes. I was bored stiff by those I did well in, utterly disinterested in those I didn't do well in. My escape was the school newspaper. That provided freedom to roam the halls and a journalism office to go and hide out in. I wound up the main writer of the school newspaper, and received an award from the Quill and Scroll Society. It's possible our best stunt was publishing the photographs from a Midnight Tour Of Richfield that I and another kid, Jim Korkuska, organized, sold for $5.00 a person, loaded up two cars full. Not much to see in Richfield at midnight. The closed, dark library. Closed, dark drugstore. Closed, dark auto parts store. And closed, dark post office. The report on this excursion with very,very dark photos in which people and buildings were barely discernible was meant to be sardonic.

Our high school principal hid in his locked office with the lights out. A lot.

I dodged the prom, and took a date to the track instead. She lied to her parents, so I picked her up in a tux, she was dressed in gown, her parents took the usual photograph. We changed clothes in the car, in the track parking lot. Unfortunately it poured rain that night and my car leaked like a sieve, so her gown was soaked, and I brought her home looking like a drowned rat. Even more unfortunately, even though it was a first date, she gave me plenty of signals which I ignored, and I was later informed by a very reliable third party that she was really p.o.'d we hadn't had sex that night.

I had one close friend throughout high school, who might best be described as my evil non-twin. Mike was "trouble." He used and sold grass - I've never once tried it. He had a very cool car, a 65 T-Bird. Puke green with black leather interior. He had his house to himself most afternoons and nights - his parents owned a bar. That combination led to a continuous house party of loose girls who liked free marijuana, hangers-around, card players, a few ostracized intellectuals. He spent a lot of time zoned out on grass, with girls who gave him crabs. We had almost nothing in common except a shared passion for getting our hands on money. We were in sales businesses together, ran blackjack games, went to the track, schemed and hustled.

Our high school football team was a disaster. I have reason to believe the principal negotiated deals to play at other schools' homecoming games - for money. The quarterback lived diagonally across the street from me. He'd had quite a few concussions and wore a jerry-rigged, oversize helmet with some kind of water filled bags.

I had a Psychology class taught by a woman we all quickly figured out was nuts. A few of us would very, very carefully tilt all the pictures on the wall just a teeny, tiny smidgen to one side, all the same. Put crimps in the venetian blinds. Put little wood wedges under one leg of every student's desk, so everybody sat tilted an inch or so off-kilter. Then we'd watch her get uncomfortable, anxious, distracted. A couple times she suddenly burst into tears and ran from the room.

I've never been to a high school reunion. Never been invited, but never made any effort to let anybody know where I was to get invited. I wonder how many of the kids I went to high school with grew up to be published author, semi-famous speaker, harness racing driver. I did go back to the school on two different occasions to visit the geography teacher who was co-owner of the bar I tended bar at. What was amazing was nothing, and I mean nothing changed. Same tile floors, same lockers, same dim light, same floor plan, same everything. I can't imagine being one of those teachers. Going there every day for four years made me nuts. How could you go there every day for *forty* years?

I'm occasionally asked where I went to college, by people who presume I did, and would be unable to wrap their brains around the idea that I do what I do without a college degree. There are three answers to the question. I give the truthful one most of the time. But every once in a while, to amuse myself, I give one of the tricky ones. The truthful answer is, I didn't go. At all. Ever. I'm a graduate of Revere High School.

One of the tricky answers is: Akron University. I did "go there" - to meet my first wife for lunch, occasionally to pick her up after work, and once to have sex in her boss' office. She was the assistant to the Dean of the School of Engineering. Another tricky answer is: Notre Dame. I did go there, on two occasions, to speak and do question-answer sessions in my friend Herb True's management classes. I went to go to a football game, too. I even have a Notre Dame sweatshirt. If I am asked "where did you go to college?", these answers are completely truthful and, of course, completely deceptive. And there's a lesson there. It is usually possible to construct an answer to just about any question that is simultaneously true and false.

Politicians do it, journalists with bias and agenda do it too. It's why you definitely dare not believe what you read in the paper. Or hear from Dan Rather.

I once felt very disadvantaged by not going to college. At the time, when I couldn't go, it felt unfair, felt like I was being deprived, and I believed it would be a significant and lasting handicap. I recall my high school guidance counselor and a couple teachers expressing horror and disappointment at my decision. One told me I was "wasting my God-given ability." I've since had a lot of experience with a lot of college educated folks. MBA's. Multiple MBA's. Without exception, they seem disadvantaged to me. Literally mentally handicapped by their education. I'm often reminded by them of a favorite saying of James Tolleson's about the over-educated fellow who could spell 'horse' in seven languages but was so dumb he bought a cow to ride.

I've never had to prepare a resume, because I've never sought a job from anybody but myself, other than my first and only job as a sales rep with Price/Stern/Sloan, for which I had no resume. Recently, though, I was invited to take a position on the Board of Directors of a new bank being formed, and contemplated doing it. I was amused by the forms given to me to fill out. There was a whole lot of room for educational institutions and degrees to be described, memberships in professional associations, and I'd have given a few bucks to see the looks on the bank regulators' faces when they looked at all that blank space and saw only 'Revere High School'. Of course, I'm in a position to plunk a few hundred thousand dollars into such a deal without blinking and no one judging my qualifications would be.

My step-daughter attended Arizona State, then Syracuse, then got an advanced degree from the Maxwell School of Public Policy. The liberal indoctrination was monstrous, but she seems to have grown out of its grip, and wound up with a reasonable balance. Liberal, but not hopelessly so. And an independent thinker, smart as a whip, capable.

Anyway, I long, long ago stopped thinking of my lack of college education as any sort of disadvantage or loss. In fact, I'm very, very grateful that I did not go. Except to Akron University for lunch with my wife.

CHAPTER 17

What Life Was Like When I Graduated High School

An Arabian oil embargo created long lines at U.S. gas stations. I repeat: long lines at gas stations. Whole lot of people reading this who've never experienced such a thing. To prove what great mileage it got, Datsun had a newsman drive their Datsun 1200 from L.A. to New York on less than $30.00 worth of gas.

Secretariat won the Kentucky Derby.

Farah Fawcett. Need I say more? If you're my age, you can see that poster in your mind's eye. Bet you know what color her bathing suit was.

Farah wasn't the only celebrity appearing in ads and commercials for hair care products that year. Incredibly, so did John Wayne. Honest. 'Hair Trigger' shampoos and - oh my God! -*conditioners* for men.

A major technology breakthrough: the PhoneMate answering machine.

Average household income, $12,965.00. Brand new car; $3,950.00. As I recall, I bought my loaded Javelin for $4,400.00, on 48 payments, co-signed by my girlfriend's father. New house, $32,500.00. You could buy a nice house the year I graduated from high school for what a luxury car costs today. When I told my Dad what I paid for my 1997 Ford Explorer, he said "Damned thing should come with a porch."

My first job with Price/Stern/Sloan Publishers paid $850.00 a month, a bonus on sales volume, and I got a company car. I was also making about $300.00 a month from my Amway business. I was paying rent although living at home. And even kicking in extra money for their problems from time to time, I was r-i-c-h. I had more money than I knew what to do with.

Is there a point to that? You betcha. Inflation. Lately, there hasn't been any. In fact, there's an entire generation of adults who've never seen gas lines, double digit inflation and double digit interest rates. But they will. We will. So don't underestimate the amount of money you need to amass. And don't take a good economy for granted, not for a minute.

CHAPTER 18

Viet Nam

I never had to face the Nam or Canada choice. I drew a very high number at the end of 1972, and we started withdrawing troops in 1973. It was all over but the shouting when I graduated from high school. But the shouting has continued all the way into the 2004 Presidential election, and I imagine it'll still be heard when the 2008 election rolls around.

In my junior year in high school, I had hair down to my waist. Politically I was what is now described as social liberal, fiscal conservative. I campaigned for George McGovern in 1972, even though I knew even then he was an economic bonehead, because I was vehemently opposed to - and very frankly, frightened by - the Viet Nam War. But my opposition was never Jane Fonda's opposition. It was more akin to Barry Goldwater's opposition. I could not find any justification for putting our young men and women into that godforsaken, horrible place and requiring they fight a war as if it were some kind of polite, Marquis of Queensberry Rules game. The two steps forward, one step backward, shoot the bad guy but not the civilian, take the hill then retreat bullshit that was Lyndon Johnson's war was, to me, a ridiculous, criminal sacrifice of lives and waste of money.

I've had the very same misgivings today about the Bush II war in Iraq. I do not argue with going in. I have a very difficult time supporting what we've done once in. If I had been running this show, there'd be a parking lot with a huge, very deep hole in its middle where a rat's nest called Baghdad used to be.

Anyway, Viet Nam was the issue of my high school years. It was argued, sometimes violently, at our dinner table, in my classrooms, at the bar, everywhere, endlessly. I lived within 20 miles of Kent State University. Those riots weren't something I saw on TV. That happened on my home turf. I knew people who went to Nam. I knew people who went to the protest marches. And I knew people who went to Canada.

That war was fought based on Eisenhower's "domino theory", that we either stopped the spread of Communism or Communism would soon arrive at our shores, with too much power and momentum to stop. Early, not late, was the idea. President Bush has partially articulated, and I think more totally believes a similar idea about Terrorism. Go change the dynamic of its breeding ground or it will grow in strength, power and momentum and ultimately be unstoppable. 9/11 would suggest he's right. Whether his daring actions based on his convictions ultimately prove to be one of the most important, beneficial interventions in world affairs or the biggest disaster in our history, it's probably going to be quite some time before we can judge. I totally agree with

President Bush that 9-11 changed everything. We now face a kind of enemy and a type of threat we've never dealt with before. The debate and disagreement and confusion about how to correctly deal with it is, for the most part, waged by honest, sincere, serious people.

Our country has gone to the brink of destruction through division on several occasions. The Civil War. The 1960's racial wars. We had the Hough riots in Cleveland, and we looked like Iraq. The Viet Nam War. Our present red states, blue states, liberal vs. conservatives culture war. It is true, a nation divided cannot stand for long. We somehow found our way back together as a country post-Nam. Maybe we will again.

CHAPTER 19

Bartending At The Bowery

I had a really great weekend job in my junior and senior years of high school - so good I occasionally filled in even after that, sometimes dropped in and worked free.

The joint was owned by one of my high school teachers, and a local optometrist. 'The Bowery' was open only Friday and Saturday nights, and it was one big, drunken party. The act was a singalong band, usually led by Bill Parthe, a banjo player, singer, and world champion beer drinker. Mostly we served beer by the pitcher and boxes of peanuts. We did have booze, but wine alcohol level due to license restrictions - so Ben Franklin Bourbon, Count Dracula Vodka, brands like that. Rotgut. Floor covered with peanuts, long tables, group seating and most regulars came in groups, many every weekend. There were two or three of us taking turns behind the bar and out on the floor. Pay: $8.25 per night, tips, and all you could drink. Which was a lot.

Our optometrist owner, Doc, married, had his girlfriend with him when he came to The Bowery, and watching her jiggle was another perk. The hiring test for girls was: stand facing the freezer door. If nose or toes touch first, you ain't hired.

You need to get a mental picture of me in straw hat and bow tie, tending bar, waiting tables, and getting up on stage to chug a mug of vodka while the band chugged beer, and even singing. After eight or ten chugs, I was a very uninhibited fellow.

There was a camaderie amongst everyone who worked there that I have never experienced anywhere else, at any other time in my life. The group at our stable at the track comes close. But, there's no music, no booze. The camaderie of a close group who works and has fun and carries on together is a big missing element in entrepreneurial life. Our coaching groups provide some watered down substitute. My Platinum group has this feeling to a degree. Still, there is a very significant loneliness, aloneness and isolation unique to the hard-charging entrepreneur. I miss The Bowery , even after all these years.

Unfortunately, it made a significant contribution to my becoming and being a very heavy boozer, undoubtedly an undiagnosed alcoholic. I wouldn't blame it. But it opened the starting gate.

It is the place I found my second girlfriend, who I then had a very enjoyable two years with. In retrospect, she holds title as the most pleasantly agreeable woman I've ever been with. Essentially, I dropped her in exchange for Wife#1, and that's a trade that got made for some very immature, ill-considered, narrow reasons. Nancy, incidentally, is the girl in my "Irresistible Offer Story" that I sometimes use in speeches, included later in this book. I'm pretty sure I owe her an apology for the way I ended that relationship -- and owing women apologies seems to be a life theme. I also owe her a thank you for the material. That "Irresistible Offer Story" has served me well.

I urged the Bowery's owner, my teacher, to franchise. In fact, the owner of three Holiday Inns in Pennsylvania wanted to buy franchises. I don't know this for sure, but my retrospective belief is that turning The Bowery into a national chain and getting really rich was so far apart from Dave's self-image, he could-n't embrace the opportunity. I see this a lot; people with the raw material and opportunity to do something really big and great, and to make a ton of money, who stop themselves. Nothing stops them. There's really nothing in their way. They just can't see can't see themselves operating at that level.

What enables one person with a small, local business to envision nationwide or even global expansion while across town, another person with a similar, small, local business never has such a thing enter his mind? To reverse paraphrase Napoleon Hill's famous quote, almost anything can be achieved by just about anybody, if they can conceive and believe themselves achieving it. Psycho-Cybernetics illustrated. Had Dave had a different self-image, different vision of himself, and maybe I a little older with more influence, we might today be presiding over a nationwide chain of Friday and Saturday night only night clubs. And, if grandma had wings and wheels we'd be in the airline business. The longer you live, the more might-have-been's you accumulate. And there darn sure aren't enough lifetimes to capitalize on all the opportunities that present themselves, once your eyes are opened to opportunity. Mine were opened at a very early age, so I have a very, very long list of those might-have-been's.

SECTION TWO

Adventures in Business

CHAPTER 20

My One And Only Job

Many say, and I have said - we're entrepreneurial because we are unemployable. Actually, that's a lousy reason to go into business. You may wind up with a dysfunctional employee you can never fire. Nonetheless, I have only had one job in my entire life, and within the first year, my sales manager, Chuck Gates, and I came to a mutual agreement that I shouldn't be an employee. His. Probably anybody's.

I held my one and only real job, , as a territory sales rep for a book publishing company, for slightly more than one year. I was responsible for Ohio, Michigan, Pennsylvania and Kentucky, for Price/Stern/Sloan, long since merged into a bigger company merged into yet a bigger company. When I worked for PSS, its most successful product was the *Mad Libs* series of padded word games, but we also had a million copy bestseller, *The Pushbutton Telephone Songbook,* a book from comedian Shelley Berman, a satire on astrology, *You Were Born On A Rotten Day,* poetry books by Peter McWilliams, and a marijuana cookbook. One of the founders, Leonard Stern, was a TV producer, with hits including *'McMillan and Wife'* starring Rock Hudson. All I remember about Larry Sloan is that he was a nice guy who had a house right on the beach in Malibu that flooded once every year - to which his response was: just replace the carpet.

I quit but would certainly have been fired had I not quit.

I saw the ad in the *Cleveland Plain Dealer*, indicating that a book publishing company's national sales manager was in Cleveland, interviewing for a sales representative for the territory, to call on bookstores, department stores, gift shops and other accounts. The ad specified experience, college education and car required. I had a basically blank resume, was just exiting high school, and a barely running car I was sharing with Dad - certainly nothing I'd dare travel far from home in. So I went to the interview determined to get the job. I employed three strategies: one, passionate salesmanship. Two, lying my ass off. Of course I had a good car - using my own car during a 90 day probation period before qualifying for a company car, no problem. I presented a resume showing myself two years out of high school, employed as Key Account Manager for an advertising company, neglecting to mention I was also its founder, owner, CEO, CFO, Director of Human Resources, one of its two typesetters and paste-up artists, copywriter, and janitor. Three, I offered to work with no salary for three months, entirely on "free trial".

To be fair, Chuck didn't exactly tell me the whole truth and nothing but the truth either. He neglected to tell me that the last rep quit four long months ago and accounts promised frequent services had gotten none. The effect of this is described in my NO B.S. SALES SUCCESS BOOK. It wasn't pretty.

Now I want to talk about: <u>lying</u>. I lied to get this job.

Only several years later, I had in my portfolio of samples supposedly of my work that I showed to prospective clients for my advertising business a brochure I thought was extraordinary. I had nothing to do with it. And I unwittingly showed it to its rightful owner. He never said a word about it, and we did business. Later he told me he figured the good judgement to pick it and the hutzpah to use it outweighed the lie.

The dirty little secret behind the start of a lot of hugely successful careers and enterprises is that they were ignited by lying, or at least stretching the truth, padding the resume.

I assure you, I'm not alone. If you read autobiographies and interviews a lot and look for these admissions, you'll discover plenty of successful entrepreneurs confess lying to get ahead. Hugh Hefner, one of my entrepreneurial heroes, tells of starting out in business with two different letterheads. One for the fledgling magazine that preceded Playboy, called Stag Party, the other for his fictional distributing company boldly named Nationwide News Company. When he needed to be the publisher or editor or V.P. of Advertising of the magazine, he used the first stationery. When he needed to be the President of the magazine distribution business, he used the other. His actual business consisted of a typewriter on a card table, vision, balls and not just one, but two big lies.

My good friend Lee Milteer has, for as long as I've known her, had a mythical staff person. I watched Jim Tolleson deal with people by phone as his much tougher, much more hard-nosed, much more bottom line oriented alter ego, appropriately named Jake Stone.

The shocking (?), rarely mentioned, nearly universal secret behind all great successes: they're liars. They have deliberately, intentionally lied to gain advantage. I don't think I've ever heard anyone actually endorse or advocate this. But it is a reality. Make of it what you will.

Of course, I *prefer* truth. Telling it, selling with it, hearing it. But I'm honest enough to tell you, there are times when nothing but a lie can do the job. Any entrepreneur who insists otherwise, well, he's a liar.

Now, if I may, I'd like to return to the other gambit mentioned: offering myself on a 90-day free trial. It was something I could ill afford. In fact, immediately after being hired, I discovered my expense account was reimbursed only twice a month. I had to get a family friend, Tom Barth, to let me have and use his American Express card just to put gas in the car, stay in motels as I traveled my five state territories, and to make a trip to Chicago, to work the Gift Show. But I had desire, determination and confidence. To Chuck's credit, he started my salary after only one month.

I had read about this idea in *Think And Grow Rich,* by the way.

Years later, after hearing me speak at a SUCCESS event, a young woman named Lucinda sent me a terrific, multi-page sales letter, expressing her desire to learn to be a marketing wizard and direct-response copywriter, and offered to move to Phoenix and work for me for free for a year, just for the opportunity of hanging around, observing, maybe getting to do some writing. She had just graduated from Cornell. Her family owned their own business. To try and make sure she wasn't a loon, I interviewed her, spoke with her parents and had a friend whose judgement I trusted, Kathy Tolleson, also interview her. Lucinda worked for me about a year and was the best personal assistant I ever had. If you told her to move a wall, she figured out how to move it herself and got it moved. She was a tough, good salesperson, and got better. She also had copywriting ability, and got good. I have lost track of her, but she was recruited away from me by Dan Pena, and was also doing freelance copywriting. If I were to wager, I'd place a heavy bet on Lucinda doing very well for herself.

Everytime I hear some putz whining that he can't find any career opportunities in his chosen field that he was educated in, that there are no jobs, blah, blah, blah, I shudder. If you want to break in and get going in any field, somewhere there's a big winner in that field who'd let you work for nothing.

I once did quite a bit of work for comedienne and entrepreneur Joan Rivers, and I was very, very impressed with her as a person. In fact, she's the most impressive woman I've ever been around. In person, she's smart, funny, sexy. Among her many admirable qualities, personal toughness. After her husband Edgar committed suicide, there was no work for her. Anywhere. No one wanted someone whose husband recently killed himself to come and be funny. She needed work. Joan says: *you push through any door you can.* She did. She took one of the lowest-rung jobs in show business, a Hollywood Square, working for only a few hundred dollars per show. You push through any door you can.

My very first copywriting gig was a 'pay after test' - I did the work free, and got paid only after it was tested and the client decided to use it more than once. I haven't done any work that way, nor have I done beat-the-controls without fees, in more than 15 years. But I did it once. My first paid speech was for $500.00, to be paid only after I spoke and the client was satisfied. I've never done that since either. Two things changed my modus operandi in this regard dramatically: Ringer's book *Winning Through Intimidation*, and an offhand remark by Gary Halbert. But I did these things. And I still think it's better to do them than to do nothing. It is better to get started than not. It is better to push through some door than no door.

Why I Could Never Hold A Job

Office Prayer

Grant me the serenity to accept the things
I cannot change,
the courage to change things
I cannot accept,
and the wisdom
to hide the bodies
of those people I had to kill today
because they pissed me off,
and also, help me to be careful of
the toes I step on today
as they may be connected to the butt
that I may have to kiss tomorrow.

CHAPTER 21

And He Huffed And He Puffed And He Blew The Air-Supported Building Down

Before I opened my ad agency, after leaving P/S/S, I was freelancing, doing some typesetting and commercial art out of the basement, selling some printing, and still with a functioning Amway business. An old neighbor offered the opportunity of taking over marketing for his struggling start-up, into which he'd poured a small fortune, Environmental Structures, a maker of a revolutionary kind of clear-span building with an inflated vinyl cover, something like a blimp cut in half.

Its appeal was the large clear span, so you could put it over multiple tennis courts or swimming pools, even over an entire construction site and work inside it protected from weather. Its cost was a fraction of more traditional buildings. Even substantially less than pre-engineered metal buildings. The company was run by scientists and engineers. The advertising and marketing was abysmal. It appeared to me it would be relatively easy to crank up demand. Even working with a severely limited budget, I saw a number of opportunities. I signed on.

Here's what I wasn't told and didn't know, until I was in neck deep: the deal that brought the major rubber company whose name I won't mention in as prime investor also bound ESI to using only vinyl products purchased from that same major rubber company whose name I won't mention. Unfortunately, none of the products they produce could long withstand

UV rays. Thus the roofs deteriorated and literally dissolved, causing the building covers to sort of deflate and come down on top of whatever was inside. Or worse.

By the time I had written and run ads that flooded the company with good leads, sold several projects, and gotten face-to-face with Kemmons Wilson at Holiday Inns and convinced him to fund the engineering work, to test putting our air-supported structure over a Holiday Inn pool to create a "Holidome", I was fully aware of and thoroughly frustrated with one unavoidable fact: our buildings would come apart like a cheap suit in a rainstorm every single time. It wasn't if. It was when.

I dare not set foot in east Texas. There, a gigantic building we'd installed over a huge crop of expensive black roses had partially dissolved, leaked its air support, and not so gently deflated on top of the roses, crushing the entire multi-acre field. In Ohio, a dome over tennis courts weakened and ripped loose of its anchors on one side, caught wind like a sale, and flipped over on top of the house and office next door, crushing both into a pile of toothpicks. This, I told our engineers, ain't good.

You really haven't lived until you've taken a 7:00 A.M. phone call from a deranged, foaming-at-the-mouth Texas rose grower who has just walked out his front door, morning mug of coffee in hand, to survey his kingdom only to find a million dollars or so of his roses flattened by your collapsed building. If there ever was a contest for stitching cuss words and death threats together creatively, in every conceivable combination, that boy wins hands down.

The pipe-smoking, cardigan-sweater-wearing, over-paid, under-brained, pompous-ass head scientist at this company grudgingly admitted that the building's skin was, quote, marginally and unpredictably unstable, but that we marketing people shouldn't trouble ourselves with such complex technical matters that were most certainly beyond our comprehension.

I am fond of movie magnate Sam Goldwyn's famous quote "It's an impossible situation but it has possibilities." This, however, was an impossible situation with no possibilities.

It was my first personal experience with the extraordinarily stubborn stupidity of big corporations. Here was a company with millions of its dollars invested in this building manufacturer refusing to let the manufacturer out of a contract requiring it to use disastrously defective vinyl, thus issuing its death sentence, thus flushing said millions down the toilet. The powers that be believed they could more easily hide the loss of millions from their shareholders than defend investment in a successful business that used a competitor's vinyl as its raw material. Incredible? Normal. In every single experience I've had since with a big corporation, I've encountered comparable stupidity, similar sacrifice of successful results and doing what works in favor of other priorities. **The bigger they are, the dumber they are.**

I have, throughout my career, gone to extremes to avoid consulting with or otherwise working with big, dumb companies. About a dozen times I've set aside my own foreboding and taken large fees from such companies, and attempted to assist them. It has never worked out well.

With the sole exception of Lee Iaccoca, I have never spent time with even one CEO from the world of major corporations that I would hire to run my lemonade stands. I thought that Michael Eisner was sharp and competent, and I made money as a Disney stockholder thanks to his leadership, yet the disclosures coming out about his most recent years at the Disney helm sure make me wonder if he stopped taking his medications. I've met and had dealings with a couple dozen such CEO's and I'm unimpressed.

The other lesson I experienced with the air buildings that collapse adventure, is that people quite often lie by omission. There are often things unsaid, that are unsaid for the very simple reason that saying them would send you running away, screaming.

When I took over General Cassette Corporation, I knew it was screwed up royally, and most of its dysfunction was no shock to me. Still, a little item of information omitted from the Board's and officers' disclosures to me (and to their bank) was that their loans were secured by assets they didn't own, with financial statements based on the fiction, audited and signed off on by Arthur Andersen. That was a nasty little surprise. Full disclosure didn't occur about the extent of its product quality problems either. Our manufacturing process was akin to God's for snowflakes: each item off the assembly line different!

I prevented one client from buying a company where sales were from fictitious accounts set up and funded by the owner/seller. In preparation for selling the company, he had created other fake companies that bought product from the company to be sold.

Another client raced ahead with an acquisition without doing the due diligence I urged, because he and the seller were long-time colleagues and friends, and everybody was in a helluva hurry. Later, we determined that the seller had made the company's profits artificially large by paying for about $200,000.00 worth of postage for the previous two years' direct-mail out of the coffers of one of his other businesses.

Those two cases, obviously outright fraud. More often, there are less creative maneuvers, concealed only by neglecting to mention certain facts. Equally damaging and dangerous, though. I've learned to be very cautious and curious about what I'm not being told. You should too.

I often work with clients who omit relevant but unflattering information about themselves and their businesses even as they come to me for advice and wise counsel. When I smell the rat, and probe and probe and probe with pointed questions, they eventually, sheepishly 'fess up.

I also often work with clients who are being lied to by omission by their employees, and making all sorts of bad decisions as a result. I vividly recall the owner of a chain of weight loss clinics who told me they'd gotten virtually no new patients from the advertising campaign I'd provided. Every week for six consecutive weeks, the doctor asked his office managers how many new patients came in from the advertising, and was told none or one or two. He never asked how many phone calls occurred in response to the ads. Since he never asked, his office managers chose not to volunteer the information. You know the punch line. Turns out, the ads produced almost a hundred calls that the staff failed to convert to appointments and, motivated by their dislike for the ads, deliberately did not capture names, numbers and addresses from. That same campaign, used again, with a new staff in place post-firings produced a return on investment of $11.00 for every $1.00 spent.

Some years ago, a woman client told me of catching her husband of some 20 years cheating, and after professional investigation, determined he'd been involved in serial affairs for years. She had often asked him if he was faithful and he had always assured her he was. She was bemoaning her husband's relentless lying to her divorce attorney, and the attorney asked, "Well, did you ever once ask your husband for his definition of 'faithful'?"

Following pages: the first ad I did for the air building company, which appeared in a tennis industry trade journal. The magazine was mostly filled with beautiful full-color glamour ads featuring tennis celebrities, so this ugly ad stood out like a sore thumb. Flooded us with leads. Also here: a letter I received from Kemmons Wilson, the original co-founder of Holiday Inns. Had those buildings actually stayed in one piece, today I might be CEO of a giant air-supported building company, in partnerships with Holiday Inn and major construction companies worldwide. Refer to earlier comments about the might-have-been list. Of course, that company might have become a major supplier to construction companies re-building Iraq, and I might have been over there supervising something, taken hostage, tortured and beheaded, live, on television, too. Some might-have-beens are better left as might-have beens.

the second largest cover up

CLEVELAND -- Documents have been uncovered that link Environmental Structures, Inc. with a plot to cover up what many people believe to be the country's leading recreation sport -- tennis.

These shocking materials come to us from an informed source within the ESI complex itself. Our source further revealed that this plot is directly related to the formation of a new company marketing department.

Details of the ESI modus operandi follow:

- An ESI structure costs from 1/4 to 1/2 the price of conventional buildings.

- ESI uses a double layer film wall unique in the air supported field. This produces up to a 40% savings on heating and cooling costs and eliminates condensation.

- ESI structures are clear span from side to side and end to end.

- If the need arises, an ESI structure can be readily moved to another foundation or even increased in size.

Although Environmental Structures would not comment on specifics, they did state that edited copies of the documents are available to the tennis industry. Call or write:

Dan S. Kennedy, Director of Marketing

Jeff B. Rios, Sales Manager

ENVIRONMENTAL STRUCTURES, INC.

CLEVELAND, OHIO 44125

KEMMONS WILSON
CHAIRMAN OF THE BOARD

Holiday Inns INC. 3742 LAMAR AVENUE MEMPHIS, TENNESSEE 38118 U.S.A. 901/362-4435

October 10, 1974

RECEIVED OCT 1 1 1974

Mr. Dan S. Kennedy
Director of Marketing
Environmental Structures, Incorporated
~~████ Street~~
Cleveland, Ohio 44125

Dear Mr. Kennedy:

In reply to your letter of September 16, I am enclosing a front page
cover of one of our Holiday Inns that shows the inside of a Holiday
Inn Solar Dome. We are taking some of our Holiday Inns that are shaped
as L's or U's and building an additional wall and then putting a roof
over it. The average size would be about 15,000 square feet. We would
not be interested in it coming up from the ground, but if there is a way
that it might be held up from the roof we would be interested in talking
with you.

I am awaiting your reply with interest.

Sincerely yours,

HOLIDAY INNS, INC.

Kemmons Wilson

Kemmons Wilson
Chairman of the Board

KW:st

Enclosure

CHAPTER 22

Water, Water Everywhere. Let's Go Have A Drink

P ete Lillo and I met when my little ad agency was next door to his storefront print shop. Our offices shared a small hallway and bathroom. My photographer partner ran pipe from bathroom to his darkroom, which ruptured and flooded Pete's entire shop. Building ran downhill a little. He arrived in the morning to find reams of paper and completed print jobs floating in a pond.

These many years later, there's a whole lot of water under the bridge of our relationship, and we are the best of friends and business partners.

This friendship exists because we have each forgiven the other much.

We have favorite, oft-told, entertaining stories. We also have things that will never be mentioned by either of us, ever again. We have a history which we have conspired to rewrite, to be more satisfactory, even though neither of us have ever enunciated the conspiracy. Presumably, hopefully, we will grow old and grumpy together, sit on a porch at sunset, sip a Scotch, and take comfort in having shared the greatest achievement there is in life - a true friendship. **Wives, dogs, horses may come and go, money and health may ebb and flow, but true friendship is constant and certain.**

For a number of years, together, we kept several local watering holes in business, and made a major contribution to the coffers of the makers of

Chivas Regal. One snowy, miserable night, warmed by a couple hours' imbibing at the improperly named Dry Dock, we decided to go to the dog races. Since there are no dog tracks in Akron, Ohio, we drove to the airport and flew to Miami. Without clothes, hotel or rental car reservations, or notifying our wives. Unfortunately, we picked Orange Bowl parade week to do so. There were no rental cars available so we wound up renting and driving around in a Ryder rent-a-truck. Staying at a resident hotel populated by 109 year old prunes. A good time was had by all.

The most revealing story I can tell you about Pete's personality dates to his print shop's first location, at the opposite end of the strip center from where he wanted to be, at the other end, adjacent to the busy post office. When he spotted that tenant doing a midnight move out, he did not go home and wait until the next day to call the landlord. He singlehandedly drug his printing press on a hunk of carpet out the door, down a long sidewalk, to park it squarely in the doorway of the desired space, making it virtually impossible to enter. This precluded any likelihood of that space getting rented until he and landlord had the opportunity to negotiate.

These days, Pete is a printing broker, with a local clientele he's built up and maintained over many years, but also serving a lot of my clients located all over the United States, Canada and several other countries. You might wonder why somebody in California or Edmonton or Tokyo would rely on a printing broker in Akron. In some cases, the clients save a little but in some cases they actually pay a little more. What they get is a smart, diligent project manager who "gets it"; understands our kind of marketing, who manages hundreds of vendors - different ones right for different jobs, makes certain deadlines are met (and much of my clients' direct-mail campaigns are deadline sensitive), and, as above story illustrates, refuses to let anything get in the way of getting the job done.

Pete is also the publisher of two publications I write. One, *THE NO B.S. INFO-MARKETING LETTER,* is specifically for information marketers --authors, speakers, seminar promoters, consultants, coaches. The other, *LOOK OVER MY SHOULDER,* is for professional direct-response copywriters as well as entrepreneurs who write a lot of their own copy for their ads, mailings, web sites and so on. It allows people to literally look over my shoulder, and see the copywriting work I do for my private clients progress from ideas to completed work. Since I am, to the best I can determine, the most expensive copywriter in the entire field, this opportunity is worth a lot - and we charge a lot.

Everybody develops different skill-sets, and the path to high income and wealth has to include determining what yours are (and aren't), finding or creating a role for yourself that leverages your best skills. Like all of us, Pete has many talents and abilities and extensive and diverse knowledge. In my mind, his greatest skill is --- and mine isn't! --- implementation. Getting things done without making or accepting excuses. If you are lucky enough to find such a person, you want to do business with him, even create opportunities to work with him. They are as rare as hen's teeth.

RESOURCE!

You can find information about the publications just mentioned as well as Pete's full range of services at www.petetheprinter.com.

CHAPTER 23

Millionaire Entrepreneur Needs Writer Who Has Read And Believes In The Principles Of 'Think And Grow Rich', 'Magic Of Thinking Big' And 'Magic Of Believing'

This is a very difficult chapter to write.

First, because I must condense, abbreviate and omit, or devote an entire book. Second, because this involves a very difficult chapter of my life with a very unhappy ending. Although also a life-making chapter from which many benefits, arguably my entire life direction came.

There is nothing quite like the experience of sitting in the first row, behind the defense table, your closest friend and associate the defendant, as the jury enters, a verdict is read, the defendant is remanded to custody. While still feeling as if I had no air in my body and couldn't breathe, I was taking the wristwatch he'd removed and was handing me, and watching him led away in handcuffs.

Let's back up and start where I started with James Tolleson.

Actually, even before that, with some brief background. James was born in the tiny town of Boaz, Alabama. He was fond of telling country boy humble beginnings stories, such as delivering newspapers on the back of a mule. His story is that, if you stayed in Boaz, you were either a farmer or a factory worker. If you got out, you got out by selling your way out. He tells of ruling out college after traveling to investigate the University of Alabama, where his idol 'Bear' Bryant coached, only to discover they offered no course in 'How To Become A Millionaire.' He began buying cars at auctions, hauling them home, rehabbing them, and selling them. He became a big-time car wholesaler with his own car carrier, couple employees. Then he found his way to Ohio, I forget how, with wife and sons, and entered the retail used car business, with a 'Station Wagon Ranch', where only station wagons were sold. This was a successful business, supporting him, his younger brother Rodney, both families, several employees. Barring the incident I'm about to describe, he might have stayed in the car business for life. Maybe eventually bought a dealership. Maybe slowly become one of those 'ordinary millionaires next door.'

But a car dealer came by, and invited James to a meeting where the most incredible business opportunity ever devised would be presented. James went. He was brought to a Koscot opportunity meeting, the multi-level marketing company (later re-defined as a 'pyramid scheme') created by hare-lipped, funny-speaking 8th grade drop-out, Glenn W. Turner. I'm not going to take time and space here to give you the Glenn Turner story. But I will tell you, I know him personally, as a result of my relationship with James, consider him a friend, have studied him, and rank him as one of the five most powerful speakers I've ever seen or heard, although listening to him on tapes, like the infamous *'Dare To Be Great'* tapes isn't easy. Thanks to his speech impediment, it takes a bit of work to get your brain in sync with his speech. Didn't stop him from bringing over 500,000 people into his companies in less than 40 months with each ponying up $5,000.00 for the privilege.

Anyway, James went from that meeting to his car lot, called everybody together and told them they were in charge and he was going to be absent a lot, as he was going to build the biggest Koscot cosmetics sales organization in the world and become a millionaire.

He did that. In fact, he made over one million dollars taxable income in 36 months. That doesn't sound like all that much today, but in the early 1970's, it was a lot of money.

After the Turner companies were destroyed in an amazing, unprecedented, coordinated blizzard of lawsuits filed by 48 of the 50 states' attorney generals, all having to be defended simultaneously, closely followed by federal, criminal charges filed against Glenn and several top guys, the leaders scattered, and literally hundreds of new multi-level marketing companies sprung up, most patterned after either Koscot or Dare To Be Great. James Tolleson's was a brilliant makeover of Dare To Be Great called 'Exciting Life', combining a series of personal growth courses based on Think And Grow Rich materials exclusively licensed from someone who turned out to be a con man with no rights to license, seminars, a travel club, and, of course, a multi-level sales structure with the pyramidal fast-money features, notably a $5,000.00 buy-in. At blinding speed, it skyrocketed to millions of dollars a month.

As an aside, a funny it's-a-really-small-world twist-of-fate, the terrific woman I'm involved with as I write this book, was recruited into one of those spin-off companies, started by a guy who got his start in 'Dare To Be Great'. She followed him to yet another company, built a huge organization, left the whole industry and spent two years on sabbatical in France, and has most recently bought the multi-level marketing company. I met her through introduction by a mutual friend, knowing none of the back story. There is that Kevin Bacon game. The idea that we are all only three people away from everyone else, connected in odd and surprising ways.

Back to chronology. I did not know James then, but I attended an Exciting Life opportunity meeting he and his troop of performers presented at the Richfield, Ohio Holiday Inn. I had never seen anything like it. My MLM experience was Amway, which was plain vanilla, while the Turner-trained Tolleson style was 52 flavors. It was controlled chaos, a circus of successful distributors parading across stage getting ever larger bonus checks, then cashing them and being handed armloads of hundred dollar bills . One guy stood on his chair and threw a mountain of money into the air. A moneymaking plan was drawn on a blackboard at rocket speed. It was incomprehensible yet persuasive. The big promise of rapid wealth, freedom from jobs, travel, was seductive. The overwhelming enthusiasm and energy in the room was hypnotic. In fact, there was actual mass hypnosis occurring, by deliberate intent. I was not swayed, but about half the hundred or so in the room were, instantly paying deposits or writing out checks to join. I took note of how well choreographed everything was, even though it appeared totally spontaneous.

This company was also destroyed, by the Pennsylvania attorney general's office.

And that wipe-out was severe. He did not quickly or easily recover. He bounced around several states, wound up back in Ohio, working as a sales guy for an oil and gas lease promoter. From him, and others, he assembled some capital to launch Success Education Corporation. He secured rights to sell the old $5,000.00 Dare To Be Great Course through mail-order, for whatever price he chose.

He ran a little ad in the *Akron Beacon Journal,* identifying himself as a self-made millionaire entrepreneur looking for a writer who had read books like *Think And Grow Rich* and *Magic Of Thinking Big,* who might create advertising for a mail-order and success training company. I saw that ad by utter accident, but it might have been written precisely for me. I was at a coffee shop counter when it leapt out at me. I went immediately to the phone booth and called, only to be told the position had already been filled. I explained I probably didn't want a 'job' anyway, but that I wanted to meet the man behind the ad, and that he would want to meet me. After a few minutes on hold, I was told he was in a meeting, and my message would be passed on. An hour later, back at my office, I called and was stonewalled again. I called five or six times a day every day for the next four days. I also delivered a letter by messenger. I made a monstrous nuisance of myself. I often note, by the way, how little determination and persistence most people have. How many people would decide they wanted to meet a stranger, based only on an ad, and call and call and call for days on end and refuse to take 'no' for an answer? **It does not take a mountain to stop most people in their travels. A pebble in the road will do.**

Probably to some fault, I usually get what I want, complete whatever mission I set out to do. I rarely take no for an answer. I will get restaurant reservations when there are none to be gotten, get a hotel room after being told there are no rooms at the inn, get concessions in deals no one else would get. You do not want to be at the other end of my aroused bulldog determination.

Finally, he agreed to meet with me for 15 minutes.

The meeting lasted five hours. It included a fascinating "test" involving fetching cheeseburgers which I've often talked about in seminars. I recognized him from the Exciting Life meeting. Shortly into our meeting, he began pitching me a lot harder than I had been pitching him. He moved very quickly to the insistence that I should shut down my ad agency, drop everything else I was doing, exclusively work for him, and I'd become a millionaire many times over so fast it would blow my mind. In spite of some misgivings, I was fascinated, excited, and it so happened I needed money. We agreed to start with me creating full-page ads for his course as well as classified ads to attract investors for the company itself, for a fee of $5,000.00. We were to meet the next night at a restaurant near my apartment to consummate the deal. At the moment he wrote out and handed me that check, unbeknownst to him, I needed it badly and intended to be at my bank when its doors opened the next morning to deposit, in hopes of covering checks I already had out; unbeknownst to me, he had no money in the bank, handed me a bad check, and hoped to somehow cover it before it hit his bank.

I wrote two different full-page ads which he instantly placed in over a dozen magazines, spending over $100,000.00 (of credit) with no testing.

Fortunately, my ad was a big, fat winner. Sold hundreds and hundreds of $399.00 courses. Flushed out of the bushes all kinds of very successful people who knew of Glenn Turner and were eager to get their hands on the *Dare To Be Great* tapes. One buyer was the CEO of a very large, national weight loss company, who ordered 15 courses for himself and his top executives. Another was a doctor running a giant, fast-growing practice management firm, later to be featured on '60 Minutes.' It was incredibly exciting, as the results started coming in, and James was hellbent on fast growth, more ads, direct-mail, telemarketers filling cubicles, seminars.

He was spending an incredible multiple of the gross revenues coming in, by leveraging open accounts and credit, and borrowing money from individuals at $10,000.00 to $50,000.00 a clip, using a personal promissory note with an option to convert debt to stock in the company at a future date. I knew next to nothing about securities law then; I know a lot now. And I didn't fully appreciate the fact the James had a target on his chest, in the sights of the entire regulatory community. His name, linked to Glenn Turner, was to folks in regulatory agencies what a huge red flag is to a bull.

In actuality, there were things in his past that he deserved getting hit for, and certainly things he did later that he deserved getting hit for, but this particular activity - probably not. After all, it's as common as snow in Alaska for entrepreneurs to finance their unproven new businesses by borrowing money or selling ownership or both, with family, friends, neighbors, co-workers and, often, strangers found by various means. If you put everybody in jail doing that this year, most of the subscription copies of 'Entrepreneur Magazine' would be delivered behind bars. And when this is being done on some kind of publicly visible or extensive manner, the offender is almost always dealt with by 'polite' law enforcement, typically state or federal securities agencies, administrative judges, settlements. That would be the norm for most, but not for James Tolleson. His past controlled his future.

So, in a Sunday edition of the *Akron Beacon Journal,* in the Business Opportunities section, he ran a little investors-wanted ad I'm sorry to say I wrote. It instantly attracted a dozen inquiries, eight of whom became investors in a matter of days. I met with several of them myself. The ninth, after a lengthy phone discussion, set an appointment to meet James for lunch, and hand over a $10,000.00 check. I had intended to go, but got waylaid by something else at the last minute. The next thing I knew, I had a call on my answering machine that James placed from jail.

The man who made the lunch appointment was an investigator from the Summit County, Ohio prosecutor's' office, who was spending his time responding to opportunity ads in search of consumer fraud. When he heard James' name he got all excited, as he had studied the Exciting Life/Pennsylvania and the Koscot cases. He believed he had a career-maker on his hands, evidenced by the news media having been called, and waiting at the police station when this clown arrived there with James. At lunch, he handed over the check, sat back and lit a cigar --- the signal for five officers with guns drawn to surround them. And a photographer to take pictures.

It was obviously unnecessary stagecraft and grandstanding by a tinpot bureaucrat weasel, may he rot in hell.

The prosecutor never attempted a fraud charge. Instead, they based their criminal charges on the promissory note being an unregistered security, and thus its "sale" the sale of securities without a license. Again, this would ordinarily be handled by the state's securities agency as a civil matter, typically resolved by fines, agreement not to continue, refunds to investors. But this was the local prosecutor, it was criminal, not civil, and it went to a jury trial. Had there been a true jury of peers the outcome would have been different. But the jury was made up of unemployeds, retirees, a postal worker, a 20 year old comic book store clerk. None capable of following an argument about what is and isn't a 'security', exemptions to registration, and the distinction between borrowing and selling securities. They zoned out during that portion of the three day trial. The prosecutors put an Akron University law professor on the stand, showed him the document and asked if it was a 'security.' He said that it was. When they had James on the stand, he was asked if he had registered it as a security and forced to respond only yes or no. He said no. He was shown each document from each investor and the one the investigator pretended to buy, and asked if he had taken the monies noted on them from the individuals named on them, and he said yes. That made them unregistered securities. A state securities agency bureaucrat testified gravely that Mr. Tolleson was not registered in Ohio to sell securities. The big blow that sealed the lid on the coffin was the prosecution's winning a debate in judge's chambers to introduce information about James' prior misdemeanor conviction, a negotiated plea deal, in Pennsylvania - where the Exciting Life distributorship itself had been classed as an unregistered security. That was a favored tactic post-Turner for years in prosecuting pyramid selling sic multi-level marketing companies. With that, the prosecutor was able to tell the jury: he's done this before. Actually he's never stopped. He's not going to stop. The business isn't real, it's cover for this scheme to sell unregistered securities. A leapord won't change his spots.

James' defense attorney was a complete twit. The judge was biased beyond all belief. He refused to allow a newspaper reporter to testify, who would have testified that the investigator had called him prior to the arrest, and said he'd caught a "big fish" that would make his career, and that ordinarily a "mickey mouse thing like this" would never be criminally prosecuted. His testimony was ruled irrelevant. None of the "victims" were permitted to testify, all of whom were happy with their arrangement. They all came to court and sat with me, right behind the defense table, but could never be identified to the jury. The judge's instruction to the jury affirmed that the document in question was a security. That was, he said, not in question. James' attorney was impotent as cross-examiner, and his summation was a strange, meandering monologue about a bakery. I could have done better drunk, with a sock stuffed in my mouth.

The jury was not permitted to know the sentence that would result from conviction. I'm sure they thought it was the kind of thing there'd be a fine for. They found guilty on five counts of sale of unregistered securities and five counts of sale of securities without a license. Each transaction becomes two crimes. And each guilty count equals one year, thus ten years. And this isn't federal, like Martha Stewart or Michael Miliken. No soft time at a white collar prison. This is hard time in the state penititentiary. James got concurrent rather than consecutive: five years, Ohio State Penitentiary.

Which brings me to being handed his watch and cigarette lighter, and watching him led off, my jaw hanging open.

The next time I saw him, he was in orange coveralls. I was his minister, with freshly acquired $50.00 Universal Life Church credentials. Only a convict's lawyer or minister can visit the first three months he is incarcerated.

James stubbornly refused to acknowledge to anyone he had done anything wrong, which ruled out applying for "shock parole", commonly granted to non-violent, white collar offenders sentenced to five or fewer years in the Ohio state penitentiary. The attorney was certain he'd get it. James was adamant he would refuse it. Neither I, Rodney, his ex-wife or his mother could sway him, even as weeks, then months of day labor and survival in with violent drug dealers, robbers and murderers wore on.

A top criminal attorney we found in Michigan agreed there were plenty of grounds for appeal, based both on prosecutorial and judicial misconduct. He required $50,000.00 up front to do the appeal - and the deadline to file on or forever hold your peace was rapidly approaching. Rodney and I sold stuff, drained our personal resources, and ran up credit to cover that, and to live on. At the time, you could rather easily obtain a lot of Master Cards and VISA's from different banks, especially if in different counties. I remember driving over 300 miles one Saturday picking up credit card applications at different banks, driving the same route Monday to drop them all off, so all the inquiries would occur simultaneously, before the quantity of cards applied for revealed itself. By the time this mess was all said and done, I'd buried myself in over $150,000.00 of credit card, Beneficial Finance, Household Finance, City Loan and other consumer debt, at 18% to 26% a year interest rates. My income was low due to my spending huge amounts of time and energy preparing his appeal, visiting him, and borrowing. The appeal bill, including the lawyer's fee, transcripts, photocopying, etc. topped $80,000.00.

On the day of the appeal hearing, the attorney had stopped overnight to sleep with a flight attendant, and never arrived in time. Shot at appeal, gone. Money gone.

I moved to Phoenix with three years left on James' sentence, and flew back once to twice a month to visit him.

He was paroled -- into my custody. Which brought him to Phoenix. Broke, beat up emotionally, psychologically and physically. But it only took six months for him to rise like the Phoenix.

I had started a retail Self-Improvement Center in Phoenix, intended to be a pilot operation for future franchising, I was speaking, and consulting. But the retail business never worked well. Otherwise, although I was generating $20,000.00 or more in income per month from speaking and consulting, the store was sucking money, the debt was sucking money, and I was juggling, always robbing Peter to pay Paul, never to get ahead of it. When the day came that I went personally bankrupt, a lot of the debt was thanks to the Tolleson legal nightmare, and my struggles in its aftermath.

Following page; the original ad I wrote for James Tolleson, that appeared in more than thirty different magazines.

Season's Greetings
From the Chairman of the Board

A Christmas Story
By Dr. Norman Vincent Peale

How to Live the Good Life
By Commander Whitehead

The Secret Behind My Success
By Carol Burnett

YOU, A MILLIONAIRE?

"It Is Still Possible,"
Says This Century's Greatest Business Empire Builder

"THERE IS A MILLIONAIRE EXPLOSION GOING ON IN AMERICA!" In the past 24 hours, 27 more Americans have become Millionaires. This year there will be at least 10,000 new Millionaires. These Millionaires are just average people who thought and believed they deserved their fair share of this nation's wealth. Millionaires are from all walks of life and all age groups.

Unless you're a negative, know-it-all loser . . . when you compare your life to the life of any Millionaire, the first thing you will think is: "If he can do it, why can't I?" **The answer is that you can.**

If You are a salesman . . .

If You are a small businessman . . .

If You are an executive, climbing the corporate ladder . . . or just an ambitious man or woman . . .

YOU CAN TAILOR-MAKE YOUR OWN BUSINESS EMPIRE.

Read this amazing, factual story with an open mind:

In 1967, a 9th grade dropout with a harelip borrowed $5000 to start a rare, unusual business. It was his 4th attempt at succeeding on his own. **24 months later his business was worth over $100,000,000.00.**

And that was only the start. This man continued to develop his own business empire. In 3 years, he had 60 companies. His business covered 50 states and 11 countries. He employed 500,000 people . . . and was worth more than 200 Million Dollars.

"Yes," says Glenn W. Turner.

You can use the same success techniques he did to improve your own career, finances and personal life as much as you desire.

You may have read or heard about the highly unconventional, uncommon, controversial businessman Glenn W. Turner. But you may not have heard the whole story. Mr. Turner's story is important to your future. So I am going to send you two full-length books by Pulitzer-Prize winning investigative reporter John Frasca . . . two exciting books that describe Mr. Turner's shack-to-castle; mule-to-Lear jet; rags-to-riches empire building story!

BUT RIGHT NOW, AS I TALK TO YOU . . . THE IMPORTANT FACT IS THAT GLENN W. TURNER HAS KNOW-HOW AND METHODS WORTH MILLIONS. Of course, you may not want to build a multi-million dollar international business empire. But you can use these unique methods in whatever you are now doing, or to start the new career or business you've dreamed about.

You'll learn from Mr. Turner how to—

• Cope with problems
• Think bigger
• Recognize the right opportunities
• Manage yourself and others easily—get things done!
• Own the grocery store instead of worrying about the price of a loaf of bread!

"To spend just One Hour with Mr. Turner would be worth $1000 to me," wrote an Ohio businessman familiar with the Turner methods.

We know you'll soon feel the same way. Our firm, SUCCESS EDUCATION CORPORATION, is a highly respected, professional marketer of the finest business and personal self-educational programs ever produced. But the fortune-building know-how of Glenn W. Turner is the most valuable and powerful material we have to offer!

LET ME TELL YOU WHAT HIS TEACHING HAS BEEN

WORTH TO ME, JIM TOLLESON. I was raised on an Alabama farm. I left the farm at a very young age and went into business, buying and selling used cars. When I first met Mr. Turner, I was earning $50,000 a year. In fact, I had made over $9000 the month before! You'll agree, I think, that I was doing pretty well.

But Mr. Turner blew my mind! When I saw what that sharecropper's son was accomplishing, I felt like a money-making bum by comparison. I said to myself: "Jim Tolleson, that Glenn Turner sure does know something you don't. And if he's willing to train you, you have got to be willing to learn. All I have to do is learn what he knows, and I can do everything I've ever imagined!"

37 MONTHS LATER, USING THE METHODS REVEALED IN THE EMPIRE BUILDER'S PROGRAM, I HAD EARNED OVER ONE MILLION DOLLARS! I even made $54,050 in a single month! Great things have been happening ever since! Today, I am President of SUCCESS EDUCATION CORPORATION. I enjoy a level of personal freedom and enjoyment in my work that most men only dream about. I've dedicated myself to showing those open-minded enough to listen . . . those not too old for a new idea . . . those not too "smart" . . . **just how amazingly easy and simple it can be to really take charge of their lives.** Will you listen? You can live as you want to . . . not as others say you have to live.

SUCCESS EDUCATION CORPORATION has purchased exclusive rights to market Mr. Turner's and Dare-To-Be-Great, Inc.'s most valuable materials. I've hand-picked from them and put together the **Empire Builder's Program.**

The Empire Builder's Program includes a full **fifteen hours** of intensive cassette-tape training—7 hours of Glenn W. Turner. Live! There are also step-by-step written supplements. Together, these materials can help you "design and build" your own empire of personal and financial freedom . . exactly as you see it in your mind . . . freedom from worry about bills, rising prices . . . from wasting your life on things you don't enjoy doing. **The Empire Builder's Program** is a **must** for the person **ready** to reach out for the financial success and security that does exist in great abundance.

The only difference between the new Millionaires and you is their use of certain basic success principles best taught by Glenn W. Turner in "The Empire Builder's Program." Just a week or so from now, you can know what they know.

The price for the complete **Empire Builder's Program** is only $300. In one way, that's a big price. (In fact, this is the most expensive success program ever offered privately by mail.) But in another

way, **The Empire Builder's Program** is the greatest buy of your life. To have the man who averaged $20,000-per-hour in his career as your private, personal consultant for only $300, makes that a very, very small price, doesn't it? Of course it does.

America is the richest country in the world, but most people go through life never learning how simple it is to step up and enjoy the wealth that exists all around them. **The Empire Builder's Program** gives you, and the members of your family, that ability . . . for a one-time cost less than 3 college credit hours or a good TV. There is no other program like **The Empire Builder's Program.** I know that **only 2% of the readers of my message are ready** to accept its challenge and make an investment in themselves. 98% of the people say, "I wish I could . . . I'd like to . . . I may someday." One excuse after another! **If you are one of the 2%** who will say, "Man, I'll bet I can get thousands—maybe millions of dollars worth of great ideas from that Program!"—then, I have a unique Guarantee for you:

I PERSONALLY GUARANTEE YOUR HAPPINESS WITH THE EMPIRE BUILDER'S PROGRAM BY GIVING A FULL REFUND ON REQUEST. But more than that . . . I urge you to experience **The Empire Builder's Program** in your home or office for 30 days. If, at that time, you don't feel it will be worth at least 100 times its cost . . . or $30,000 . . . to you in the next 5 years, return it at once. SUCCESS EDUCATION CORPORATION is in the Results Business. Your prosperity is our business. If you're not going to profit . . . greatly . . . from **The Empire Builder's Program,** we simply do not want you to have it.

I know you've never heard of a Guarantee like that. But then, there has never been anything like **The Empire Builder's Program** before, either. SUCCESS EDUCATION CORPORATION will have no part of any get-rich-quick, something-for-nothing gimmicks. We endorse and market only proven methods that require honest effort on the student's part. When you apply yourself to **The Empire Builder's Program,** you'll profit more than you ever believed possible.

So order now. Mr. Turner has said, "Show me a person who can make an immediate decision, after getting the facts, and I'll show you a winner every time." You have heard the facts and the strongest guarantee of results ever offered. Now make the right decision.

Emerson said, "A wise man investigates what a fool takes for granted." **Are you ready** to investigate your potential? Do you dare to compare your abilities and future with the man who became a money-making legend? Can you accept this challenge and **Dare To Be Great?** Sure You Can—**Do It Now!** Order **The Empire Builder's Program** at once.

Yes

Jim, have Success Education Corporation send me my own **EMPIRE BUILDER'S PROGRAM** now! I know it worked for you—it can work for me. (And if I don't feel it will be worth $30,000 or more to me in 5 years, I'll return it, get my money back and keep the books for my trouble.)

Name _____

Address _____

City _____ State _____ Zip _____
Send order to:

Success Education Corporation
980 W. Lafayette Road, • Medina, Ohio 44256

Telephone your order by calling, Toll Free, **800-824-5136, Operator 55A** — California residents call **800-852-7631.**

☐ $300 check or money order enclosed
☐ Charge my ☐ Master Charge ☐ VISA
☐ I am enclosing $5.00 to cover shipping and handling Air Mail —Please **Rush.**   SU-12

Card # _____
Bank I.D. # _____
Card Exp. Date _____

■■■■■■ **The Future Belongs To Those Who Prepare For It.** ■■■■■■
See Response Coupon

CHAPTER 24

The Comeback, The End
(James Tolleson, Part 2)

A bout six months post-parole, while I still had the retail self-improvement store, James picked off a few of its customers, began coaching them, got money from them to begin running ads for free seminars, and began teaching Saturday, then weekend, then four day trainings - and in a matter of months, went from a dozen 'disciples' to a hundred to two hundred to five hundred in the groups. He recorded the hours and hours and hours of these sessions to turn into product. Gradually, this morphed into a $5,000.00 *"Future Millionaires Home Study Course"*, a product that grew at its max to over 300 hours of audio and an unlimited series of seminars.

I began working with him early on, speaking, helping with marketing. When he went on TV with a primitive infomercial and began giving away free tapes, *'The Free Enterprise System Still Works Today - Why Not For You?'* and *'How To Get Out Of Financial Prison'*, growth suddenly spiraled out of control. Almost overnight, there were ten of us leaders speaking at Thursday through Sunday marathon seminars combining EST-like long, long hours on into the wee hours of each morning, sleep deprivation and many psychological break-down-and-control techniques with get-rich motivation, recognition, and intense pressure to multiply through referrals, what EST's founder, Werner Erhard called 'sell it by zealot.' Not multi-level, because no one was paid. But working like one otherwise. We had 1,000 people per week, we were using a giant theater in the round. I didn't, but the other nine leaders went out during the week on separate tours, running small seminars every day and every night all over the country, feeding the weekends in Phoenix. A tape factory was in place, staffed half with volunteers dedicated to James and his "mission". In a two year span, over a million free tapes were reproduced and distributed. I have no idea how many $5,000.00 courses were sold. Hundreds and hundreds every month. A multi-layered organization of speakers, recruiters spanned the country, with area leaders on the ground in at least 100 cities. Hundreds of thousands, maybe millions of dollars were flowing in every week - and in classic James Tolleson fashion - out , like floods of water. The ten top leaders, me included, were being paid $5,000.00 to $10,000.00 every weekend. Money was spent willy-nilly without plan, budget, or even accounting. This entire operation was an amazing exercise in controlled chaos.

It appeared to me he might be able to sustain this, make it a totally legitimate success training business safe from legal attack, and we were having serious discussions about stabilizing acquisitions, such as, possibly, trying to buy Nightingale-Conant or Success Motivation Institute or Success Magazine or all three, as well as vendors like a travel agency, a printing company. I was arguing for siphoning off cash flow to buy "real businesses." James was wholly unconcerned with any distinction between gross and net, unconcerned even with such nuisances as accounting, paying taxes, creating cash reserves.

Trouble began brewing quickly when sales and cash flow started slipping. James' initial reaction was spend more not less. But next, it was irresistible to him to pervert the whole thing into a pyramid scheme. Maybe this was inevitable. Maybe he'd always intended it. I don't honestly know the answers to those questions.

Slumping sales were easily heated back up by turning every Course owner and buyer into a seller, receiving $1,000.00 on each Course sold, $1,000.00

on each Course sold by somebody they recruited, and $1,000.00 on every Course sold by anybody brought in by somebody brought in by somebody they brought in. People were instantly making $10,000.00, $50,000.00, even $100,000.00 a month....gross commissions of course, not calculating all the money they spent sending out thousands of free tapes by FedEx, putting on seminars, coming to seminars. We actually had FedEx parking trucks outside the seminars, to take all the hand-addressed FedEx packages prepared by everybody attending the seminars, sent to their friends, family members and acquaintances. If you actually calculated all that, the ugly truth James would never acknowledge was hardly anybody was making any net income. In fact, many were piling up debt, maxxing out multiple credit cards, in pursuit of the millionaire status James made their every waking moment all about.

I protested, argued, screamed, stomped. I secured his agreement that a new order form would be used with a long list of disclosures including all of his prior legal problems, his prison sentence, and a statement signed by the buyer that they were buying the Course for its merits, not solely to get the right to sell it. Even so, I knew this thing was disaster waiting to happen. People who wanted refunds were either talked out of them or refused them. Claims were made in seminars, on tape that were beyond outrageous. The breaking point for me was discovering umpteen sales made with no signed forms, contrary to James' promise to me.

We had a knock-down, drag-out screaming match. I left, and subsequently demanded he cease use of my name, likeness, story, recordings in my voice, printed matter I'd written.

It only took a few people refused refunds to march together into the Attorney General's office to tip over the first domino. The rest fell very quickly. Less than a month later, the Arizona Attorney General's office filed an action against James' American Free Enterprise Institute, a S.W.A.T. team descended on the office, confiscated all files and records, computers. Bank accounts were frozen. In this case, the government was satisfied with merely destroying the business and him personally, but no criminal case of any kind was ever pursued.

There has not been another comeback. To the contrary, James' health is bad, he has no business to speak of, and is basically destitute. He is completely estranged from his brother, from me, and as far as I know, from any of the old team members.

I attempted to be of help to him once, and we entered into an agreement that would have had him only speaking and conducting seminars, and creating products, for a re-constituted Doers Club of America, linked to a publication I created and briefly published, *Philosophy Of Success Magazine*. We got going, had one big event, but he wouldn't, couldn't stay within his defined role.

There are four main things I'd like to say about James E. Tolleson.

First, he may well have as much innate, raw talent in persuasion, recruiting, motivation, at creating excitement as anybody I've ever seen or studied. I was there, up close, inside as he took improbable people and turned them into masterful speakers and field leaders, built an organization, built a movement. I sat in the rooms as this movement's versions of ten commandments were created, disciples created, essentially a godless religion built from scratch. I watched him spend hours and hours taking a guy who mowed lawns for a living and literally building him into someone he could send out into the hinterlands and have him return like a pied piper, leading first dozens, then hundreds, then thousands. I saw him speak nonstop for ten, twelve, fifteen hours and hold the attention of thousands.

I watched him literally will a giant enterprise into existence. He has, as Turner had but more so, the unique ability to see something in a person no one else would see, that the individual himself is clueless about possessing, to seduce and recruit that individual, to transform that individual. He is a builder of people, to the nth degree.

Drawing the analogy very, very cautiously, I'll tell you, having seen him build this thing from nothing, from the ground up, I can comprehend how Jesus Christ started with just twelve disciples, wandering around barefoot giving talks, and built Christianity.

Second, he is testament to the fact that talent alone is of little value, and even dangerous. His talent, his greatest asset and worst enemy. Because he could make so much happen through sheer use of talent and exertion of effort, he never matured in his knowledge of business, finance, law. He was what I call a "militant positive thinker", so extreme he refuses to honor reality, to admit mistakes, to learn from mistakes. Stubborn far beyond persistence to delusion.

Third, he was right about 95% of everything he believed and taught. I learned an enormous amount from him. There's seldom a day I don't use something I learned from him, and recall the source. There are principles I came to understand and adopt, from my time with him, that have served me extremely well. The *Future Millionaires Home Study Course* is an extraordinary body of work few could ever equal even if they set out to do so, in part because its hundreds of hours of recordings are mostly unscripted and spontaneous.

However, the 5% of things he has always been totally, severely wrong about are killers. The lesson, which I've paid a great deal of attention to, is that it's not enough to be 95% right. W. Clement Stone's saying "little hinges swing big doors" has two sides. Little leaks sink big ships.

The truth of the man, as I see it, he was --- and I say 'was', because the James Tolleson that I knew has long ago ceased to exist, although he is still alive ---- was an incredibly gifted, talented, intuitively persuasive individual, a masterful motivator, a remarkable developer of people, and a wise person in many ways, but also a severely, desperately, irredeemably flawed, dangerously stubborn, in some ways delusional individual.

I frequently point out to people that Napoleon Hill identified 17 principles of success and presented them <u>not</u> as a cafeteria but as an integrated collection. A lot of people like ignoring one of those 17, 'Accurate Thinking.' No one I've ever met ignored it with more consistency, greater zeal or more resolute determination than James Tolleson. As a result, his extraordinary grasp of the other 16 was fatally sabotaged.

Ultimately, he became not only a danger and toxin to himself, but to anyone and everyone around him.

He feels deserted by people he 'created', people who should be beholden to him, but in truth, he gave them no sane option but to desert him. One of the things I've felt compelled to do in my life that I feel badly about is continuously urging his son to have no contact with him.

This is all sad for me. I admired him, learned from him, went through trials by fire and extraordinary successes with him. It is quite possible I would not have proceeded in any of the directions I did, in speaking, in developing the Inner Circle business, in creating my products, without the experiences with him. It would have given me enormous pleasure to have invited him to see me speak at the SUCCESS events, to have him see and be part of all that I created. But it long ago reached the point that I dared not let him even meet anyone I was doing business with; he would instantly hustle them for money, to invest in a comeback that would never come. It became impossible to have a frank and sensible conversation with him. He could not be trusted. He could not be helped.

I am good friends, and involved in business activities with James' brother, Rodney. We were once so broke we shared a wristwatch. Rod wore it if he was going to an important meeting with someone or vice versa. Today, Rod and I are working on an interesting business, www.OwnAFlorida-Business.com.

I am also very good friends with James' son, Tracy, and Tracy's wife, Vicky. In fact, they sort of came to my rescue immediately after my divorce from Carla, and Vicky stepped in to run the office and be my desperately needed support person. Working for me is no stroll down the lilly path, and she has been a godsend. Tracy and I are in business together, providing a marketing system to mortgage brokers who work with real estate agents, which can be seen at www.PinnacleClubFor Realtors.com, or you can FAX inquiry to 602269-3113. So, a lot of good came out of my time with James Tolleson. A lot of pain and suffering and loss, too. I'd call it the most mixed bag of my entire life.

Over the years, I've worked with a handful of great entrepreneurs beset by numerous personal demons, who keep their demons caged, who are aware and conscious of the need to do so, and who are able to sustain success in spite of them. I've gotten very adept at "smelling" the people who cannot cage their demons, and at getting and staying the hell away from them at all costs. Everybody has a closet in which thoughts and emotions and seductive addictions and behavioral dysfunctions and even evils live, and millionaire entrepreneurs are no exception. The actor Jack Nicholson once said that for every five bankers or agents you meet who spend their days pissing on people, one of them, at night, secretly pays somebody to piss on them. Whatever your personal, private, secret "black" impulses and habits you wrestle to control, you might think you are alone in having them, but you ought to know, you most assuredly are not. You shouldn't even feel ashamed of them, even if you wouldn't want anyone to know about them.

Maybe one of the most difficult tricks to a successful life is living a self-aware, conscious life, of being honest with yourself. It's the denial and rationalization and defensiveness, the need to appear perfect to others, the refusal to ever acknowledge error or admit weakness, that gets us into trouble. I watched a very talented man approach the fork in the road and veer off, from a path to likely global prominence and celebrity and lasting wealth, to ignominy, oblivion and poverty, I believe solely because of dishonesty with self. It wasn't pretty. I paid a financial, emotional and time fortune for the experience, so I've tried to learn from it, try to keep reminding myself of it, and also feel I bought and paid for the right to talk about it here, even though it paints an unflattering portrait of a living individual. If we were speaking, I would apologize to my old friend for any hurt this chapter might cause, but I would still feel compelled to write it as I have, and to include it here, otherwise writing a dishonest book, if only by omission.

The more successful we become, the more important it is to constantly question ourselves -because others grow more hesitant to do so, and it is easy to equate a rising tide of prosperity with an unwarranted certainty of being Right with a capital 'R' about all things, easy to permit the flow of money pouring in to blind us to, or make us insistent on not seeing the flaws in our thinking or actions.

CHAPTER 25

Unjustly Accused

Presently, you can be detained in any U.S. airport purely because you are carrying a lot of cash - five to ten thousand dollars will do it. They can confiscate your cash and you then have to go to court to get it back, if you can prove its source. Your bank also works for the IRS, and is required to report any single transaction of $10,000.00 or greater, a series of cash transactions within a 24 hour period that add up to $10,000.00 or more, and is encouraged to report any of your banking activity it considers "irregular" or "suspicious." Your CPA works for the IRS too, as he is subject to fines and other penalties for failing to verify any information you provide or filing returns subsequently determined to be "false." In many cases, the federal government can invoke the RICO Act, originally created only to prosecute organized crime ie. the Mafia, and use it to confiscate all your assets in one fell swoop, when you are charged with a crime, long before you are convicted -- leaving you homeless and defenseless. As Martha Stewart learned, you can be imprisoned just for lying to investigators even if your lies are not covering up any crimes. Under The Patriot Act, the FBI can enter your home or office, download the entire hard drive of your computer, install tracking bugs in your computer and phone and premises, all without ever notifying you or presenting you with a warrant. The FTC, FDA, IRS, etc. track visitors to their web sites and, in turn, investigate them.

Most people shrug their shoulders at all of this. Their belief is, if they're not doing anything 'wrong', they have nothing to fear.

Such naivete is charming but foolish, ignorant, hazardous.

The average small business owner violates at least ten different laws by noon each and every day.

Many statutes are written so over-broad, just about anybody can be prosecuted under them. FTC rules are particularly impossible to actually comply with.

I have seen firsthand a person wrongfully accused of a crime, over-zealously prosecuted, unjustly sent to prison, and ruined for life. I have seen first-hand another business owner unjustly attacked by the FTC and quite literally hounded and harassed to death; a massive coronary. I have seen a SWAT team descend on an office, herd staff up against walls, handcuff principals, and load file cabinets, computers, and records into pick up trucks. I have seen over 25 business empires toppled, more than 25 millionaires and multi-millionaires quickly stripped of every penny and left ruined. A few deserved it. Most didn't. But most did bring it on themselves. For most, it could have been prevented.

Such events in business are like burglary, fire to homeowners, rape to women, a parent's teen becoming a drug dealer or committing suicide; everyone thinks such things only happen in someone else's family.

Retroactive prosecution is among our most interesting legal oddities. Michael Miliken was heralded as a hero in business, an innovative venture capitalist who devised a revolutionary way to finance new, risky start-ups. He was on the covers of FORBES and FORTUNE. A darling of Wall Street. Subsequent to all this success, the term "junk bond" entered our language. Laws were passed. And under new law he was prosecuted for acts that occurred prior to the existence of the laws - and sent to prison.

This is not new or all that unusual. My friend Glenn Turner was prosecuted for "pyramid selling" under new laws written to outlaw his business methods five years late. This is also commonly done with tax law: what is legal today is made illegal five years from now, retroactively, so what you did that was legal is still penalized.

Double jeopardy is another oddity. You may hear that double jeopardy doesn't exist, that you cannot be prosecuted and tried for the same crime twice.

O.J. Simpson is example this is not true. Agree or disagree, he was prosecuted for murder and acquitted by a jury. NOT guilty. However, the Goldman family subsequently filed a civil action and took the case back into civil court, where the standards for proof are much looser. Generally speaking, in a criminal case, the burden to prove is on the prosecution and if you are the defendant, you are presumed innocent unless proven guilty. In civil court, the opposite. You are presumed guilty and it is your burden to prove yourself innocent. Thus, in Simpson's case, and many others, the defendant judged not guilty in criminal court is subsequently judged guilty in civil court, assets confiscated, life ruined.

Most people feel strongly that justice was not served by the 'not guilty' verdict in the O.J. Simpson case. What most people do not recognize is that justice was not served (either) by the subsequent civil prosecution of the acquitted Simpson for the same crime.

In business, entrepreneurs need to be cognizant of their true legal risks. The more visibly successful you are, the greater the danger. The more 'renegade' you are, the more jealousy and ire of peers and competitors you arouse, the greater the danger. An Inner Circle Member, Dr. John Barrett, puts it this way:

*"The higher up the tree you climb, the more
your naked pink ass hangs out."*

If you happen to be in a genre like mine, telling people they can get rich, the danger is multiplied 100-fold. Personally, post-Tolleson, I have avoided telling the great unwashed masses they can be millionaires, instead focusing only on people who already own businesses, focusing on teaching 'marketing.' But I have clients who play on a bigger, broader field, and I frequently give them cautionary advice they generally do not welcome.

My first piece of advice is to avoid anything that might land you in a criminal situation, as opposed to civil, or regulatory agencies' enforcement. This means, for example, not drinking and driving, not consorting with strange women, not engaging in exotic tax avoidance schemes, not lying to investigators. If you wish to engage a prostitute, it's best to go to a legal Nevada brothel; don't be Hugh Grant picking up a streetwalker. If you want to drink while on the town, hire a limo and chauffeur. If you cannot stand seeing your ex-wife carouse with drug users and engage openly in promiscuous sex, even in front of your children, hire the best lawyer money can buy and sue for custody, move to the opposite end of the world, but resist the impulse to murder her. If your company is worth a billion dollars, resist the temptation to jerk around with insider trading deals for $40,000.00. In your business life, avoid high risk activities subject to criminal prosecution, such as securities fraud.

My second piece of pure business advice is: prevent unhappy customers from complaining to anybody. Sell with unconditional guarantees. Honor them without caveat. Never make it difficult for a dissatisfied consumer to get a refund. Refund even when warranties have expired, product is returned damage or the consumer is otherwise "wrong." If you cannot unconditionally guarantee what you sell, stop selling it. If the people you sell to abuse such guarantees to such an extent you cannot operate your business profitably, stop selling to them, find more honorable people to sell to. Do not permit emotional response to complaints or refunds. Manage it as math, within acceptable range. Banish the customers that cannot be satisfied. But never, never, never, never refuse or delay a refund.

Please re-read that last paragraph.

The man who was hounded to death by the FTC ignored my advice on this subject. We argued about it once a year, when we had dinner together, for five years. Had he unconditionally given refunds rather than requiring his dissatisfied buyers to meet certain conditions for refunds, it would, at most, have cost him a million dollars of the nine to ten million dollars he was making each year. Instead, he lost his entire business, his family lost a fortune and he lost his life.

My friend and client who had his entire business destroyed and narrowly escaped a stay in the Arizona State Penitentiary attracted the attention, then ire of the Arizona Attorney General's office as a result of five very aggressive, vocal, unhappy customers denied refunds. $25,000.00, total. Saving that $25,000.00 toppled a 25-million dollar a year business, and did so much damage to him personally, he's never recovered. He lives in poverty and will likely end his life in poverty, ill health, and alone.

I could continue. I could fill more than 50 pages of similar situations I have witnessed firsthand or have very close, personal knowledge of.

Still, people ignore my advice on this, argue, fight, insist they are different, and they are right. But being "right" has absolutely nothing to do with this. I am not talking about right or wrong. I am talking about survival.

In general, you want to do everything you can to avoid lawyers, regulatory agencies, and the courtroom. No one wins there. At best, you may be less damaged than the other party. But no one wins.

To quote Glenn Turner:

> *"if you want justice, go to a whorehouse.*
> *If you want to get screwed, go to the courthouse."*

Finally, avoid dangerous people or associations. My time with James Tolleson only put me into bankruptcy, helped destroy my first marriage, and put me through years of extreme emotional trauma. It could have been much worse. I could have gone to the lunch that led to jail. Ever since I've been very, very quick to judge someone self-destructive, irrational, delusional, toxic, or actually criminal, and to get and stay away from them. I err on the side of caution.

I am quite often surprised at the risks some entrepreneurs are willing to indulge in, when it's not necessary. It is one thing to risk association with dangerous people or to engage in high risk activity when you have nothing to lose. But once you have some road under your tires and mileage on your odometer, you have reputation, you have success, you have wealth, then it is inexcusably stupid or stubborn or arrogant.

"*Talk Is Cheap, Until You Hire An Attorney.*"

CHAPTER 26

Shakespeare And I Agree

He wrote: "First thing we do is kill all the lawyers."

Quick preface: my apologies to the few attorneys we have as Inner Circle Members. Several in my Gold/VIP coaching groups. I like you guys. I really do. Harry Williams, Bill Hammond, Mace Yampolosky and Ben Glass specifically come to mind, but there are others. At coaching meetings, I say you guys have to sit together - because nobody else wants to sit next to the attorneys! But my impression of you guys really is positive, and you are a credit to a much maligned, mostly deservedly maligned profession. It is my opinion you are as rare in your profession as diamond-studded hen's teeth in chickens who look like Elvis and drive Buicks. I'm sure there must be other exceptions hidden in the legal profession, lawyers not worthy of my scorn. To them, apologies as well.

With that said, America would benefit more from the following three changes than from anything else anyone could dream up, invent or enact:

#1: Close all the law schools for 10 years. Re-open for one graduating class per decade.

#2: Prohibit attorneys from breeding with other attorneys. This produces especially evil spawn.

#3: Prohibit lawyers from being elected to Congress. Letting the lawyers get control of our government has been a disaster.

Lawyers have ruined our health care system, paralyzed business, steal millions yearly from business owners and investors, and are a gigantic drain on our productivity. As example, consider the actual letter an Inner Circle Member, Phil Campbell got from McDonalds, after submitting his book to them, suggesting it might be provided to franchisees. This letter (shown at end of chapter) is representative of the chill on innovation imposed on our entire economy by lawyers.

Here are a just two of my unfortunately numerous stories:

A top U.S. criminal attorney, paid $50,000.00 by me and James Tolleson's brother to handle James' appeal, arrived so late for the hearing the judge ruled against him in his absence, permanently denying appeal. Instead of coming in the night before the 10:00 A.M. hearing, the lawyer stopped halfway from Detroit to Cleveland for a night of sex with a flight attendant he'd met the week before, then trying to drive in the morning of the hearing, his Mercedes blew a tire.

My business attorney for General Cassette Corporation was having sex with, more accurately getting sex from an ex-employee and stockholder suing the company.

In total, I have met three types of lawyers:

1. Competent criminals, completely devoid of morality and humanity

2. Reasonably honest, with some humanity intact, unfortunately, utterly incompetent

3. Incompetent criminals

With the exceptions noted at start of this chapter, I've met none I would trust without supervision for even 10 minutes with wife, daughter, small animal or silverware.

I once told my step-daughter: please, never bring home a lawyer. If your choices of boyfriends or husbands come down to (a) a scumbag drug dealer who is covered with prison tattoos and, as a hobby, runs cockfights for bikers or (b) a Harvard law grad --- by all means, bring home the drug dealer. I was serious. (And, ironically, at one point in her teen years, she took me up on the suggestion.)

Unfortunately, there are times and instances when using a lawyer of your own is unavoidable and essential. My advice is: never forget you have in your hands a snake.

Over the years, I've done more and more and more of my own legal work, dealt with lawyers less and less and less. I do everything possible to avoid them, in business, socially.

The letter from McDonalds illustrates the paranoia every successful business owner must possess, to survive in a society overrun with litigation. We have more lawyers per capita than any civilized nation and they all want get just as rich as John Edwards did ---- he famous for actually acting out in front of a jury as if channeling the spirit and voice of a dead child. Classy guy. Paranoia must color your every business decision, important or day to day trivial, from important contract to being alone in your office with an employee of the opposite sex for even ten minutes, one time. So, I end with four pieces of advice:

"Be paranoid."

— Donald Trump

"Just because you are paranoid doesn't mean they're not out to get you."

— Dr. Charles Jarvis

"Paranoia is essential."

— Harold Geneen, former CEO, ITT

"Trust. But cut the cards."

— Ronald Reagan

McDonalds Corporation
McDonalds Plaza
Oak Brook, Illinois

November 27, 2004

Mr. Philip Campbell

Dear Mr. Campbell:

Thank you for contacting McDonald's recently with your idea for a product or service you believe would be of interest to us. We appreciate your interest in McDonald's, but we have to return the material you sent because it is our company's policy not to consider unsolicited ideas from outside the McDonald's system.

It's not that great ideas cannot come from outside of McDonald's. Each year, however, McDonald's receives thousands of unsolicited ideas and proposals for products and services from individuals as well as companies. Because of the volume of unsolicited ideas and the difficulty of sorting out what is truly a "new" idea as opposed to a concept that has already been considered or developed by McDonald's, we must adhere to a strict policy of not reviewing any unsolicited ideas that come from outside the McDonald's family of employees, franchisees and approved suppliers. We realize that we may be missing out on a few good ideas, but we have had to adopt this policy for legal and business reasons.

As a result, we must decline your invitation to review your submission and hope you understand the reasons for this decision. Enclosed is your original submission. Your material has not been reviewed and we are retaining no copies.

Nacy Larr
Representative
McDonald's Customer Response Center.

CHAPTER 27

The Greatest Sale I Ever Made

I've never had a good, succinct, publicly comprehensible answer to the question of "what do you do?" My occupation is a combination of occupations, individually or combined, indefinable. But one of the things I definitely am and have been for more than 30 years is: a salesman. A damned good one. I can sell face to face, to a boardroom of ten, or to an arena of 10,000. I can sell tangibles or intangibles, low priced or high priced, under the worst of circumstances. I can also sell with virtually any media, from the simple sales letter to the television infomercial.

My speaking colleague of ten years, Zig Ziglar, labels selling "the proud profession." I think it is more than that. I think it is **the *essential* skill for a successful and happy life.** Napoleon Hill wrote a book titled *"Sell Your Way Through Life."* I have a story about selling my way to life.

On two separate occasions, I came close to committing suicide.

Once when I was a teenager. I got as far as driving through a blinding rainstorm to a bridge I intended leaping off of. Maybe you recall the song 'American Pie.' It has a line, "I drove my Chevy to the levy." That I did. For no good reason other than that both the radio and 8-track were broken, I clicked on a motivational tape in the audio cassette player on the seat next to me, just for noise. The voice on that tape shamed me out of my suicidal determination by the time I got to the bridge.

The other, much more recently, the week I signed divorce papers. I got as far as purchasing the necessary plastic pipe and duct tape and driving to the garage of my Phoenix home (which I no longer inhabited), ready to put myself to sleep. I talked myself out of it, sitting in my parked car, in front of the house I was barred by court order from entering.

You might call either of these the greatest sale I've ever made. But I would differ.

At my ill-fated retail store, The Self-Improvement Center, a man walked in late in the day, shortly before closing,. I was there alone, finishing some work at the desk. He sat down in a chair across from me, pulled out a gun, and proceeded to tell me a story of woe, culminating with his intention to blow his brains out.

I confess, what flashed through my mind was totally self-centered. I saw the headline in the newspaper:

Man Blows Brains Out At Self-Improvement Center

It occurred to me: this would not be good for business.

So I sold. Real hard. For forty minutes. My success was his putting his gun back in his briefcase and walking out the door, down the street. I have no idea of the subsequent life or death of the anonymous fellow. I only know he was out my door and out of sight.

According to a Harris poll reported in 2003, 7% of all adults - about 15million Americans - have actually tried to commit suicide. Another 21% have seriously considered it. More than one in ten young people, age 18 to 24, have attempted suicide.

When I was a kid, my grandmother's third husband, my non-paternal grandfather, killed himself with the running car in closed garage method.

I was so young I don't actually remember much about him. His name was Leonard, and he was an accountant. Retired, I think. I do remember the car. A huge white Pontiac with blue interior, which he had meticulously maintained in pristine condition. I remember not wanting to ride in that car after his death.

One of the neighbors I grew up with on Schaaf Road, one of five sons, hung himself in one of the family's greenhouses, in his 20's I believe. Long after we'd left. In fact, I don't think we knew until I brought Dad back to Ohio from Phoenix on a vacation, and drove him around to visit old neighbors. The one who hung himself was the only son of the five who stayed and went into the family business. He lived next door to his parents, with his wife, in what had been his grandparents' house.

I tell you this for two reasons.

First, I know bald-faced, strong, oppressive despair. I have heard the persuasive voice promising peace, insisting life's not worth living, death will be welcome relief. My father's favorite movie was 'It's A Wonderful Life' -- the original, not the truly horrid remake with John Laroquette or somebody like him in the Jimmy Stewart role. My guess is Dad used that movie to keep talking himself into not quitting, at his worst times. Should you ever face such despair, maybe you can recall this Chapter, and maybe you can use it to talk yourself out of it. No matter how awful the situation is that you find yourself in at the moment, there are three things that are absolutely, certainly true about it. One, it seems and feels much, much, much worse in the present than it will when it is history. Two, killing yourself is the only way to lock it into permanence at its worst. Three, there's at least a chance that you will pass through your darkness and emerge into some new life well worth living. Why not roll those dice? You can always kill yourself. No rush. Need not be today. Wait a few months and see how you feel about it then. As far as I know, you can't change your mind after the fact and come back. I'm all for being decisive but a truly irreversible decision deserves a lot of patient thought. If in any doubt at all, don't.

Second, be alert. The vast majority of teen suicides and young adult suicides come as a shock to the parents, grandparents, girlfriends, boyfriends, spouses, co-workers. At first. But over days after the event, on reflection, it's very common for people to recall 'warning signs' in the suicidal person's demeanor, utterances and behavior. The statistical odds of someone in your family or circle of friends deciding to end life are quite high. You could save someone's life. Err on the side of caution, of interference, of confrontation, even at risk of making a fool of yourself or thoroughly pissing somebody off.

CHAPTER 28

Congratulations Captain, Here Are The Keys To The Titanic

I took control of a company called General Cassette Corporation at a time in my life when I believed in my own infallibility and invincibility.

Not long ago, I got around to reading the book *"From Worst To First"* by Gordon Bethune, the CEO who turned a sick Continental Airlines into a winner. Continental had gone through two bankruptcies in ten years, nine CEO's in ten years, and was on the verge of extinction when Bethune took the controls. He knew he had to gain the trust, support and involvement of his 30,000+ disgruntled employees if he was to save the company. I was struck, As I read the book, by the many things he did that I had done in 1979 and 1980, when I took over General Cassette.

Bethune, for example, yanked the security devices off the doors to the executive suite, stuck a wood wedge in the door and announced "open door communication." He implemented incentive plans linked to solving the air-line's biggest problem: on time performance. He implemented another incentive program to cure excessive absenteeism. He sliced off parts of the business - in his case, unprofitable routes - in order to re-focus resources on the most profitable parts of the business. And so on.

When I took over General, it had burnt through all its capital and was in a daily cash flow crisis; the quality of its goods and services had reached rock bottom; it was losing money; employee morale was non-existent.

Like Continental, General was the worst. I did take it from worst to best, but in this case, that wasn't enough.

I yanked the door off the executive offices and mounted it on the wall sideways, to announce the end of closed door management. I don't know how this actually worked out for Bethume, but I wouldn't recommend it. It invited an endless, daily parade of people with petty problems and complaints and its initial symbolic value was quickly lost.

I had better luck with new incentives. I implemented one incentive program along with a tougher quality control program that, in 90 days, took the production error rate from a whopping 80% down under 5%. I created another incentive program that cut rampant absenteeism by 90%.

I slashed unnecessary costs as well as unprofitable business. I cut from 47 to 12 employees, yet increased output. Incredibly, the company, while hemorrhaging money, negative cash flow in excess of $30,000.00 a month, had a full-time Human Resources Director (mostly hiding in her office making vacation charts), a full-time Comptroller (counting what, I can't imagine), and a full-time Marketing Director (whose appointment book actually had his nap times inked in). We had expensively leased mainframe computers in a special climate-controlled room, with two full-time computer operators generating reams of completely inaccurate reports on giant green paper put into giant notebooks. One day, the two computer operators got in a hair-pulling fight, one pulled a knife on the other, Pete Lillo broke it up, and we fired the two of them on the spot. The next day, the Comptroller said in horror: "But they're the only ones who know how to operate the computer system." Pete solved that problem by yanking the plug on the computers out of the wall. I fired the Comptroller.

Pete and I managed to keep this company running for a full year without once having a positive checking account balance. On several occasions, I negotiated additional credit from vendors that should have cut us off. We never missed a deadline or a delivery for a client, we never missed a payroll (other than holding our own checks), and we were ever so slowly navigating the wounded, leaky Titanic past the icebergs to open seas.

I made some mistakes. For example, I let the company become overly dependent on just one sales rep, so we soon had the tail wagging the dog. I promoted one person to his level of incompetence. But overall, I played the corporate turnaround game pretty damned well. In a short period of time, I took the company trough a Chapter 11 Reorganization (without an experienced corporate bankruptcy attorney) and got a Plan approved by the creditors and the federal court. I sold the least lucrative portion of the company's business to a competitor for a needed infusion of cash.I had the company moving forward on a fast track toward a new, healthy life.To accomplish this, I, and my wife, sacrificed mightily.

The ultimate destruction of this company was unnecessary. We were victimized by a sleazy, alcoholic bank vice-president who (illegally) kept extending our credit line every two weeks by advancing just enough to meet net payroll but not enough to cover payroll taxes, while promising that a comprehensive refinancing package would be completed "any day now" - and asking for kickbacks. The corporation's second largest creditor was a Catholic Diocese, and we had secured their agreement to that refinancing plan, including providing a substantial amount of new operating capital, contingent on the bank's participation. Just about the time all this was to occur, unbeknownst to me at that time, the bank began a process of merging with a much bigger bank. Our bank's president decided to bury its worst loans and most questionable dealings. They renigged on all commitments to us overnight, made the veep we'd been dealing with disappear, and in the space of 48 hours, we went from daily communication to being unable to get a phone call returned. We also had two stockholders: one a vengeful ex-employee, the other an irate ex-client file actions against the company in bankruptcy court. I even know now that our attorney was "sleeping with the enemy"; literally; having sex with the ex-employee suing to derail the reorganization.

All of this was made worse by the simple fact that I had done the right things with this corporate rescue operation. In short, the operation was a success, but the patient was murdered before getting out of the recovery room.

As I read the book about Continental's turnaround, I'm reminded of just how much was done right at General, and just how wrong the outcome was.

This was as close as I'll ever come to building a big business. Since then, I've avoided having to deal with bankers, corporate attorneys, brokers, and other parasites, and I have no interest in operating in that environment. I also developed my distaste for having employees, and have kept my employee count to the barest of minimums in my businesses since then. For a number of years 8, then 6, then 1. Someday soon, none.

With 20/20 hindsight, it is possible to see that much was gained from this experience. I mastered every aspect of "information product development", I made many good contacts and friendships and alliances in the speaking world that continue today, I got great clarity about how I wanted to live my life and how I didn't, I became fully committed to applying my energies to a few things I do very well and to minimize my involvement in things I don't do very well, and I developed a nearly bullet-proof mental attitude. Overall, I view the experience as a necessary "zag" in the zig-zag progress toward today's success.

CHAPTER 29

Hey Dude, Where's My Car?

I have had two cars repossessed. In the same year.

The first time this occurs, you are surprised and dumfounded, even if months behind in payments as I was. I came out to a snow covered apartment complex to find an empty space where my car should be. I called the cops to report it stolen. The cop who arrived asked "Wouldn't happen to be behind in your car payments, wouldya?"

The second time, my Lincoln was parked right smack in front of The Self-Improvement Center where I was milling around with about thirty people waiting to go into the back room, to my seminar. The Center had floor to ceiling glass windows. When somebody yelled to me "Hey, somebody's stealing your car", all eyes turned to the car, and me racing out the door. This time I knew. The repo person, a woman, had the car started, window rolled almost entirely up, undoubtedly fearing a physical confrontation as I rushed to the car. With a big flourish, I got the last $50.00 bill in my pocket out and shoved it through the window to her, while quietly asking to be allowed to retrieve my briefcase and books from the back seat before she drove off. Which I did.

I walked in with my stuff in my arms and loudly explained that my car was off for a badly needed wash, wax and detailing. I told everybody "Next time you see it, you won't even recognize it."

I'm betting that woman's the first repo person ever to get a $50.00 tip.

Later, I called Carla, to get her to come pick me up. "Good news," I said, "I'm getting a new car."

CHAPTER 30

Chapter 11 And Chapter 7

I have had my corporations go bankrupt, and I have been through a personal bankruptcy as well. Sitting on a witness stand in bankruptcy court, being quizzed by attorneys for credit card companies, is the least amount of fun you can have in front of an audience.

I've never made a secret of this, so I've had quite a few very successful entrepreneurs tell me of their own past bankruptcies. These are the kind of war stories that, for the most part, you only share with others who've suffered the same tragedy.

Quite a few famous and successful people have gone through bankruptcy, too. Here's a very small sampling:

Politicians

Daniel Webster (U.S. Secretary Of State, 1841)

George McGovern (U.S. Senator, Presidential candidate, bed 'n breakfast owner, briefly)

Entrepreneurs

P.T. Barnum

David Buick (Founder, Buick Motorcars)

Walt Disney

William Durant (took control of Buick by, in part, forcing David Buick into bankruptcy. Started General Motors)

James Folger (Founder, Folgers Coffee)

Henry Fod William Fox (Founder, 20th Century Fox Film Corp.)

J. Heinz (without whom, no John Kerry For President)

Conrad Hilton

J.C. Penney

Roy Raymond (Founder, Victoria's Secret)

John Ringling (Ringling Brothers' Circus)

Charles Schwab (Andrew Carnegie's associate; Founder, Bethlehem Steel)

Sam Walton (Founder, Wal-Mart)

Celebrities

John Wayne

Morton Downey Jr.

Larry King

Jackie Mason

Pat Paulson

'Wolfman Jack'

M/C. Hammer

Merle Haggard

Wayne Newton

Kim Basinger

Jerry Lewis

Athletes

Dorothy Hamill (Ice-skating star)

Johnny Unitas

Danny White

Others Of Interest

Susan Powter ('Stop The Insanity' Infomercial Star)

Richard Bach (Author, 'Jonathan Livingston Seagull'- which sold 30 million copies)

L. Frank Baum, (Author, 'Wizard Of Oz')

Samuel Clemens, aka. Mark Twain

Al Lowry ('father' of get rich in real estate movement)

Frank Lloyd Wright

Alexander Bain (Inventor of the FAX machine)

George Washington

Gale Ferris (Inventor, the Ferris Wheel)

Charles Goodyear (Inventor, usable rubber)

Johann Gutenberg (Inventor, printing press)

Charles Stahlbrg (Inventor, alarm clock. Go ahead, enjoy a revenge smile.)

Bruce Vorhauer (Inventor, the contraceptive sponge - without whom a Seinfeld episode would not exist)

The fraternity to which I belong: those who've gone through one or more business failures and bankruptcies before creating a sustained success, and its neighboring fraternity: those who've gone bust after a success, some making another fortune all over again, others not.....these are very large fraternities spanning centuries, adding new members daily.

It's nothing to be proud of. In most cases, many others are harmed besides the bankrupt. Henry Ford had investors who lost a fortune in his first, failed car company, investors who must have snarled and spit and cursed every time a Model-T chugged past them on the road. I had some investors, who must have knashed their teeth, and maybe still do, with each visible success of mine that has occurred --- although several of the investors who lost every penny invested in my earliest business remain as Inner Circle Members today!

One of the most interesting lessons I took from bankruptcy is: *it ain't fatal.*

In fact, I became nearly fearless --- intelligently paranoid but not fearful --about losing money or even being wiped out as a result of discovering how readily replaceable money is, how generously forgiving the free enterprise system and marketplace is, how little the "stain" matters to anybody. When I lost half of everything I owned to the divorce only a few years ago, I can't recall even a moment of fear response. No "how will I ever replace all that" thoughts.

It's my belief that a lot of the entrepreneurs who go through this, and then go on to subsequent, enormous success, actually owe credit to the bankruptcy's removal of their fears about money. The bankruptcy recovery experience buys them a certain kind of confidence unobtainable from any other source.

Still, this fraternity never has a reunion party.

CHAPTER 31

He Doesn't Play Well With Others

I got in trouble in kindergarten. There were these large, hollow wood blocks you could build forts or other buildings large enough to crawl around in. Apparently I preferred these blocks to any of the other toys and activities, and I wasn't much into sharing. When another kid insisted on plopping himself down in the middle of my construction site, I took one of the blocks and hit him on the head, hard enough to knock him half unconscious, draw blood and produce a big, fat bruise.

I still don't play well with most other people.

There is only one trade/professional organization for professional speakers, the National Speakers Association. It was originally organized by Cavett Robert, who became a speaker after retiring from law -- he worked with Elliot Ness in prosecuting organized crime. When Cavett retired to Arizona, he invested in real estate and got rich. His entry to sales training was developing the sales presentations for in-home sales of burial insurance and cemetery plots, and he got rich again. Cavett was one of the warmest, most pleasant, most encouraging individuals to walk the planet, who loved speaking. I produced his audio products when I had General Cassette.

While the National Speakers Association gives out a Cavett Award each year, its relationship to Cavett pretty much stops there. It is an intensely political group, dominated by cliques and infighting and juvenile foolishness, mostly driven by people who are not doing well as speakers and get their sense of importance through bureaucratic bullying of others, having their butts kissed by people who buy the illusion that the thing has any importance or significance outside itself. Which it does not.

My first NSA experience was a real breakthrough, a terrific confidence builder. I have told the story often, and it's in my book about speaking, '*Big Mouth, Big Money.*' Suffice to say I went to my first NSA workshop after grinding out over $100,000.00 my first year, expecting to find people doing much better than I. While I found many who were far better speakers, I found hardly any earning six figures, and most clueless about effectively promoting themselves, let alone using speaking to fuel and build a real business. After my initial disappointment passed, my confidence soared. In fact, at the airport, waiting to board the flight home, I got into a conversation with another first-time attendee who'd been shocked by the lack of marketing and business know-how he'd encountered. He hired me on the spot to consult with him and make over his marketing materials. He was Buster Crabbe, originally 'Tarzan' and 'Buck Rogers' in the movies.

At one point in my NSA membership, I wound up filing suit against the association, and engaging in a nasty, ugly battle. The lawsuit was unfortunate. I was thrown out of NSA by its Ethics Committee, based on complaints by a disgruntled ex-employee and an unhappy stockholder of General Cassette, on the grounds that I represented myself as a "successful entrepreneur" while presiding over a company in Chapter 11 reorganization. This was, of course, utter bullshit. However I had made some enemies in NSA, notably a few very prominent members who owed General a lot of money when I acquired the company, who I pursued very aggressively for collection. So there was some ill will.

Just for the record, no General Cassette Corporation client was ever affected by its Chapter 11, or ultimately, its Chapter 13. Everybody got all their product, everybody got their master recordings, no one lost a penny. Furthermore, I was a 'successful entrepreneur' as well as a successful speaker at the same time General was playing out, as I always maintained separate businesses, and never made less than six figure personal income from those other interests. So there.

When I was refused right to be represented by an attorney or to have a court reporter to transcribe a record of the Ethics Committee's hearing, I refused to participate, so I was convicted in absentia and tossed out. At which point, I sued.

The association spent a small fortune defending itself, using a high-priced, multi-named, prestigious Phoenix law firm. I used my attorney, and did most of the work myself. At the first hearing, the judge told them they were fools, and ran risk of not only losing in court, but having their entire ethics procedure challenged and voided. He strongly suggested they settle. We agreed not to disclose the financial nature of that settlement, so I won't. But I was reinstated, and if you look in an NSA Directory you'll see me listed as a member since 1978, with no interruption.

There's a pompous little twit who was a Board Member at that time, who kept this silly thing moving forward all the way through interrogatories and depositions to courtroom. When I was speaking on the 'Success' tour, he started greeting me at NSA functions as if we were buddies. At one point actually asking me how to get on the tour. If he happens to read this, let me tell you something: every time you walk up to me and smile and do the hale-and-hearty routine, I walk away thinking about what a piece of crap you are and privately laughing at you. Oh, and there was a discussion about you getting an infomercial deal from a client of mine. I made sure I killed it.

Does that seem mean-spirited? It is.

CHAPTER 32

The Case Of The Disappearing Real Estate Speculator

I used to love Perry Mason novels by Earle Stanley Gardner, and they all had titles like this Chapter's. The Case Of The Long, Lovely Legs. The Case Of The Lady In The Red Dress. The Case Of The Midnight Intruder. That sort of thing. Well, I have one of my own. The Case Of The Disappearing Real Estate Speculator.

One day I had a long-time friend and off-and-on business associate call and ask me to meet him for lunch. At lunch, he told me an obviously cockamamie story about why he needed $20,000.00 for just a few days. Although he was involved in real estate speculation, he did not use that to justify his request. While I believed his story to be false, I chose not to embarrass him by pressing him. I agreed to help, and gave him the $20,000.00.

Two days later, I learned that he was gone. I mean: *intentionally* disappeared, he and his wife. House stripped and empty, nothing left but trash and the business card of the company that apparently came and bought all the household goods for cash on the spot. BMW and Jeep, gone. At his company, large sums drained from the bank accounts, checks bouncing, banks calling, staff bewildered.

Weeks later, a clue: the finance company linked to the Jeep had a guy calling anybody who had known him, and he let slip that they had found some bounced checks passed at Price Club locations in California near the Mexican border.

This guy and I had been very good friends, and had been through a lot together. We owned a multi-level marketing company, a cosmetics company, and a mail-order awards and trophy business together. He and his wife and Carla and I vacationed together. I'd brought him in to the SuccessTrak seminar business I created, where he'd made quite a bit of money. His gig running the real estate company came about, in part, through my introduction. I have never heard a peep out of him since the $20,000.00 lunch. I suppose I never will.

You've probably never thought about it, but there are tens of thousands of people who intentionally disappear each and every year. Some successfully establish new identities and secretly live out their lives, some half a world away, some only a few towns from where they lived. Most get caught or give up and surface. Some of these people are involved in attempted insurance fraud or organized crime or whatever. Some disappear into the Federal Witness Protection Program. But most are just unhappy spouses or people diagnosed with fatal diseases or embezzlers, etc., who, for their own reasons, walk away from their lives. There are even books written about how to do all this. I've never known anybody who did it. You probably haven't either. Now I do.

This fellow and his wife lived in a very nice home, drove nice cars, lived well, and he had excellent sales ability, so he was able to make a good income via any number of options. In years immediately preceding his abrupt disappearance, he'd been working at establishing himself in community affairs. He was on the boards of two local charities, ran one's annual telethon, active in a political party, and active in helping its candidates raise funds.

Unknown to most but known to me, they tended to live far beyond their income, juggling credit, but this was nothing new. He was running a real estate syndication business that constantly flirted with illegalities - in fact, its former CEO was serving five years in a federal "white collar" prison - and, often, some of its investors were unhappy and filing lawsuits. But again, this was nothing new. If something related to that business sparked his run, it seems that he overestimated the severity of the developing difficulties as, in the aftermath of his disappearance, no investigatory agencies of any kind came looking for him. So I can only speculate why he ran. I do not know.

His wife eventually surfaced. She tells of being unable to handle the separation from her family, the pressure of life on the run, underground, and of running away from him in Mexico. She claims she does not know why he suddenly engineered their disappearance and does not know where he is or where he might have gone after she left him.

Their marriage had long been volatile. A mutual acquaintance speculated that, somewhere in a Mexican desert, she killed him and left him as vulture food. She has previously demonstrated an truly astounding ability to "snap" under stress and then act as if nothing had happened; a couple years earlier, at a time when they were under extreme financial duress and were keeping a failing business breathing by "kiting" checks between banks, one day, she drove over to the bank branch nearest her home, walked in with a toy gun in full view of the security cameras, held up the bank, then drove home. She then acted as if nothing unusual had occurred. The FBI agents told her husband they'd never dealt with a bank robber quite like her. So the idea that she might have murdered her husband in his sleep, methodically cut him up in pieces, and buried the parts in the desert is not impossible to imagine.

In any case, she returned, served some jail time for violating her parole, went home to her parents in California, and recently, married. We do not talk or visit. We exchange Christmas cards.

He has never been seen or heard from again. The only person anybody is aware of hunting for him, from the car finance company, has given up. The Jeep they drove into Mexico has never been recovered. No one he knew has admitted having any contact with him. I certainly have not.

My best guess, from various conversations, and from his wife's speculation, is that he put together no more than $150,000.00 in cash when he left. $200,000.00 at the absolute most. Even in someplace like Mexico, the interest on that sum, if somehow legally invested, would not be enough to live on. If eating up the principal, maybe you could buy three or four years before being out of money. Maybe he had or found a way to make money with the money. Again, I can only guess. Maybe he is sitting under a thatched umbrella on a beach in some obscure village somewhere in Mexico or Costa Rica or wherever, sipping a margarita, watching the sun set into the ocean, at peace with himself. Maybe he has become a day-laborer or a bartender. Maybe he has created a new identity and is selling time shares somewhere. Maybe he has become a criminal or con artist, preying on tourists or widows. Maybe his skeleton is lying out in the desert, the bones picked clean by the vultures, bleached white by the wind.

It is oddly unsettling to know someone so well and have them deliberately disappear. With each passing year, I think about this less, less often. Occasionally somebody asks about him. Or recently, while cleaning out some boxes in the garage, I found old photographs.

I have no reason to think I'll ever know the answer to his self-created mystery. It is unsettling because, every once in a while, I can't help fantasizing about the best case scenario. There is the tiny temptation: what would it be like to suddenly pile up all the money I could get my hands on and disappear, leaving every stress, every responsibility, every obligation, every relationship, every routine behind, to create a whole new existence from scratch, possibly in a distant sundrenched, oceanside locale. It is unsettling because, every once in a while, I can't help but speculate about the worst case scenario.

CHAPTER 33

Inside The Infomercial Business

For several years, my front license plate said HOLLYWOOD, because "television" had become such a big part of my business life. Not real television. Infomercials. Those annoying half-hour fake shows that sell you stuff late at night, when your resistance is low. It's amazing how sensible that food dehydrator or folding chair that turns flab to rockhard abs looks at 2:00 A.M.

Actually, there is no infomercial business. This is a commonly made mistake; confusing a 'media' with a 'business.' Similarly, the Internet is not a business. Even speaking isn't a business. These things are 'media' which can be used to develop businesses. You ought to lock this idea in, because it's very important business advice. Confusing 'a business' with 'a media' is dangerous. I'd add, by the way, that very few people actually understand what business they are really in.

Anyway, I started working with infomercials, as I started many things in my life, by accident. After completing the sale of General Cassette's manufacturing operations to Bill Guthy, for his company, Cassette Productions Unlimited, he invited me to take a look at his first infomercial, *Think And Grow Rich,* which had been airing successfully but was petering out. Cost per sale was creeping up, and it was obvious the show would soon cross the line from profitable to unprofitable. I did nothing to the show itself but suggested changes to the product and offer. I created the new bonus reports to be added to and emphasized in the offer, rewrote the

CTA (call to action) and the show enjoyed another 18 months or so of profitable life. And I was in demand as a seer.

Guthy-Renker's next project was *Personal Power*, the first of a series of Tony Robbins infomercials. The first was hosted by Fran Tarkenton, who had hosted *Think And Grow Rich*. My contributions to *Personal Power* were small yet significant.

I continued working with Guthy-Renker for 20 years. The biggest thing probably pushing them into their acne product field. That began with a nonGuthy-Renker project, rewriting and co-producing a show for a product called 'Acne-Statin', for its owner, Dr. Atitida Karr. I'm not going to personally offer any opinions about Dr. Karr. I will tell you, all you need do is mention her in a room populated by writers, producers and others in the infomercial field, and somebody will grab their head and start moaning. She has a reputation. She is generally regarded as difficult, nasty, rude, impossible. Many say: insane. I am not saying any of those things, only reporting what others say. The show we shot featured soap star Gloria Loring as host. Gloria also has a reputation as difficult, easily annoyed, and I found that to be true, but she's also a pro, and we got along okay. In fact, I later hired her to host another show I produced. But Gloria and Dr. Karr got along so well Gloria stormed off the set and I had to talk her down out of the parking lot, back to work. Soon, Karr and Gloria wouldn't even stay in the same room with each other, so we had to shoot their interview in two separate parts, then put their heads in two boxes on the screen, sort of like two politicians being interviewed on a Sunday morning news show, each in a different city. It was an ugly, unpleasant , tense, long day, one of the three worst I've ever experienced on a shoot.

Dr. Karr has been at war with the FDA and FTC for decades. One of her earliest Acne Statin commercials led to precedent law, where celebrity hosts could be sued and prosecuted for claims made in commercials in which they appeared. This involved Dick Clark.

Partly thanks to my work on this project, I became convinced that the acne product category was an enormous opportunity. There are huge numbers of adult acne sufferers, not just teen-agers. Most treatments don't work. If you supply one that does, it is the next best continuity product, behind cocaine. Because, if the person stops using the glop, the acne returns. It later took me a couple years of nagging and prodding and pushing to get Guthy-Renker interested in this category. The result is the Pro-Active business, generating hundreds of millions of dollars a year. I am very sorry to say I failed to approach this entrepreneurially, to get equity. Had I handled this differently, I might very well be worth 50-million dollars as a result.

As an aside, there is an equivalent opportunity in another product category which I've repeatedly suggested to Guthy-Renker but, for various reasons, they've chosen to ignore. It could easily be a 100-million to 200-million dollar business, fueled by infomercials. It would take a $300,000.00 to $500,000.00 roll of the dice to determine if I'm right and possibly launch the business. I have no interest playing with my chips nor in running the business, but I could be interested in consulting --- for considerably more than I received from Pro-Active. You know where to find me.

One of the shows I did, that I was very proud of, even though it was a very modest base hit, was 'The Mental Bank Breakthrough' with Florence Henderson and her husband, hypno-therapist Dr. John Kappas. I later hired Florence to host another show for a client, too. And she is the best, most talented, most professional, most cooperative celebrity I've ever worked with. The Mental Bank show, selling a self-improvement product of that title, was the third or fourth reincarnation of the product and prior infomercials. I wrote the script, and controlled every aspect of the show's production, working with a very good producer, Stan Jacobs. And I put some unusual and interesting elements in the show. An opening involving a giant bank vault that Florence walked out of, making the bank analogy visual. I had Florence holding a real, live baby as she delivered a little monologue about us being born with only two fears, then learning all others. There's a funny, inside story about the baby I'm going to leave out here. In the second take of this, the baby suddenly reached up, grabbed onto Flo's big gold hoop earing and yanked down with all its weight and strength. To her credit, the surprise and pain never showed on her face, her delivery never wavered. That's a pro.

Unfortunately, Florence switched agents, and the last time I attempted hiring her for a project, the agent and I had a major conflict. One of the challenges of working with celebrities is often their agents, who some-times speak for them, turn down offers they celebrity would accept, even outright lie to the celebrity. I've dealt with my share of lying, thieving and incompetent agents and lawyers who are not serving their celebrity clients well at all.

I also did a lot of the work on a Guthy-Renker show done with Entre-preneur Magazine, for a product called 'The Be Your Own Boss System', including me, Tony Robbins, Fran Tarkenton and the magazine's writers as authors. For a variety of reasons, this was a difficult project, there was a lot of three-way conflict between the folks at Entrepreneur, Guthy-Renker and Tony, and I was wedged in the middle. I also had more of a temper than I do now. I no longer even recall the details, but I know that Entre-preneur Magazine's editor, Rieva Lesonsky, still bears a grudge against me dating back to this fiasco. It's entirely one way.

Ironically, my biggest success was the cheapest infomercial I ever produced. There's a very big marketing lesson in this, and I'll tell you the lesson in advance of the story. Lesson: it is all about the pitch, the proposition. When you have a really terrific pitch and can present it with people who are authentic and believable, you don't need celebrities, beautiful settings, Hollywood production values, or other trappings.

The show was a lead generation show, for the Gold By The Inch business opportunity, which I wrote, produced and controlled from a to z, from start to finish. The first version was produced for under $15,000.00 at a time when the average infomercial budget was ten times that much. Frankly, it looked it. In fact, we later re-shot the exact same show with slightly better lighting, sound and set, to get it on a couple national cable networks that refused to air the ugly one.

The Gold By The Inch infomercial aired non-stop for eight years, a record for this type of infomercial that still stands today. It made the client rich, able to retire.

I've had lots of interesting experiences both consulting in this industry and producing shows. I went to Switzerland to shoot testimonials for a weight loss show --- and, incidentally, getting people to perform well, delivering their testimonials to the camera is a very difficult "art" that very few people are any good at, and too many clients take for granted. I've worked on a show for a company owned by the same movie production company that produced all the James Bond movies with Sean Connery. I've worked with countless celebrities, minor and major. Fun, but also the most difficult work I've ever done in marketing. Getting one of these things written, rehearsed, filmed, edited and made to work is extraordinarily complex and time-consuming, and at best, a longshot proposition. It is far easier to put words onto sheets of paper.

One opportunity missed or bungled by a lot of marketers is the use of an infomercial-formatted video that sells, to be used in direct-mail. A lot of companies make video brochures but fail to use one of the proven infomercial formats. What they don't understand is that TV is TV. When the person puts in the video tape or DVD and turns on the TV, their brain expects to see certain things presented in a certain way on TV. Their attention is held or lost depending on those expectations being met. A few years ago, I produced such a video for Paul Johnston, for his Shed Shop business, that builds and installs upscale backyard sheds. It is not a video about sheds, but a video about the people who own them, the different ways they use them, their feelings about them. It has a format like a TV show, with anchor set, host, and man-in-the-field reporting. And it has proven very, very, very effective.

RESOURCE!

I am available to consult or turn-key produce videos that sell or infomercials, but there's no point contacting me unless you are committed to a substantial investment. You can FAX 602-269-3113 with your inquiry.

CHAPTER 34

On The Road Again, I Just Can't Wait To Get On The Road Again

If ever there was a two word lie, it is "hospitality industry."

I've always flown first class. Even at age 20. When I first started flying on business, it was coffee, tea or me. Now it's a strip search and a snarl.

I remember having eight businessmen and four stewardesses in first class. On long flights, playing cards and flirting with the stewardesses. Having a good meal served on real plates with real silverware. Never an argument about carry-on luggage.

I went home with a stew once, in Chicago. She had her entire cupboard stocked with mini-bottles. Swizzle sticks, cocktail napkins, dishes, glassware, everything purloined from the planes.

It was a different, better time.

I've grown to passionately *hate* travel, and these days have to fight physical nausea when driving to the airport. I resent putting on my cheap plastic travel belt, carrying no pens, no money clip, and then taking off my cowboy boots in order to pass through the completely ineffectual security line. I hate being herded like cattle. I hate the trained liars who work for the airlines. I hate everything about it.

Hotels aren't much better.

For many years, I spent nearly as much time on the road as I did at home. I honestly believe it has shortened my life by at least ten years. No one who has-n't lived on the road can possibly understand the physical and psychological toll it forcibly extracts. The experience eroded my already limited intimacy skills, perfected my aloneness skills. The people who stay home actually think you're out there living the high life while they toil in a dark cave. When you call the office or call home, you can hear it in their voices, the irritation, the certainty you are being pampered, enjoying gourmet room service, fluffy pillows, foot massages by nubile servants, while they are left to cope with endless problems and irritations.

Well, for the record.....for many years, I couldn't go to sleep without hearing "put your tray in its upright position." One shoulder was 4" lower than the other from hauling the Hartman. I ate my salads last, so the other food might still be at least lukewarm after the room service waiter apparently wandered aimlessly through the hotel, hopelessly lost between kitchen and my room. I caught colds and flu frequently, inhaling recirculated airplane toxic air. I steamed shirts in showers, washed socks in sinks, paid to watch movies I had no interest in, slept next to my hanging bag, hauled my exhausted ass out of bed at 4:00 or 5:00 AM to go to airports, shuffled into hotel lobbies late at night after delayed flights, stood in pouring rain and freezing cold waiting for airport shuttle buses, ate nachos with melted Cheesewiz on them, argued and battled with airline and hotel sadists, waited for limo drivers who never showed up, sat in cabs with no air conditioning smelling of vomit stuck in traffic -- oh the glamour of it all!

One day, I was flying from Phoenix to Seattle to speak on a SUCCESS Event. Ben or Jerry, I forget which, of Ben & Jerry's Ice Cream was flying with me, for the same reason. We were to leave at 3:00 P.M. I planned on having a pleasant dinner with friends, getting a good night's sleep, and getting in a productive day writing before speaking the following afternoon. Our first America Worst plane had not one but two mechanical problems for which there were no parts. After being herded on and sitting on the runway for two hours, we returned to the gate to be herded off, and hang around listening to lies for another hour, then board another aircraft, which also had a mechanical. We finally departed on a third plane at 9:30 PM. On the flight I had the incredible pleasure of being lectured on the evils of capitalism by Ben or Jerry, when he wasn't eating his airplane meal with his bare hands. Even the gravy.

This sort of incident was not abnormal.

I decided to cut way, way, way back on my travel a few years before the 9-11 attack on America. I quit the SUCCESS tour, sharply cut back on other speaking, and nearly stopped going to consulting clients, instead requiring them to travel to me. These moves were fortuitous, given the post 9-11 travel environment. I cannot even conceive of maintaining my travel schedule of the 1990's today. It would be fatal, or I'd be jailed for murder.

If you want to get me to do anything these days, it's a good idea to start by putting it in Cleveland, Ohio.

The road warrior has my admiration and sympathy.

I cannot begin to tell you how happy and grateful I am that my resignation from their ranks has worked out so well.

A Hotel Is A Place

A hotel is a place where you will find a phone on the bedside table and a second phone in the bathroom ----but none on the desk.

A hotel is a place where you get teeny, tiny little soaps. One for your face, one for each armpit, one for your privates, one for your butt, and one for your feet. If you carry an adult sized bar of soap with you, as I've done, and use none of the little soaps, the maid will still leave a second pile of little soaps. I imagine if you stayed for a month and never used even one of those tiny little soaps, the maid would keep pilling them up, until the pyramid of little soaps blocked the entire shower.

A hotel is a place where it costs $47.86 a minute to make a phone call.

A hotel is a place where the bed is two feet shorter than your bed at home.

A hotel is a place where your free copy of USA TODAY put outside your door results in a $2.99 delivery charge on your bill.

A hotel is a place where there are five front desk clerks working during the slow mid-day time, one working at check-in rush hour at 6:00 PM.

A hotel is a place where there's a 5-foot high shower head.

A hotel is a place where all meeting rooms are designed and built by people who have never put on a meeting in their lives.

A hotel is a place where the most expensive suite may be located next to the elevators, may be located at the furthest end of the hall 12.6 miles away from the elevators, but will never be in a really convenient, quiet spot.

A Holiday Inn is a place where...

The remote control is screwed to the table.

The restaurant closes at 10 P.M.

The towels are see-through.

Room service food is covered with saran wrap. Which melts onto the food.

There's nothing anywhere in the world quite like Holiday Inn room service nachos. Stale chips with hot cheez-whiz and melted saran wrap.

Where there is one local, desperate, drunken housewife at the bar on weeknights who will, by closing, go to the room of one of the desperate, drunken traveling salesmen. On average, your odds in this joyless lottery are one in nine. In the small trowns, where the Holiday Inn is at the freeway exit, there may be a few secretaries or dental assistants in pairs or groups, too. One in four of them will also wind up with one of the traveling salesmen. The lighting in the lounge is very, very dim. For good reason.

The room will likely be heated and cooled by a separate in-room unit, not central air. This unit can make the room either too hot or too cold, with the added appeal of rackety noise.

CHAPTER 35

Being A Published Author

I wanted to be a writer for as long as I can remember.

I *love* books. I love their binding, their covers, their smell. I love seeing them on shelves. Having them around me in stacks. Going to a bookstore to find new ones. Re-reading old ones.

If you accept premises of Psycho-Cybernetics , then you can say that a magnet was implanted and ingrained in me from earliest memories, to be involved with books. I gravitated to it every way I could.

I started writing, seriously, not casually, very young. My first and only job was as a sales rep for a book publisher - a job I was absolutely determined to get when I saw it advertised. In a way, at General Cassette Corporation, I was a publisher, although of audio rather than written product. I've wound up writing a veritable mountain of material and been fortunate to develop a loyal audience. Other non-fiction business authors hit higher spots on bestseller lists, but few enjoy my kind of sustained success and longevity. I've had multiple books on bookstore shelves without interruption since 1991.

When I left my first and only job at Price/Stern/Sloan, I very seriously thought about getting myself a bookstore, and I've come close on several occasions. When I opened the retail Self-Improvement Center in Phoenix in 1978, I almost bought an existent bookstore downtown , adjacent to the San Marcos Hotel. The only thing that stopped that deal was their lack of a customer mailing list. But - other than the money - I would be quite happy owning a little neighborhood bookstore.

I'm grateful to my parents for getting me into reading from the git-go. I had every Seuss book, then every Hardy Boys book. We went to the library once a week, every week to get books. I got books as gifts. Our house was full of books. My mother was a voracious reader her entire life, with a broad variety of interests, fiction and non-fiction. Dad was a great reader as well, although more narrow in interests. My homes have always been full of books and I'd rather spend two hours filling a cart at a Barnes & Noble than just about any other entertainment. My current home has an upstairs reading room where my personal library resides, a large downstairs library just for business books, a reading table in the hall between living room and master suite for the readingin-progress books, and, frankly, there are a dozen or so cartons of books still waiting to be unpacked in my garage, shipped from Phoenix now 3 years ago. And I belong to two book clubs, buy books everywhere I go. I just bought a $17,000.00 table, hand-carved to look as if constructed of books.

I'm a self-taught speed reader. Actually, I don't remember ever learning it at all. I just became a speed reader. Last time tested, with 80%+ comprehension. As I've gotten older, I've gotten a tick slower, but more significantly I can't keep focused reading for extended periods of time as I once did. Ten years ago, I'd get on a three hour flight, read three novels, and often give them to the stews as I left. Now I can read for 40 minutes or so but then I need a nap.

I think you need to read a lot.

I am dismayed that a lot of entrepreneurs I know don't read much. I just can't imagine how you can stay current, stay motivated, stay mentally vibrant without reading a lot.

The Virtue Of Bookselling

My working life has mostly been devoted to selling information --- in the form of books, recordings, other media. I believe this is a virtuous profession. When you sell someone a book, you don't merely sell them a half-pound of paper and ink and glue. You sell them a doorway to a different world, or at least a different world view. You sell them opportunity. Inspiration. Sometimes consolation and comforting. Sometimes reassurance. Hope and encouragement. You help them develop their own life philosophy. You cause them to question and reconsider some of their beliefs, reaffirm others. You make them laugh, cry, feel. You introduce them to people, you take them to places they might otherwise never meet or visit.

Mark Twain said any man who writes but for money is a blockhead and, basically, I agree. While I have created, assembled and sold information intended to be useful and valuable to people, I would not have produced a page of it, if not for profit. I am a devout capitalist. Ironically, writing this book is the exception. There was no economic need to do it, no publisher for it, and it won't directly produce much money. This is the first thing I've ever written solely because I had things I wanted to commit to pages.

I have made authors and information purveyors out of hundreds of people who, before meeting me, never dreamt of writing anything, never conceived of being in the information business. Many of these people have followed my example, and, in their own fields, positive influenced thousands, tens of thousands, even hundreds of thousands of people. Our combined influence has been enormous, and I am very proud of that.

What's It Like, Being A Semi-Famous Author?

A lot of people dream of being published. As I did.

In truth, it ain't all it's made out to be.

Not much is.

In the unremarkable movie 'Down With Love', Renee Zwellwegger plays the author of a book bearing the movie's title. When it is released, her agent drags her to a New York bookstore, gushing with enthusiasm, so Renee can see her book in the store. It's not in the window. It's not in the bestsellers. The agent leads Renee through the store maze, to a rear section, to the relationship books section, where way up on a high shelf, one copy is visible spine out. Dismayed, Renee says: "But there's only one."

The agent brightly, happily, enthusiastically says: 'But here you are, on the shelf, right here in Doubleday Bookstore."

Renee says "But if someone buys it, there'll be none."

To which the agent bravely says "There's one copy across the street at Bretanos too."

Well, that's the reality of being a published author. There's one. If someone buys it, there'll be none.

I have a similar, true life story. In an airport bookstore, when a guy comes in and buys the three copies of one of my books, one copy of the other. And then there were none.

The book publishing industry is possibly the most dysfunctional, idiotically managed, screwed up industry on the planet, and the distribution side of the business is the worst. It's actually amazing anybody of any stature is willing to invest their energy in writing books, because the authors are so badly abused by both publishers and booksellers. Selling books through this system is like trying to push a strand of spaghetti through a tiny pinhole in a sopping wet piece of plywood in the dark - with three nitwits on the other side pushing back.

So what is it like, being a semi-famous author? Frustrating as hell, that's what it's like.

My Writing Life

I was first published in 1972, when a junior in high school. I sold a manuscript to Kirkley Press, for a flat $500.00. I thought that was a very good deal. That company published little motivational booklets that companies bought in quantity, to use as paycheck stuffers. About ten years ago I checked in with the publisher and was told that sales had topped three million copies.

My first book published by a 'real' publisher was *Ultimate Sales Letter* in 1991, by Adams. They also published *Ultimate Marketing Plan* in 1993. New editions of these books are being published by Adams in 2006, in conjunction with my own national Ultimate Marketing Plan/Ultimate Sales Letter Contest, where you can earn some terrific prizes. Information will be posted online beginning in December 2005, at www.ultimate-sales-letter-contest.com, or via www.dankennedy.com.

My three NO B.S. books were first published by a Canadian book publisher, Self-Counsel. I approached them, met the President, Diana Douglass, pitched her and did the deal on the convention floor at ABA.

And she was very entrepreneurial and creative and cooperative. If I had known then what I know now, I could have gotten more done with them,. But it was a good relationship. Most recently, I re-wrote all three NO BS books for Entrepreneur Press, the book publishing arm of Entrepreneur Magazine. The editor there, Jere Calmes, was the editor at Adams in the 90's. He, and their marketing director, Leanne Harvey, really tried to "get it" and "get me" and cooperated as best they could with the efforts I pulled together to promote the books. I am doing two more NO B.S. books for them, for January 2006 publication. You can access info about all the NO B.S. books at www.nobsbooks.com.

I have also self-published a lot of books, including *The Ultimate Success Secret* and *Why Do I Always Have To Sit Next To The Farting Cat?*

I write almost every single day, for at least an hour a day, for my own books, other information products and newsletters. I can't recall ever having 'writers' block', although I have a square wood paperweight with a drawing of the brain on it that says "Writer's Block." The trick to writing is: to write.

Can I Have Your Autograph?

One of the things people think is cool about being an author, or, for that matter, a speaker is getting asked for autographs.

I've probably signed about 30,000 books in my lifetime. By comparison, Colin Powell told me he signed over 100,000 books in 90 days, on his book tour. People lined up and got 30 seconds of quality personal time.

At the old SuccessTrak Seminars for chiropractors and dentists, I gave everybody a copy of my *Money/Business/Success* book, wrote their one year goal in it and signed them. People do come up to me at events, even occasionally in airports or restaurants, books in hand to get an autograph, and I appreciate it. I do not appreciate the occasional super-cheapskate at a seminar who brings up a blank sheet of paper for an autograph. Just for the record, I hate doing anything free. Even signing my autograph.

I have signed things other than books. I've signed covers of my products, the cloth bags that *Magnetic Marketing* was packaged in, T-shirts with our logos on them, and once - alas, only once - a young woman's bare breasts. She said "You're a rock star to me" and pulled up her shirt. Revealing a very nice pair of breasts indeed.

I wrote "My eternal gratitude" on one and signed the other.

UPDATE!

In 2018, I passed the benchmark of one million copies of my books sold, all titles, all editions, domestic and foreign, combined. And titles snared several high positions including #1 on Amazon bestseller lists. Over years, the books have gotten top list spots or other recognition in BusinessWeek, INC., SUCCESS, USA TODAY. The review I like best is from Rich Karlgaard, now Publisher at Forbes, years ago, when he compared my writing in the No B.S. books to the great novelist Tom Wolfe's.

I'm not done. In 2019, in the NO BS series, a new 3rd edition of the *No B.S. Guide to Marketing to the Affluent* is being released by Entrepreneur, and a new book, *ALMOST ALCHEMY: How Any Business Can Make More With Fewer & Less*, by ForbesBooks. There will probably be several more to follow, before I finally, completely retire.

All titles currently in print can be found at Amazon or BN.com.

CHAPTER 36

Thoughts About Books

"A man's reading program should be as carefully planned as his daily diet, for that too is food, without which he cannot grow mentally."
— *Andrew Carnegie*

There is a lot in Carnegie's statement. First, to credibilize Carnegie, I'll remind you he came here an immigrant from Scotland and became one of our greatest industrialists, by many accounts, America's first billionaire. He was a champion of practical education. In his later, philanthropic years, he provided funding to Carnegie-Mellon University, and our public library system. His greatest contribution to education, in my opinion, was sending Napoleon Hill on his 20 year research mission that birthed the famous book *'Think And Grow Rich'* and other works.

In Carnegie's quote above, the first thing to note is the words "reading program".

This suggests that you actually have a commitment to a planned reading program. I'm certain few people do. Most read at random, if or when they read at all. I budget time to read, I am typically reading three to five books at a time, taking notes or, in some cases, tearing out pages to keep and discarding the bulk. I read the new book release information in *Publishers Weekly* and the Harrison's *Radio/TV Interview Report,* to spot new books to read. I visit and browse a big Barnes & Noble at least once a month. I read on several "tracks." I read business, marketing and self-improvement books predominately to extract fodder for my own writing, speaking and coaching, as well as for personal benefit. I read biographies and autobiographies of both historical and contemporary people worthy of study -- from Donald Trump to Dolly Parton - predominately for personal benefit, but also for ideas and anecdotes to share with my readers, audiences and clients. I re-read books in my own library to strengthen my understanding of philosophies and ideas I consider especially important and meaningful. Finally, I read fiction for entertainment and relaxation, but also for dialogue and character studies and ideas I might use in copywriting work. On average, I read one new book every week. I used to read two or three a week, when I traveled more. I also read a lot of magazines. Point is, I do have a "reading program." I do plan it carefully.

Two more words from Carnegie's statement: "grow mentally." This presumes people intend to grow mentally, and do grow mentally. Again, sadly, only a small percentage do. Most people stopped deliberately growing mentally when they graduated high school or college. Sure, there's accidental growth, unavoidable growth produced by experience, or forced learning, such as that mandated by taking a new job, or acquiring new technology. But I'm talking about volunteering, taking iniative, and making strategic choices.

I like to ask entrepreneurs what they know today that they didn't know yesterday or last week or last month about their craft, their business, their industry, their competitors, their customers.

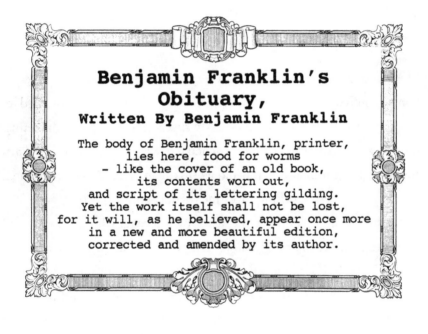

Benjamin Franklin's Obituary,
Written By Benjamin Franklin

The body of Benjamin Franklin, printer,
lies here, food for worms
– like the cover of an old book,
its contents worn out,
and script of its lettering gilding.
Yet the work itself shall not be lost,
for it will, as he believed, appear once more
in a new and more beautiful edition,
corrected and amended by its author.

CHAPTER 37

Intellectual Equity

I t is true that **just one great sales letter - or its equivalent - can support you in grand style for life.** I've written many such sales letters, ads, speeches or infomercial scripts for myself or clients, each producing at least a million to millions of dollars.

My record with speeches that sell is very good. The SuccessTrak presentations I crafted, one for myself, one for Foster Hibbard, combined to produce over seven million dollars. My speech for 'Magnetic Marketing' supported me for ten years, directly generated over eighteen million dollars, and brought customers into the fold worth much more. A speech I created recently, for a person selling investment education to doctors, generated $400,000.00 the first time it was used, by a speaker who had never sold from the front of the room before. A new presentation I developed for use by Tracy Tolleson, for selling an expensive program to small groups, has, as of this writing, been used twice, closed 12 of 13, and produced $240,000.00. I have created at least eighteen different platform selling presentations that have produced millions of dollars for their owners. And, actually, one of the smartest things to do, to hire me to do, is to re-engineer and improve a platform selling presentation, although, ironically, I've been retained to do this only about a dozen times compared to being hired hundreds and hundreds of times to write ads and sales letters.

In other media, I've had even more such successes - literally too many to catalog here. Sales letters I've written for clients including Craig Forte, Craig Proctor, Joe Polish, to name a few, have had lives of ten years and longer. Many more, for many more clients, have been for short-term projects and had briefer lives, but brought in hundreds of thousands to millions of dollars. One of the full-page ads I wrote for a client is in its 7th year of continuous use. A dozen or so have had 5 year life spans. The TV infomercial I wrote and produced for Gold By The Inch holds the longevity record in its category of 8 years, producing millions. For my own purposes, I've written more than 50 sales letters that have each been worth hundreds of thousands of dollars. A couple had continuous use for five to twelve years.

At least fifty different information marketers, each to a niche of their own, now possess a "bank" of sales copy they recycle, rotate, mix 'n match in their ads, sales letters and web sites, to provide themselves with 7-figure incomes each year.

This all leads up to a very important business and wealth secret:

The real value or equity in any business is not in the product, products, service, services , or skill or skills of the professional. None of those things have any value without the sales copy used in media that attracts, retains and optimizes the value of customers.

This is especially true in the information business, yet possibly less understood by most authors, speakers, educators and artists, than by anyone else. What's viewed as intellectual equity by such people - the book, the play, the course, the speech - actually has negligible if any value independent of its marketing.

I have purchased two different famous authors' entire bodies of work and all rights to it for peanuts, once there was no marketing attached to it. If I had the ambition, there are two others' available at the moment I know of. These people, their heirs, their families all thought there was enormous equity and value in these intellectual properties. They were all wrong. There are rare intellectual properties that have lasting marketplace value without marketing, notably including literary classics kept alive by the academic world, such as Shakespeare, Hemingway. But in percentage terms, these represent a fraction of a fraction of a fraction of 1% of all the literary works ever published. Not a good bet, as a strategy. **The only sane business or wealth strategy will be based on an understanding that there is no value in the 'thing'; the value is in the process devised for successfully selling the 'thing.'**

I cannot describe how fortunate I am, and how grateful I am, to have been sales and marketing oriented from childhood, and to have come to this understanding early.

Most people think the Ford family wealth is based on Henry Ford's Model-T, and more important, his assembly line that made it possible to manufacture an automobile affordable by the masses. Actually, the assembly line would have been completely worthless without the invention of the franchised dealership system, to get cars advertised, demonstrated and sold to the masses. Which is more important, Ford's chicken or Ford's egg? The egg.

My loved sport of harness racing will be extinct in the not too distant future thanks to stubborn ignorance about this reality by all the involved parties. While the breeders have foolishly focused on breeding faster (and more fragile) horses, the horsemen focused on better training techniques and high tech equipment, and track managements focused on making up for declining revenues from live attendance with simulcast and slot machines, *nobody* has focused on developing a successful strategy for selling the sport to the public. They have a fine chicken. But no egg.

In my years in consulting with authors, speakers and publishers, I have seen countless and I do mean countless books, courses, newsletters and other intellectual properties in which enormous talent, time, energy, blood, sweat and tears, and money, was invested, lying dead, covered with the dust of dashed dreams, because their creators thought the thing itself represented equity and value. Consider something recent like the controversial movie produced, funded and brought to the market by Mel Gibson, 'Passion Of The Christ.' To the surprise of the Hollywood elite, it made hundreds of millions of dollars and was a blockbuster success. However, the movie itself would have had zero value without Mel's savvy, behind the scenes marketing strategy directed at evangelical churches, without his clever stimulus of massive publicity and manufactured controversy by leaking advance information about the movie to influential religious leaders certain to protest it. Mel created a "banned in Boston" atmosphere for his movie, knowing that whatever is banned, people are eager, even desperate to see. The equity here was in the marketing, not in the film.

Unless and until you get a firm grip on this reality, you'll find it very, very difficult to get rich. Except by the slowest of means, the millionaire-next-door grind, as user and implementor of others' intellectual equities. Most authors, artists, publishers, inventors and other creative types are most severely handicapped in their belief in intellectual equity existent in their 'things' rather than the marketing of their 'things.'

The most valuable asset is the 'thing' that sells - be that ad, sales letter, infomercial, speech, seminar, web site, publicity. The value in all other assets is illusion. The most valuable skill is the ability to sell. The value in all other skills only exists as welfare recipient of the sales skill.

CHAPTER 38

You Can Either Agree With Me Or Be Wrong

I've been in the advice dispensing business for 31 years.

It is an odd business.

I currently get paid no less than $800.00 an hour or $8,600.00 a day to sit in a room or get on the phone with someone and suggest advertising, marketing, sales and business strategies, ideas and solutions. I have had as many as 53 clients in coaching groups, paying as much as $14,000.00 each per year, to meet three to four times a year. I have quite a few clients who have spent more than $100,000.00 to $250,000.00 each over years, getting advice from me. Throughout my career, I have been paid millions and millions of dollars by CEO's of Fortune 500 corporations, entrepreneurs, small business owners, even my peers in my own fields; professional speakers, authors and consultants. Lately, I am in more demand than ever before, a demand that seems to keep growing.

There is something a little surreal about the experience of being a high paid advice giver. When you consider that the average psychologist or therapist may sell his time for $75 to $100 an hour, attorneys $100 to $200 an hour, my ability to create abundant, constant and continuing demand for my advice at eight times their fees is impressive even to me!

Some years ago, when Carla and I went to a marriage counselor, and he discovered what I charged per hour for my time vs. what he charged, and he discovered I had no college education or academic qualifications, he was, at first, horrified; quickly fascinated and asking for help. In teaching others how to create their own consulting and coaching businesses I have occasionally run up against 'professional norms and guidelines' dictated by some association or certifying organization, and had my fees and the fees I recommend others charge criticized as unethical or scoffed at as impossible. Nevertheless, I'm fully booked with demand left over. And people I've guided in this business routinely command $5,000.00 to $25,000.00 per year per person for group telecoaching and coaching in group meetings, $500.00 to as much as $5,000.00 per hour for one on one consulting. This sort of opportunity exists for a whole lot of people who it never occurs to, or who could never conceive of themselves in such a role, commanding such compensation.

In case you are curious about the secret, here it is:

Being in such a business requires a great sense of certainty that I am right. Or at least a show of certainty.

Equivocation is *not* what these paying clients want.

You can't be John Kerry, with the I voted for it before I voted against it stuff.

A lot of advice giving fortunately does <u>not</u> require superior knowledge. It only requires the ability to raise questions. A lot of people know the answers to their problems, know what to do and how it ought to be done, and if prompted, they'll find their own way. I believe this follows Socrates' method of teaching. At the very least, this can narrow things down to a multiple choice situation. The client tells me he doesn't know what to do about 'x'. I say: what do you think you should do? Or: what are your options? The client then spells out two or three or, at most, four possible alternatives. I pick one. Genius.

Fortunately, advice doesn't have to be right. General Norman Schwarzkopf told me that leadership has less to do with making right decisions than with making decisions right, and I get it, and I agree wholeheartedly. If I can get a client to start, to move forward, even if it's the wrong direction, the movement will lead to figuring it out and ultimately moving in the right direction. But without movement, they never get anywhere.

I *have* provided a lot of advice that has made a lot of money for a lot of people. It is *not* exaggeration to refer to me as a 'millionaire maker.' However, I've also dispensed some really bad advice. I've been very, very, very wrong.

I do have a caution about being a consumer of advice. In my booklet, *'Why Do I Always Have To Sit Next To The Farting Cat?',* there's a chapter about getting financial and business advice from your unemployed brother-in-law. That's one common mistake: paying attention to completely unqualified, even ignorant advice from friends or relatives or co-workers. Another is giving undue credence to advice from a legitimate expert about subject 'x' even though his expertise is in subject 'y.' When we find a guru who proves helpful with 'x', we are eager to view him as equally expert in 'y', 'z', 'a' and 'b'. Caveat emptor.

One of the biggest lessons I've learned about the advice business, that applies to all businesses, that I teach is: there's never a long line to consult with the wise man at the bottom of the mountain. The less accessible, the better. The less the supply, the greater the demand.

CHAPTER 39

If You're Going To Screw Me, At Least Wear A Condom

S
ome people have an exceptionally mercenary, ruthless, one-sided, scorched earth approach to business and business relationships. They are not happy after a negotiated deal if the other person leaves with anything but a bloody stump. These people lie, cheat, steal with impunity. Most are pathological. They are to be avoided at all costs. Even though there is often enormous temptation to do business with them.

I have a simple litmus test, I teach in *The Renegade Millionaire System,* for successfully avoiding involvement and entanglements with these people, and I urge you to adopt mine as yours.

Fortunately, I have been ripped off or abused only a few times in my entire career -- because I've taken great care not to permit it.

One of those few involved a very well-known infomercial pitchman and producer, who a client of mine involved in his business. I had deeply discounted fees and gone to herculean lengths in producing an infomercial for this client, a long-time friend. When my client did his deal with this devil, known by him and pretty much everybody else in direct marketing to be a devil, he neglected to protect my interest. His new partner circumvented our contract, re-shot the show for no good reason other than to screw me out of my royalties, and ignored the contractual requirement to pay royalties even if a replacement show was done but the creative concepts retained in significant part. My client later got royally screwed by this guy, too. **When you knowingly invite a snake into your sleeping bag, you really have no right to complaint about having your testicles bitten.** I would never have done business with this crook had it been up to me. Greed often erases good judgement.

I have, on several occasions, gotten a royal screwing by attorneys, including my own. Each time I've been disappointed, but not particularly surprised.

But, overall, I've been nailed very, very, very few times.

I have, however, frequently had my intellectual properties stolen, my information products illegally copied and sold, and it is a real irritant, and something that continually takes time away from more productive enterprise. On average, I pursue several such rip-offs and abuses every month, have to send a number of cease-and-desist letters every month, track down people hiding behind the internet while committing these crimes, and, occasionally, proceed with litigation.

I have a big bone to pick about this with ebay. It is my firm opinion that ebay is engaged in a criminal enterprise, profiting from the sale of stolen goods and electronic and print products illegally copied, in violation of federal copyright law. If a pawn shop owner deals in stolen goods, he can be, and often is prosecuted. So far, ebay's been getting a pass.

A while back Napster was trafficking in copyright violation, mostly with music and entertainment product, but a few speakers' recordings, mine included, were in their mix. They were stopped. I have hope that ebay will be too. In fact, I'm actually surprised that a consortium of authors and publishers have not joined forces to tackle the ebay problem.

I am always amused when some nitwit buys some info-product authored by me from somebody on ebay, at a ridiculously cheap price, only to discover he got only pieces of the product --- and has the audacity to contact me, looking for the missing parts. And I am saddened by the few boneheads who get a product and illegally copy it, in order to resell the original via ebay. It's a shame somebody puts so little value on their time and lacks integrity.

There is no telling how much of ebay's prosperity is linked to fraud, copyright infringement, sale of stolen merchandise, sale of illegal replicas of brand name products like designer name shoes, handbags and watches, and other criminal enterprise. It is my guess, and I admit, a guess, that the amount of ebay sales that involve these things is substantial.

Anyway, here's the thing: most thieves and criminals and rip-off artists and abusive individuals ultimately, eventually do harvest appropriately from what they plant. As Jim Rohn points out, you cannot sow pumpkin seeds and reasonably expect a crop of lettuce and tomatoes. However, justice, especially karmic justice is sometimes painfully slow, and often of no direct help to the victims. For that reason, you don't want to let yourself be victimized. So I strongly suggest you memorize and use my litmus test for business associations, provided, as I said in *The Renegade Millionaire System.*

I also suggest not behaving in ways that will attract to you karmic justice. I interviewed negotiating expert Jim Camp once, and he makes the case that the idea of 'win-win' as most people think of it is actually 'lose-win'; even thinking this way is weakness, and I agree more than I disagree. I do believe, though, that what is important and represents value to one person can often be provided by the other person, while that person still gets what he wants. I have done many business deals in my life, I have provided services to many clients. I have taken great care not to abuse anybody, not to take advantage of any ignorance or weakness on their part, not to favor short-term greed over long-term relationship. I have also seen people who've followed me into the fields of consulting and copywriting unable to retain clients for more than a year or two, while I keep so many for life. Why? Mostly, because they take too much, they set up their compensation in ways that will inevitably be resented by their clients. The 'win-win' concept is tricky, as Jim Camp ably explains in his great book 'Start With No.' But you need to find ways to make people whole, to make it a positive for them to do business with you.

My final piece of advice about this is: do not ever let yourself be bullied. No deal is ever worth it. And sometimes you have no alternative but to punch a bully in the nose. Fine, turn the other cheek. Both cheeks if you like. But after that, pick up a big club and knock the sonofabitch on his ass.

I'll tell you a story, as example. In horseracing, about half the races are "claiming races" - when you enter a horse in one, it has a price on its head and can be purchased right out of the race by any licensed owners. You have to put horses in places they can compete, so often you are putting horses in claiming races even though you'd prefer to keep them. Generally, there is a professional courtesy, or if you prefer, an honor among thieves, so one horseman will come and ask the other if he cares if his horse is claimed. However, a claim is fair. However, picking on somebody, while legal, is not fair. Twice, somebody has gotten the idea it'd be a good idea to pick on me and my trainer and claim our horses, one right after the other. They know my trainer keeps his horses in good health, invests in top veterinarian care. We are also good at finding under-performing horses in other states, buying them, and getting them going, or bringing along young horses, and it is particularly aggravating to invest a lot of time and money in doing so, only to have the horse taken just as it starts racing well. So, most recently, as I was writing this chapter, we had two horses claimed by the same trainer, one right after the other. The next Saturday night, I claimed his three best horses, and spent $36,000.00, all in the one night. All three were owned by others, clients, paying him to train them, so I put an abrupt end to his paychecks.

One driver said, "Guess he got you pissed off, huh?"

"Yes he did," I said.

Another trainer said, "Well, you stepped up and made a statement."

"That was the idea, " I agreed.

The last time I had to make such a statement was nearly two years ago, and that put an end to anybody picking on us until this incident. Hopefully, this will buy another two years.

You just can't let yourself be picked on.

I work at treating everyone with respect. I expect to be treated with respect. I am willing to point that out if necessary.

SECTION THREE

Inside Dan Kennedy

CHAPTER 40

Therapy's Expensive. Jumping Up And Down On Bubblewrap, Cheap. You Decide.

P ersonally, I've only seen a "shrink" once in my life - actually, three sessions. Marital counseling during my second marriage. I wasn't impressed.

I have a good friend who goes out on her patio and throws glassware against the wall of her house to alleviate extreme stress. I find twisting bubblewrap and making it pop like popcorn rather relaxing. Actually, most docs express surprise at discovering that I do not have high blood pressure. I'm sort of a stress camel. I can take a lot. In fact, I don't get stress - I give it. (My assistant, Vicky's 2004 Christmas present from me included a hot 'n cold therapy neck wrap, little doohickeys you stick on your forehead to make migraines go away, a gigundo size bottle of Advil, and a big box of chocolates.)

Anyway, I'll bet a good psychiatrist'd love getting me as a patient. But it's not going to happen. Although I do have a few 'issues.' Telling a doc about them could take years and cost a fortune. Telling you about them here, free.

First - my problem with joy, or more accurately, absence thereof. I'm a pretty happy and contented fellow, but I'm not a celebratory guy. I tend to take my victories and successes in stride and keep moving on without taking time to revel in the glow of accomplishment. Something like getting a book deal, getting a book onto the bestseller lists, signing a very lucrative deal, hitting a home run on stage as a speaker, these get, at most, a few minutes of pleased-with-myself thoughts. From time to time, I wonder about this. It's probably not healthy.

I saw Dustin Hoffman interviewed in November 2004. Asked about his regrets, he said he regretted not taking more time along the way to celebrate and appreciate his successes. I imagine I'll someday share that regret.

Second - I live inside my head a lot. Always have. My brothers were born so much later than I, that I was basically an only child. And often anti-social. Not fully accepted into adult company, easily bored with the company of kids my own age. I spent a lot of time by myself. As an adult, in business, I traveled constantly and extensively, alone, for more than twenty years. Hours and hours and hours in a car alone, in airports and airplanes alone, in hotel rooms alone. I have a nearly constant dialogue with myself, so I have no real need or pent-up desire for conversation with others. I can go days without human contact, and I can be with someone and go hours without saying anything, and not notice. I heard a Hollywood script writer teaching a class say that he believed all writers do this: live inside their own heads. I've also heard comedians talk about it. Maybe that means, if you get a whole bunch of writers together at a meeting, nobody talks. Just for the record, when you get a bunch of speakers together, everybody talks. I've long been aware that I'm an unlikely professional speaker.

Third - I'm mostly unable to whip up - or even fake - interest in the things most people seem to spend most of their time talking about. I'm easily bored, and easily irritated. Early in my second marriage, when Carla was still a medical records supervisor at a Phoenix hospital, she was eager to "socialize" with people I wasn't involved in business with, And I tried. I really did. But I was miserable, a fish out of water, nothing in common with anyone. I recall being at a cocktail party at a hospital administrator's house. Maybe 70 or 80 people there, including doctors, executives. I found my way out the back door, across a huge yard, to a corral with two horses in it. I was missing for about an hour before being drug back. I prefer the company of horses to the company of a lot of people.

Fourth, I am compulsive. I have to be careful about taking up games or hobbies or interests, as I seem unable to do anything casually. Were I to take up golf, in short order I'd have a coach, be playing three times a week, trying to go on the senior tour and buying a country club. Were I to take up cooking, I'd wind up with a restaurant, a line of food items. Were I to take up poker with only the intent of playing in a friendly game at a friend's home, I'd soon be in tournaments.

Fifth, maybe biggest oddity, I don't experience many of the emotions most others seem to, at least not anywhere close to the degree they do. I might be diagnosed as a narcissist. Or worse.Donald Trump recommended a book, *'The Productive Narcissist.'* Fascinating. My solution is: avoid diagnosis.

Now, here's big rub. My fear - and I'm pretty much fearless, very much in control of most fears - but my big fear is:if I "fix" one of these things, I'll throw my whole system out of kilter, harm or even lose some ability or power I have. I fear a trade-off. I believe it to be a realistic fear, based on my extensive research into the psychosis of other highly successful entrepreneurs, other exceptionally prolific writers, other extraordinarily persuasive and influential people. I've made quite a study of hundreds of hugely successful entrepreneurs, and I find most have a set of really serious psychological and emotional issues. I suggest reading Gene Landrum's works for greater insight. And I would urge anyone considering intimate relationship with a super-entrepreneur to read Gene's works, for their own protection. In studying Gene's material, my other research into such people, my observations of such people, I have to ask - **if you "cure" their neuroses, psychoses, dysfunctions, do you automatically, unavoidably alter other powers, talents, skills, drives they possess?**

Two analogies. One, if you've ever owned and driven old, bad cars as I have, you know the insertion of one brand new engine part is not a good idea. The one new part is too much of a shock to the system. The other old parts can't work with it. Everything starts falling apart. Two, a lot of the greatest comedians are depressed, traumatized, insecure, deeply troubled people. The classic clown crying on the inside. Their ability to be funny is dynamically linked to their personal, private demons. If you need yet a third example, consider the truly extraordinary, celebrated writers awash in personal demons and dysfunction. Hemingway leaps to mind.

Would being "well adjusted" be Kryptonite to my superhuman powers? I have been unwilling to find out.

It is my observation that ultra-successful entrepreneurs are all emotionally and psychologically dysfunctional, and do not attempt to cure their neuroses and psychoses and bizarre eccentricities and compulsions. They only *manage* them. They privately acknowledge them, then they manage them. Like me, they secretly fear re-arranging those chairs on their personal Titanic, as superstition, with the thought that just moving the chairs might very well sink the whole damned ship. Few ever verbalize such thoughts. All have them.

Some of my clients do wind up talking about this with me. They admit this to me, when they may never admit it to anyone else, sometimes carefully concealed inside a stated business problem, sometimes openly and boldly presented. Maybe they sense we share the same angst and paranoia and risk. I tell them I have concluded that we dare not fix ourselves. We must harness our whole selves, flaws and foolishness and fears, compulsions, obsessions, as well as our powers, talents, skills and drive. Use it all. Maybe there's a better answer than that. I do not know it.

CHAPTER 41

It's 5:00 P.M. Somewhere

I believe this Chapter's title is cribbed from a Jimmy Buffet song. But he cribbed it from heavy drinkers. I can recall saying it when I hit the booze bottle in my office before lunch. Almost every day.

I was a heavy, heavy drinker for too many years. There are years that, if I wrack my brain, I can only remember two or three 'events' involving my stepdaughter. I saw a photo of her, in her high school basketball uniform, and a very foggy memory of going to a game showed itself in a distant crevice of my memory, but then I realized I couldn't recall anything else about this - did she play for one year or two? Did her team do well or not? I was in an alcoholic fog too much of that year. For that, to her, I apologize.

A lot of days I had a couple drinks at lunch, a couple drinks in the office in the afternoon, eight or nine at happy hour, then drove home, had five or six, drank to pass out. For quite some time, I averaged a bottle of Chivas at home every two days.

I believe I was what is referred to as a 'functioning alcoholic.'

Well, I may have been 'functioning.' But I certainly did not do right by my wife, step-daughter, associates. Who knows what I might have accomplished, what my relationships might have been like, had I been sober?

At some point, I stopped. I cannot tell you the day, the month, I can't even tell you the year. Or any cataclysmic event that triggered the quitting. But quit I did. And I went totally dry for several years. Then I was able to social drink without problem. Have one or two once in a while but go weeks without a drop. For the past five years, maybe longer, I've not wanted alcohol, and have had a drink only once or twice a year. Sometimes a sip, literally a sip of somebody else's cold beer at the track. I'm extremely fortunate that I can have a cocktail if I choose without it inevitably leading to a second and third and fifteenth. I realize for most recovering alcoholics, the key word is 'recovering', not 'recovered', and it's an all in or nothing proposition.

When I was packing up my stuff in the Phoenix house, in conjunction with my divorce, I encountered fourteen unopened bottles of Chivas behind the bar. They accumulated, as several people kept giving them to me as Christmas gifts long after I'd quit imbibing. They had dust on them.

I mention this from time to time, in my written works or seminars, for one reason and one reason only - the possibility that my talking about it might motivate someone else to examine their behavior, admit they've got a problem, and quit, with help if necessary. I know of one such person, now a long-time Inner Circle Member, who stopped drinking thanks to hearing me talk about it and has been sober for over five years. That one person's recapture of his business, family and self-control is sufficient exchange for every time I have talked openly about this.

It's really helpful and important to some people to discover that the successful individuals who seem to be living the lives they aspire to, who they admire, are not, in any way, superhuman or superior to them. Whatever success, prosperity, autonomy, celebrity, prominence and happiness I've achieved is certainly within anyone's reach, because I'm certainly not genetically or inherently or otherwise superior to anyone. Our bank balance might be different, but our human fallibility is the same. This is why I talk about having stuttered almost uncontrollably as a kid, but going on to be one of the most successful professional speakers of my time. It's why I talk about having gone through bankruptcy. And why I mention the boozing.

There's no red cape hidden away in my closet.

CHAPTER 42

Birthdays

Here's how I know I'm getting old. There was a time when, whenever I gave my name as "Kennedy" to anybody, they always asked if I was related to THE Kennedys. Then everybody stopped asking. Then they started asking how to spell "Kennedy."

I wrote the following essay way back on my 44th birthday:

Celebrating mid-life birthdays seems damned difficult to me.

When you're a kid, birthdays are definitely worth celebrating. There are benchmarks. Beginning with a certain birthday, you get to stay up after 8:00 PM. Date. Get a driver's license. Get a car. Drink. Have sex. Other than with yourself. For a guy, that teen birthday when your girlfriend gives in , well, is there ever another birthday that good?

When you're getting old, birthdays are definitely worth celebrating. After 70, I imagine just making it through another year is something you feel like celebrating.

But in between, to me, it's weird. I'm writing this on my 44th birthday. I don't really want to celebrate just making it through another year. To do that, I have to celebrate not being in an airline crash. But that would mean acknowledging being in a crash a real possibility, and given that I'm on two to four flights almost every week, I can't afford to think that way. Or celebrating not getting in some kind of racing accident. But that would mean thinking about that as something that might actually happen. If I do that, I'm worthless on the track. Or celebrating not keeling over with a heart attack. But that would mean acknowledging that as something that could happen. Unacceptable. So at 44, I don't see how you can reasonably be expected to celebrate making it through another year like I assume (hope?) I will at, say, 74.

Also, at 44, you really begin coming to grips with what you are NOT going to get done in your life. Fortunately, I've accomplished a lot, have garnered considerable recognition, and feel pretty good about my achievements, as well as my future plans. Still, I'm never going to run for governor or senator, which, for a number of years, I seriously believed I would do. I'm never going to build a big company, take it public and get really, really rich, which for some years I seriously thought I would do. I may never write a book that thrives for many weeks on the Times bestseller list or plunks me on Oprah. I've had eight books published already. But it's quite probable I'll never write a blockbuster. And so on. Anyway, I don't think much about these things that aren't going to happen. Except on these darned birthdays.

Also, at age 44, a lot of stuff has started going bad physically. I'm like some ageing car. Nothing major. But this week, this thing breaks. Get that fixed and a few weeks later, it's something else. Over the last few years, I've been gradually increasing the quantity and diversity of vitamins, minerals and herbs I'm taking, the magnetic back belt, thicker and thicker eyeglasses. There are more pops and cracks and creaks. On some days I can get indigestion from water. Geez. If this is the 40's, what the devil will the 50's be like? This ain't anything to celebrate.

By the way, one of the worst things about aging is how the women you lusted after in your youth are ageing. For the most part, they had about a 20 year head start. Raquel Welch has held up pretty well. But I can recall chasing all over town to get a OUI MAGAZINE when naked pictures of Adrienne Barbeau (the Swamp Thing movie; the daughter in Maude) came out. Wouldn't chase around now. And others I won't mention by name: wrinkles and sagging galore.

Well, it's about time to go to my birthday dinner, where I am required to satisfy others by celebrating something. So I'll celebrate the obvious: having a 44th birthday does beat the alternative.

CHAPTER 43

Arrested Development

"I don't want to belong to any club that would have me as a member."
— *Groucho Marx*

It seems to me a lot of adult males never emotionally get out of high school. I've really tried.

I have always been either outsider or leader - never an invited *member* of a group. The consummate mis-fit. As a child, I either formed the groups, invented the activities and led the clubs or I was left out. My grandfather built me a very good, oversize clubhouse with dutch-door and windows, and our huge house had a large 'secret' cellar underneath the carport, so I had the best facilities for group activities in the entire neighborhood. That was my ticket of entry. Without it, I know I'd have been left out a lot.

As an adult, my experience has been pretty much the same.

Although active in the National Speakers Association, more successful than 90% of its members, I've rarely been invited or welcomed into any of its cliques. Even when only Zig Ziglar and I were the only NSA speakers appearing on all the giant SUCCESS events, and I was selling over a million dollars a year from the stage, I wasn't even invited to chair a Meet The Pros table, let alone speak at an NSA Convention on the subject of platform selling. I've invited others to sit down at my tables in the bar. I've rarely been invited to sit down at others'.

In the harness racing world, even though I have more business experience and knowledge than most owners, trainers or drivers; even though I'm one of the highest paid marketing consultants; even though I've written numerous articles for industry trade publications; and even though I've offered to consult free - I've yet to receive an invite into anything; track owners' meetings or groups, horsemans' committee, or United States Trotting Association. I did receive one invite to speak, to one state's horsemens association. Frankly, it was a disappointing and unsatisfactory experience. Because I am something of an oddity as a horseman, returning after a long hiatus rather than staying in the business continuously from childhood on, because it is known that I have money, I am not welcomed into the drivers' and trainers' fraternities. There is pleasant, friendly, casual conversation with many, but hang out together at the sports bar invitations from none.

There has never been a group or society or organization that has invited me in and embraced me. One way to look at my business life is as creation of my own club, so I could be welcomed as a member. And what a club I created!

At the time I sold the newsletter/Inner Circle business to Bill Glazer, there were about 5,000 active Members from virtually every state in the union and more than a dozen foreign countries. That membership has more than doubled, incidentally, under his more aggressive leadership, and is growing substantially every month. Many Members have been with me for 5, 10, even 20 years. Member-events are routinely attended by people having to travel 15 to 25 hours to get there. It is an elite club containing a disproportionate percentage of millionaires, multi-millionaires and seven figure income earners in hundreds of different businesses. From cosmetic surgeon and CEO to chimney sweep and auto repair shop owner, you'll be hard-pressed to name a business or occupation not represented in this membership. The group culture is decidedly entrepreneurial, libertarian-conservative, committed to direct marketing, early adopting of innovation, and committed to continuous education, self-improvement, business improvement and financial advancement. They are a thrill to be around and I am proud of many of them, and proud of the group as a whole.

This group has frequently stepped up to the plate, too, to raise and donate money to individuals in severe difficulty, to especially worthwhile causes. Many of these Members who've prospered thanks to this association have literally become philanthropists in their own right.

The coaching groups (ie. Gold/VIP and Platinum Membership levels) that I retained as my business, the club within the club, contain, as of this writing, by my limits, only 53 Members. All entrepreneurs, from diverse businesses, many in information businesses as primary or secondary activity. Combined, they generate more than 250-million dollars in annual revenues. Many are in their 3rd, 4th, 5th to 9th year in these groups with me. We meet in mastermind groups, go on fact/idea/resource finding field trips, share information, engage in joint ventures, even occasionally invest together. This really is *my* club. It will be hardest to let this go, in retirement.

Unfortunately, most professional and trade associations and similar organizations, community groups, and church groups are all run by people suffering from arrested development, still emotionally in high school. I have gone to great lengths not to permit that to occur in my own Inner Circle at any level.

Ultimately, the entrepreneur cannot *need* to be a welcomed, embraced member of a group. The isolation of the successful is actually a norm, not an oddity of mine. The more entrepreneurial you are and the more successful you are, the fewer groups you can possibly fit into, unless you choose to submerge your true personality, avoid even discussing your actual experiences. I was once told by a near-billionaire that he had three friends he played golf with twice a month and poker with once a month, who he never discussed business or financial matters of any kind with.. They'd been playing golf and poker for twenty years. He engaged in what he called 'fake socializing', attending functions necessary for his business. Otherwise, he belonged to no group, socialized with no one, spent his non-work time exclusively with his wife, or alone walking in woods with his dog. I understood perfectly.

CHAPTER 44

Me and Psycho-Cybernetics

For those who don't know, Psycho-Cybernetics is a scientific approach to self-improvement through deliberate self-image re-programming, created by Dr. Maxwell Maltz in the late 1950's. Dr. Maltz was a world celebrated, pioneering plastic surgeon, inspired by observations of patients' reactions to their new faces. In many cases, the grand changes in their lives they believed would occur thanks to the changed outer image did not occur; they felt the same way as they did before. Dr. Maltz coined the term 'self-image' in response to this phenomenon. In devising his approach to re-programming the self-image, he was directed by Dr. Norman Wiener's work on guided missile technology, for which Dr. Wiener used the term 'cybernetics.' It refers to Greek language, meaning "steersman". Psycho-Cybernetics is a system for steering your mind, and for locking in targets and then automatically being drawn to them. Dr. Maltz first published his ideas for public consumption in 1960. Most modern self-improvement literature includes discussion of the self-image and owes a debt to Dr. Maltz, whether acknowledged or not.

I first paid serious attention to Dr. Maxwell Maltz' book *Psycho-Cybernetics* while stuttering severely, as a kid. I went to two different speech therapists, who put me through all sorts of exercises designed to slow speech. Trying to hear a metronome inside my head so I could speak in rhythm. That works for some people. I imagine that's why Mel Tillis never stutters when he sings but does when he talks. Painstakingly contorting my face to form each consonant. On my own, after reading about the Greek orator Demosthenes and his pebbles, I experimented with a mouth full of marbles. Passing marbles is painful. Nothing worked. Psycho-Cybernetics did.

Not perfectly. If I am incredibly fatigued, if I am incredibly nervous (rare), sometimes on the telephone (I don't like talking on the phone), I still stutter a little. It comes and goes. When I first started recording product, being in the small recording booth, watched through the glass made me nervous enough the stuttering crawled up out of the deep recesses of my subconscious and briefly had real presence. Steve Tyra actually edited out stutters. But for the most part, I don't stutter, and most importantly, I'm not a stutterer. That's an important distinction from Dr. Maltz, by the way; that you are not your mistakes.

Anyway, Psycho-Cybernetics was the tool kit that worked for me.

I've used it a lot, for a lot of different purposes, some big, some small, a few trivial.

I'm very, very skilled at "compartmentalizing", at what Dr. Maltz called "clearing the calculator." I believe I have put together a Psycho-Cybernetic Automatic Success Mechanism that works for me, overall. Not perfectly, not in every circumstance, but overall. I'm able to use my subconscious as able, hardworking servant. For example, I give it writing assignments and it writes good ad copy or content while I sleep. These are just a few of a number of ways I have internalized and used Psycho-Cybernetics.

My earliest, embarrassingly bad forays into speaking involved presentations based on Psycho-Cybernetics, beginning with a truly awful speech, and audio cassette, titled 'How NOT To Be A Robot.'

When I was offered the opportunity of working on a Psycho-Cybernetics product and infomercial for Guthy-Renker, I leapt at it. Max was already deceased, but his widow, Anne still alive and sharp and vibrant and eloquent. I worked with her, accessing extensive archives, previously published works and unpublished notes, to craft both the product and the show. The infomercial project was derailed by strident objections from a certain motivational speaker with whom Guthy-Renker had an existing relationship, whose ego knows no bounds, and ego and fear are two sides same coin, so his fears and jealousies led to his crybaby fit over this project. The product was completed and sold via Nightingale-Conant.

After Anne Maltz died, I was contacted by the small Florida university that he and Anne had assigned the rights to all his material to. They did not want to follow through on their commitments to the Maltz', and wanted to sell the rights. I and three partners bought them. Two partners have since been bought out and today, Jeff Paul and I own all rights, and license the content to various publishers, speakers and others, and publish a home study course based on the works, 'Zero Resistance Living'. We assembled a team of authors and had a book published for salespeople, 'Zero Resistance Selling', and I co-authored (with the late Dr. Maltz) 'The New Psycho-Cybernetics.' That's an interesting book, an up-dated version of the original, still written in Dr. Maltz' voice, which I believe I captured and stayed in perfectly. I also did a 'New Psycho-Cybernetics' audio program for Nightingale-Conant, which, for over a year, was their #1 bestselling program in the self-improvement category.

I'm proud of what I have accomplished, keeping Dr. Maltz' works alive, and successful in the marketplace. I wish I had accomplished and could accomplish a lot more, but the truth is, the financial rewards do not warrant enough attention from Jeff or I. It is a lot easier to make money with other types of content and information than self-improvement.

The material is timeless and, I think, important. As I write this, Jeff and I are contemplating what might be done next.

Success Rejection Syndrome

Dr. Maltz talked about the **ASM: Automatic Success Mechanism,** and the **AFM; Automatic Failure Mechanism.** Animals have their own simple ASM's. The squirrel's motivates it to gather and store nuts before each winter. Human babies are born with ASM, then learn and acquire AFM.

One of my clients, Daniel Frishburg, author of *Wall Street Lies,* called my attention to the fact that Freud believed certain people have a "secret passion for failure." Sooner or later, they turn triumphs to disaster, success to failure, happiness to distress. I have noted this without knowing that Freud did as well. I reached my conclusions about this independently, through observation of others, as well as doing battle with myself.

The self-image is the governor, restricting the amount of success allowed. Success cannot exceed sense of deserving. If it does, the person quietly feeling unworthy does something or things to bring it all back into balance. I call this the Success Rejection Syndrome.

I will never forget hearing my mother-in-law say "Oh, this is too good for me" almost every time she got into my car, and every time we took her to a nice restaurant. Most people do not express the 'undeserving programming' so clearly and vocally, but a lot of people have it installed in their subconscious minds.

Syndrome sufferers are sometimes frustrating, sometimes even dangerous to be involved with. I have been in intimate, personal relationships and in business relationships with people suffering from this Syndrome.

Dan Frishburg points out that SRS sufferers in his world of investments sometimes accomplish their balancing act by taking huge, unreasonable risks for insignificant possible rewards. Gamblers exhibit their SRS and AFM by winning large sums but not stopping play until they lose all they've won and then some. In relationships, a man or a woman does it by making themselves impossible to be in a relationship with. For example, by agreeing to certain commitments again and again but never keeping them. I've seen entrepreneurs exhibit SRS and AFM many different ways, including choosing clearly inappropriate, toxic and dangerous people to associate with or repeating certain behavior or business practices that were destructive, again, and again.

Truth is, we all have an AFM, we all have an ASM. Most people's ASM lies sleepy, dormant, their AFM stimulated and active. Most successful people have an active ASM, and are able to keep the AFM reigned in, in check.

How A Guided Missile Gets To Its Target

If there is anything I totally latched onto from Dr. Maltrz's writings on Psycho-Cybernetics, it is the concept of achieving big objectives via zigzagging, not a straight line. Few people ever get from point A to point B via the shortest, most direct path. I certainly haven't. So I try to keep the big goal clearly pictured, in terms of what I definitely do not want as well as what I do, without being restrictive about means or modus operandi for getting there. Early on, I tried controlling means. In the latter decade or so of my business life, I've gotten better and better at flexibility, evolution and change in means while staying fixated on big objectives.

A lot of people create a lot of frustration for themselves, even abandon worthy goals, because they do not understand how guided missiles and how successful people actually get to their targets.

CHAPTER 45

Why It's Really All About Self-Improvement

S elf-Improvement is damnably hard to sell. I figured that out early, and switched to 'marketing' as my topic category. First of all, it's ethereal. Second, it requires a healthy self-image and strong self-esteem to invest in one's self, something of a catch-22.

It surprises most people to discover how many very successful people have large libraries of self-improvement and success books, credit several of those books with getting them moving in right directions. The list includes people you probably wouldn't expect to find on the list. Drew Carey and Dolly Parton. Donald Trump, who now also writes them.

Comedian Drew Carey credits books like *'Power Of Positive Thinking'* and *'Think And Grow Rich'* and others of this ilk with guiding him in his career. On the Jay Leno/Tonight Show, the night of memorial for Johnny Carson, Carey described how he "visualized" his first appearance on Carson's show, then lived it deja vu exactly as imagined -- this the exact 'Theater Of The Mind' methodology described by Dr. Maxwell Maltz in the original *'Psycho-Cybernetics.'* I have it on very good authority that Carey is a regular Nightingale-Conant customer, purchasing most new self-improvement audio programs still today.

Dolly Parton cites Reverend Robert Schuller's book *Possibility Thinking*, Claude Bristol's *Magic Of Believing*, Catherine Ponder's *The Dynamic Laws Of Prosperity*.

All of these books grace my bookshelves as well.

I once met with the Dean of Akron University, to advance a proposal for a college course based on *Think And Grow Rich,* and was told "We would never permit a book with such a ridiculous title to be part of our curriculum." He displayed remarkable ignorance even for a dean of a university! In one survey done by *Inc.* or *Fortune,* I forget which, more CEO's and multi-millionaire entrepreneurs credited *Think And Grow Rich* as the most important book they'd ever read, other than the Holy Bible. I do not know of a single millionaire who does not own this book. And I know a lot of millionaires. More than that college dean did.

My long-time client Bill Guthy, who started his business from scratch, and built it from zero to 800-million dollars a year in sales, launched its infomercial driven empire producing and airing the show *'Think And Grow Rich',* because he had been so inspired by the book.

Athletes and coaches certainly know the power of self-improvement information, books, tapes and programs. Almost everyone on the Vince Lombardi era Green Bay Packers studied the book *Psycho-Cybernetics.* Football superstar Jim Brown mentioned *Psycho-Cybernetics* as an important tool in visualizing each successful run. When I spoke on the SUCCESS Events, we had top coaches like Tom Landry and Jimmy Johnson, top pro athletes like Joe Montana and Troy Aikman and George Foreman, and Olympians like Mary Lou Retton on with us frequently. At various times, I asked them if appearing on the SUCCESS event was at all odd to them - and every one answered "No", and then named success books, authors, speakers they personally studied.

Jean Nidetch based the psychological aspects of the original Weight Watchers program on *Psycho-Cybernetics.*

Lee Iacocca is one of a great many Fortune 500 CEO's, past and present, who are alumni of The Dale Carnegie Program, based on the book *How To Win Friends And Influence People.*

You will be very hard-pressed to find any entrepreneur who has started a business from scratch and built it into a substantial success who cannot turn to his bookshelf and pull out dog-eared, yellow hiliter marked self-improvement and how-to-succeed books important in their lives. In fact, I dare you to find even *one* such person.

Most of us continue our habit of feeding our minds with such books (and tapes) our entire lives, long after we have achieved considerable confidence, success, prominence and wealth.

Personally, I frequently revisit the books and tapes in my library, and continually acquire and process the newest published. The week I was writing this, I started re-listening to my Earl Nightingale programs beginning with cassette #1 of 'Lead The Field' (while exercising on my treadmill) and began reading Elizabeth Ross Kanter's new book *'Confidence'.*

Are we all fools?

Obviously not. No, it is those who ignore and criticize and make fun of these books who are foolish. They ignore empirical fact as solid and universal as the existence of gravity and man's proven ability to transcend it via ingenious engineering. To argue that self-improvement books are silly or valueless is as asinine as arguing the earth is flat.

If you aspire to exceptional success or peak personal performance, whether artist, athlete, entrepreneur or executive, you would take note of the facts about this kind of 'success literature' and the people who study it, then you would adopt the habit of building up your own extensive library of such materials and reading and listening to them studiously.

To be fair, to offer a caveat, it is important <u>not</u> to give this sort of literature more credit than it deserves. Some of it, maybe even much of it is simplistic and redundant. More importantly, much of it is mis-read and mis-used. No matter how positive or inspired or creative, thought alone is a dead-end. I have written extensively about this in my book *'How To Succeed In Business By Breaking ALL The Rules'.* You cannot actually, *just* think and grow rich. Rather, there is a particular way of thinking that facilitates growing rich through iniative and action. It is very useful, possibly essential to discover and embrace this way of thinking but it is not panaceaic to do so.

One of my primary premises in *The Renegade Millionaire System* is that success is all about behaviors. Behaviors are thinking translated to action, and behaviors can influence and alter thinking as well. There is a closed loop, and I don't think it matters much where you step into the loop and start. I do believe that deliberately, actively working on the way you think is important.

It's easy to make fun of self-improvement 'stuff.' George Carlin says there shouldn't be a section in a bookstore called 'Self-Help Books' -- after all, if it was truly SELF-help, you wouldn't need a book. Funny. But. Those who dismiss "self-improvement" as touchy-feely bullshit usually point out that the vast majority of people with shelves full of self-help books, graduates of countless self-improvement seminars are not measurably better off after than before, or when compared to peers who read no such books, go to no such seminars. And they're right. But that is a dangerous standard. Since most people never do anything with any information they get, of any kind, from any source, you can't judge the value of information by examining the results achieved with it by the majority. Instead, you should examine only extremely successful people in whatever field or endeavor interests you. You will find that focus on self-improvement is a commonality with them.

There's more pay off from self-improvement than improving anything else.

Consider a visual image of the horses I race. The Standardbred racehorse is used for harness racing. They pull little carts, called sulkies. So visualize the horse and the sulky. How would you improve its speed as a unit?

Believe me, everything that can be done to that little cart that might buy a smidgen of speed gets tried. When I was around harness racing as a kid, there was one sulky. Now there are dozens of different models and brands, engineered at different angles, made of different materials, with different wheels. A set of hi-tech, fast spinning wheels costs over $600.00. The designs are patented. Many things have been tried, including single shaft sulkies and sulkies with the seat off-center. All the focus is on the cart.

Most people would think similarly, that doing something to the cart might help the racehorse go faster.

The analogy is cart as your business or your life. You might think that changing what's in the cart or on the cart or what the cart's made of would change the results you experience. A lighter cart ie. a simpler life might make achieving goals easier. A better moneymaking opportunity added to the cart might make winning more likely. In short, all our focus is on re-arranging things in the cart.

So, one night, in the paddock, I asked one of the top drivers in America what he thought of the newest gizmo invented to improve the sulky. He shrugged and said, 'I think it might make a tiny difference - but ultimately it's what's between the shafts that matters most."

The horse.

The analogy: you.

I discovered long ago, you can equip somebody with all the equipment, information, tools and correct instructions in the world, but if that person isn't a real racehorse, in head and heart, it's mostly wasted, often futile. People who transition from "slow pokes" to "winners" in life do so inside out. It really is more attitudinal than aptitudinal.

It's more about you than it is anything else.

Having said that, I want to emphasize that ALL humans, regardless of how successful in business, finance, relationships, sports, whatever, are dysfunctional. We're all screwed up and screwy in our own ways. Unfortunately, a lot of people see this in themselves but falsely attribute perfection to others, and let that stand in their way of achieving things. I've spent my whole life around hugely successful and rich entrepreneurs and can assure you as fact, they're, we're all a massive mess of psychological, emotional and behavioral flaws and oddities and eccentricities, fears, rage, paranoia, you-name-it. The differences between rich and poor, winners and losers just is not significantly better mental or emotional well-being. Instead, there are two key, duplicateable differences:

One, we recognize and *manage* our dysfunction.

Two, we are perennially engaged in self-improvement.

CHAPTER 46

Your Dreams Should Die Hard

I'm writing this Chapter at 9:00 at night, after returning home from driving in the first race, sitting behind a trotter of limited ability but strong heart, named Glory's Potential. We finished third. I turned in a solid drive, did pretty much everything right, and I feel damned good. When things go right, these two minute races are the best times of my entire life. I would rather do this than anything.

Everybody ought to find something to do in their lives that they feel this way about. And do it. Now, not later, because you can't count on later.

I had to fight hard to be able to do this.

On October 11th, 2001, at 10:22PM, Northfield Park's Assistant Judge informed me that my Provisional Driver's License was reinstated, and I was able to drive in any races I wished at the track.

This was the result of 2 years of work, plenty of angst, fighting considerable opposition. I'm going to tell you the entire story even though it involves an "oddball" field: harness racing, because I believe it illustrates what it takes to get what you want. I'll tell it as briefly as I can. But first let me say that this incident mirrors many other times and incidents in my life when I've had to prevail against opposition, obstacles and my even my own ineptitude. Everything I've ever wound up doing successfully, I started out doing badly. You see, I believe that you should never let a dream die without extraordinary effort. Most people get stopped too easily. Most people give up on their dreams without putting up much of a fight.

Anyway, let me tell you this little story....

In harness racing, the path to a professional license to drive in pari-mutual races at racetracks is torturous and political. In Ohio, you first get a license only to drive at county fairs, and must then drive in a certain number of races without negative incident, and win a certain number, and get both drivers' and judges' recommendations before next securing a license to drive only in qualifying races at a regular racetrack. These are non-betting races, run once a week, mostly for horses coming off long layoffs, young horses, or bad-acting horses required to "qualify" before being permitted to race in real races. You must drive in a specified number of these, and get a majority of the drivers on a drivers committee and the judges to okay your next provisional license. With a provisional license, you can begin driving in regular races, at my track only on weeknights. With your "P" license, you then need at least 50 drives and at least 10 wins, no negative incidents, and a unanimous okay from the drivers committee and judges to get a professional license. While driving with a provisional license, you are skating on very thin ice; you can - and usually will have your license yanked for just about any negative incident, such as an accident, a horse out of control or interference with others. You have to drive cautiously, yet you also somehow need to get those ten wins.

In my case, the politics were not favorable. Most drivers get to their professional status beginning as a kid, with the family in the business, staying in the business, and gradually moving from groom to assistant trainer to trainer to driver. A racetrack is essentially a very small town. Its inhabitants dislike outsiders. Also, owners -- the clients who support everything -- are ironically disliked and resented by most horsemen. Someone viewed as a rich owner dropping out of the clubhouse and deciding to do what these guys do for a living and have spent their whole lives doing is not likely to be enthusiastically welcomed and embraced.

Early on, there was a lot of "cold shoulders". To be fair and complete, I have to say that some horsemen were very good to me, encouraging, helpful, supportive. The names won't mean anything to you, so I'll leave them out. But I'm grateful. But there were a lot of guys who were not in my fan club. There are still some.

It didn't help that, in my first race with my freshly inked provisional license, a horse I'd driven at the fairs many times and won with at the fairs inexplicably lost its mind right as we turned to go to the gate, took off at a dead run at 900 miles an hour as if a rocket went off in its ass, and ran under the gate -- nearly getting me decapitated. I hung on for three laps before getting the horse stopped. By the time I got out of the sulky, my provisional license had been cancelled.

I returned to the fairs and logged the entire number of required races and wins again, and re-applied for my provisional license. It took considerable arguing and cajoling to get it.

In an incredible act of stupidity, I chose the same horse for the first race and even more incredibly, a deja vu incident occurred. And my license was yanked. And I was told, there wasn't going to a third time around.

I will not lie to you. I was despondent. That night, I cried. For a few days I was ready to give up. But only for a few days. I went back through the qualifying process yet again. I got a number of top drivers and experienced drivers to watch my fair drives and sign a petition asking the judges to give me another chance. One of the two top drivers personally went and talked with them. I was allowed to drive in qualifiers. I went to each driver on the committee to plead my case for another chance. It ultimately came down to one man's vote, and I had to negotiate with him. The deal I agreed to was: if I screwed up again and lost my provisional license, I would stop, never again attempt to get licensed, not even drive at fairs.

I drove as a provisional for the required year, got the required drives, required wins, and then asked for my professional license. I was told hardly anybody gets it on first request. But I doggedly pursued and talked with each driver on the committee. I worked. And I got it. On April 5, 2004, I got my first win as a professional driver.

There is, incidentally, a limited amateur driving circuit, and people have occasionally asked me why I didn't just content myself with that. My response is that I have never done anything in my life as an amateur. What I wanted to do was drive as a professional driver at the track I was at as a kid, Northfield Park, in Cleveland, Ohio. And that is what I'm doing. If you have TVG on your cable TV, or you're in Las Vegas or Atlantic City where they simulcast harness racing, you can see me drive.

I will forever be in enormous debt to the trainer of my horses, partner in many, Clair Umholtz. He has long been a well-liked and respected horse-man at this track, and he spent all the political capital he had and then some on my behalf.

Frankly, I think the overwhelming majority of people in my boots would have given up.

But I did not.

So I get to do what I most wanted to do.

I believe you are never too old, never too young, never too poor, never too anything to be required to give up on your dreams. Most people who make a lifelong practice of giving up on their dreams, ideas and opportunities wind up mastering only one skill: excuse-making, so they have a long, comforting list of reasons why they have not done more with life. I prefer achievement.

I will tell you, incidentally, this remains the most difficult thing I've ever done. Driving in harness races has at least as much frustration as golf, with the added attractions of dirt, grime, mud, shit, rain, snow, frigid temperatures, and physical danger. Doing well is a lot harder for me than most other drivers. The top pros drive 10 to 14 times a night, 5 nights a week, while I drive 4, 5 or 6 times a week. They get a lot more reps, they are sharper. I am not in 'the club', so hardly anybody will let me have the lead easily or let me into a hole, while they do give each other such courtesies. But I am safe out there. Knock on wood, I've never caused anyone an accident and gradually, in some cases grudgingly, most have come to at least respect me as competent. I do win, I do finish in the top three positions, and I get my fair share of fourths and fifths too, for which we get purse money although bettors don't get paid.

I am extremely pleased that I did not let this dream die.

Don't Take "No" For An Answer So Easily

If you would like to know what I've decided is THE single biggest difference between successful people and 'the mediocre majority', between leaders and followers, between those who enjoy generally rewarding lives vs. those who lead mostly frustrating lives, here it is: how easily they take 'no' for an answer. If you wanted to focus on the one single behavior that has more to do with success than any other, this is it.

In his classic book *Think And Grow Rich,* Napoleon Hill tells a story about a young black girl dispatched by her mother to see the "boss", the girl who refused to take 'no' for an answer. It's a revealing, instructive and inspiring story. Most people lack the single-minded determination of this girl. Most people take the first "no" that comes along, in trivial as well as important matters.

When you travel a lot, as I have, you learn never to take that first "no". If you do, you'll be standing around airports, bumped off flights a lot. You'll have no hotel room to sleep in. You'll be bounced around, lied to and abused. I quickly figured out, traveling, that everybody was gong to say 'no' to just about everything. Because I fly first class, I feel it's reasonable to ask for my preferred beverage: iced tea. Occasionally a flight attendant will tell me they have no iced tea, at which point I order a cup of hot tea, a glass of ice and an empty, extra glass and either embarrass the waitress into doing her damned job or do it myself. These days, by the way, as soon as anyone waiting on me or selling me something says 'no' to me, I go elsewhere if I can. It's sort of my litmus test. And to compliment a hotel staff, I held a meeting at Trump Plaza in Atlantic City and, in two days, never heard the word 'no' once. It was the best hotel staff I've ever worked with anywhere at any price. There are a lot of pricey places I'll never go to, stay in or patronize because I heard 'no.'

Otherwise, I still refuse to accept a 'no.' I fortunately started learning this early - or never lost the ability; after all, kids never take no easily. Watch a kid told "no" by a parent in a store - does he give up and quietly accept the verdict? Think back to when you were a kid, asking to go someplace or on a trip or to stay up past bedtime or out past curfew, etc. - when the first parent you asked said no, what did you do?

I got my first job by refusing to take no for an answer.

I got my first wife by refusing to take no for an answer.

I got my most important mentor by refusing to take no for an answer.

I've gotten a lot in my life by refusing to take no for an answer.

Goal-setting's fine and useful, but what good is it if are willing to give up on or compromise the goals you set? The real key to success is "adamant refusal" - what conditions or circumstances or limits do you adamantly refuse to accept?

Consider financial success. Jim Rohn says - if you're broke, don't start out by sticking up happy, positive affirmations like "I am wealthy" all over the place. Not yet. First, put up a big sign next to your mirror that says "I'm 42 years old, I've got an education, a family to take care of, and I'm flat broke and I ought to be damned embarrassed to be that way in this land of abundant opportunity." You really do have to be absolutely, overwhelmingly sick of being broke, humiliated by being broke, mad at yourself for being broke before you'll muster up what it takes to stop being broke. You have to get to the point of adamantly refusing to stay broke.

I think you can tell a lot about somebody by what they refuse to accept or tolerate. You can certainly decide whether or not you want to put somebody in charge based on that.

On a Monday, at about 1:00 PM, our main business phone line went dead. Incoming calls fortunately went to voice mail, but we couldn't access the line or take it off voice mail. On Friday and Saturday of that week, 140 people from all over the world were arriving in Phoenix for a two day seminar they'd paid $3,000.00 each to attend; many would be calling with last minute questions. At the time, our published hours for answering live were Tuesday and Wednesday. People would expect to be able to get through. Further, a lot of our business was done via FAX. Orders came in mostly by FAX. And the FAX line now was dead.

First, we guessed it was a systems problem, so Carla got on the phone to AT&T service, got bumped around, finally got a commitment for somebody to come out but not until Wednesday, by 5PM. I asked: "Now what do we do?"

"I guess we wait," she said.

Now let me say that my ex-wife did an excellent job running our office. Most of the time, most of what she did was perfect. And she outworked any three people. However, there were a few very un-entrepreneurial and unsuccessful habits she had, and this was one of them; too easily accepting that nothing could be done, too easily taking 'no' for the answer.

There is that idea, that all things come to those who wait. Just not in this lifetime.

I next went to the Yellow Pages and started looking for independent tele-communics companies that serviced AT&T equipment. It took six calls to get one where somebody sounded sharp and was responsive; in fact, she got a technician on his way immediately. By 3:00 P.M., the technician had determined it was a local phone company line problem, not an AT&T equipment problem. Now I started on the local phone company. I started, naturally, on the "there's nothing we can do" square. But I fought my way up the food chain and got a service call scheduled for Tuesday, sometime between 8:00 and 5:00, and convinced them try to call forward the line, so we could do that on Tuesday and answer calls at home, until it was fixed. For Monday, I had it put back on voice mail. When I arrived home at 6:0 PM, I tested it and found: no voice mail. Now the line just rang and rang and rang. I again got on the horn with the local phone company. And I had to get a bit nasty and pushy before it was over, but I got somebody's attention, and I got the line call forwarded; and I drove back to the office to check it. And my pressing got the service order prioritized, so by 10:00 A.M. Tuesday, the problem was fixed and the line was working normally.

This is the way I have trained and conditioned myself to respond. To insist something can be done. Now. Not to take 'no' for an answer.

The lesson in that story about something you might judge trivial applies to bigger things - like making your dreams reality - but if you won't do it routinely, you won't do it when it really counts either. I didn't try just one solution; as soon as I had one in place, I kept digging for a better one. I pressed. And pressed and pressed. I refused to accept the undesirable situation.

Let's switch it around a little. You run down to the grocery store at 4:00 and leave your 7 year old home watching TV, you're back at 4:30 but your son's gone. You search the house, call the neighbors. Son is missing. By 6:30 P.M., you have determined he's REALLY missing. When you call the police, they politely inform you that he has to be officially missing for 48 hours before they can start doing anything. Do you shrug your shoulders, say 'I guess we wait", watch some TV and go to sleep? I certainly hope not. And I imagine you would decisively spring into massive action, and continue relentlessly turning over every rock and prodding everybody who might help immediately and for days, weeks, months to come.

This is the kind of relentlessness it takes to get what you want. But it can't just be your reaction to only the most dire of emergencies. It has to be your conditioned, ingrained, automatic, consistent reaction to every 'no' you ever hear.

High performers are relentless. That means they won't accept the idea that nothing or nothing more can be done. That means they keep working at it long after mere mortals would have given up. That means you think about and work at it every day if not more often. You're on it like a bull terrier with a rat in its mouth. You're gathering every ounce of relevant information you can find. You're calling, chasing down, bugging, badgering every and any person who might help, You're breaking down doors to get to them. You're calling back every hour on the hour to get through. You're, well, you are relentless.

One of the big paperweights on my desk reads: IT CAN BE DONE.

CHAPTER 47

Turning Points

People often ask me about big, big turning points or breakthroughs in my life.

Jim Rohn has a marvelous story about 'the day that turned my life around.' I'm afraid I have no such story. But there have been biggies, now and then. In fact I've been fortunate to have a lot of them. I'll try and enumerate some here that may be instructive and useful.

One came at the first of several Gary Halbert seminars he invited me to come and speak at. (If you aren't familiar with Gary, and you're in marketing, you should be.)

Anyway, I heard Gary explain that, as a copywriter, he charged a $15,000.00 fee plus a 5% royalty on the sales that resulted from the client's use of the copy. He said it as an offhand, routine thing. Not anything important, not anything he was teaching. Just how he did business. To me, it was a life changing revelation. It had never occurred to me to get anything but a fee. For consultants, copywriters, other professionals, there is a billable hours ceiling or trap. In my copywriting work, I was trading time for dollars, the only leverage re-cycling work. This provided a new and fascinating kind of leverage, and I immediately altered the way I did business, adding a 3% to 5% royalty to my fees. In recent years, I've calculated project fees based on my estimate of the number of hours needed multiplied by $800.00, plus the 3% to 5% royalty, so I'm paid my daily wage as fee, I get my profit from the results. Over the years, I've received over a million dollars in royalties from copywriting projects. One sales letter used by a client for five years: over $160,000.00 in royalties. Another sales letter brought the client over a million dollars in sales in a onetime campaign: over $30,000.00 in 90 days. Again, in total, over a million dollars I would not have known to ask for, not gotten, had I not heard the idea from Gary.

I think there's an important point there: you have to be alert all the time, with your subconscious mind conditioned to run everything heard against a master-list of everything going on in your businesses and lives, to ring a bell when something's said that might be used. Because, very often, the most valuable items will be said casually, heard in the hallway or bathroom rather than in the seminar room. For example, a main impetus for my coaching groups was a backstage conversation I had with Henry Kissinger, when we were both speaking at the same event. The title for my *'Farting Cat'* book leapt out of a nothing conversation at the racetrack.

My work with Peter Lowe was another huge breakthrough. It enabled me to acquire large numbers of ideal customers at an accelerated pace with no out of pocket cost. And that, incidentally, is the kind of breakthrough every entrepreneur needs to be on constant alert for, searching for, trying to make happen. Anytime you can solve the customer acquisition financing conundrum in any business, you can get fabulously rich.

Tony Robbins got his big break thanks to Bill Guthy and Greg Renker. Dr. Phil thanks to Oprah. And what's significant about all these examples is the breakthrough occurred as unintended, unplanned consequence, through some sort of accident. Tony was used as a testimonial in the original *Think And Grow Rich* infomercial. The success of that show, in part as result of my contributions, led to Bill and Greg deciding to do another self-improvement show, and to begin considering ideas and people. Dr.

Phil was hired as a jury consultant for Oprah, in her famous fight with the beef industry.

In my case, I was hired by Peter for a couple days of consulting. Of the many items discussed, one was the need to increase revenue at the events without adding costs to the events, a tricky proposition. Several ideas proved viable. The day's souvenir program with a sponsor and paid advertising. One idea was adding another speaker who sells in a late spot, at the very end of the day, as a "bonus speaker". This speaker would have to take the stage following the last big-name celebrity, at 5:00 PM to as late as 6:00 PM, and would be working while the road crew was starting to dissemble and pack up equipment, while a lot of people were leaving. Could this work? Who knew? I agreed to try out the difficult time slot myself in several cities, with the intent of then finding a speaker to take it as on-going assignment, if it could be made to work at all.

As a relevant aside, you should know that there are hundreds, maybe even thousands of good speakers. There are less than two dozen who are really capable at selling from the platform.

I proved the time slot could work. But then no one else could make it work but me. I wound up speaking on that tour, in every city, 25 to 30 times each year, for 8 consecutive years., then in most cities for another year and a half. Beginning in the 9th year, we started testing speakers to replace me, in my slot, in minor markets. I had told Peter I wanted to quit in the 8th year. Seven or eight well-known speakers tried, none succeeded, none came even close to my numbers.

I burnt-out on it and walked away, and have never regretted leaving. I can't even imagine doing the travel required today, under the truly abysmal travel conditions post 9-11. However, it was, as I said, a major breakthrough for me, of enormous direct financial value as well as indirect value, in credibility and celebrity.

This is not the only beneficial event in my life that is unintended consequence, an unexpected opportunity arising out of work or discussion or association for other purposes.

Re-discovering my love for harness racing, another big turning point. I had been around it as a kid, from 1964 to 1971, then a fan and spectator. But the move to Arizona in 1978 took me out of harness racing territory altogether, and for many years, I barely paid any attention to it at all, only occasionally going to a track when traveling or watching simulcast races in Vegas. I was in Cleveland for a Peter Lowe speaking engagement on a Thursday, and had east coast dates the following week, and decided to hang around rather than going home and coming back east only a few days later. On an impulse, I called the publicity people at the track, Northfield Park, and asked if there was any trainer there who might let me sit in a jog cart behind a horse, something I hadn't done in 25 years. There was. I was around the barn all day, jogged horses, came out the next morning for more of the same, and I was hooked. A quick progression followed, and I wound up re-arranging my entire life to accommodate my passion for this sport. It has been a tremendous source of pleasure and enjoyment and excitement for me. It provided motivation for me to lose 45 pounds and keep it off, and get more fit.

Not directly related, but following chronologically, my divorce was certainly a gigantic turning point. This unanticipated event changed my entire life, delayed my planned retirement, severely tested my resiliency. It remains to be seen where that sudden turn in the road leads.

I have given a lot of thought to this matter of 'turning points', while working on this book. 'Turning' is a good word, because there are so many turns taken, that it's impossible to even speculate what might have taken place had the other turn been chosen. What if, instead of randomly picking Arizona as the escape from Ohio winters, I'd chosen Las Vegas instead? (A much smarter choice for tax reasons, by the way.) What if, instead of impulsively asking Carla out, in an odd circumstance, I'd not opened my mouth? I almost certainly would never have seen her again. I'm sure that your life like mine has a short list of big turning points, but our lives are knit together and controlled more by all these day to day turns, most made without time for analytical consideration.

A speaker by the name of Joel Weldon had a speech he used for years titled "Jet Pilots Don't Have Rearview Mirrors." I always liked the title, because I'm not much for spending time looking backward. Some people go through life haunted and tormented by an ever-growing pack of "what if?" and "if only I'd" ghosts trailing along behind them, visible in their rearview mirrors. I've made a very deliberate decision not to live in a haunted house. And I've honed my skills as an exorcist. Once I'm done with something, I'm done. Once I'm done with someone or someone's done with me, I'm done.

CHAPTER 48

My Most Difficult Decisions

I've been asked about the most difficult decisions in my life in several interviews and in Q & A sessions in seminars. It's a good question, but I haven't had all that much to say in response. There have been very, very few decisions I've agonized over. I'm fortunate in that I've not been presented with many situations that seemed to me to require or benefit from long, sleepless nights. I also have rarely second-guessed myself about decisions made. I am a big believer in decisiveness. However, there have been a few.

"Who Do I Have To **** To Get Out Of This Picture?"

Tony Curtis reportedly said that, loudly, to Jean Simmons, on the set of the movie 'Spartacus.' I think I heard the story told by Robert Evans. The line stuck in my head, and there have certainly been situations I found myself desperate to get out of, when the line would pop up in my mind. During the brief 'time of hell' when Peter ill-advisedly brought Tony Robbins into the tour (a very short-lived misadventure), I said the line out loud. But I had thought it before then.

Walking away from the SUCCESS speaking tour was difficult for a number of reasons. For those living in a lead mine, this was the biggest, most publicized seminar tour in the history of the industry. More world leaders and former U.S. Presidents, Hollywood celebrities, famous entrepreneurs and authors appeared on these events than any other series of seminars, as well as every one of the most celebrated professional speakers: Zig Ziglar, Brian

Tracy, Tom Hopkins, Jim Rohn, and, in four cities, Tony Robbins. The tour was featured on CNN and 20/20, in People and Fortune magazines, in hundreds of newspapers. It pulled crowds comparable to rock concerts, football games, even the World Wrestling Federation!

For me, it was the pinnacle of my tenure as a speaker, the pinnacle the entire speaking business. Hundreds of speakers would have chewed off their own left arms to get a spot on these events - *who was I to choose to take myself out of such a spotlight?* I often wrestle with guilt over turning down opportunity, even guilt about simply not working. I did feel very guilty about walking away from this 'golden' situation I'd been so fortunate to possess.

It *was* also something of an ego trip, appearing on stage in every major sports arena in America, in front of audiences of 10,000, 20,000, 30,000, with a Who's Who of former U.S. Presidents and world leaders, sports stars, Hollywood celebrities, legendary entrepreneurs and, of course, every top speaker. See how I described that? Ego trip.

It had become an important aspect of my identity. Certainly as close to fame and celebrity as I was ever going to get.

I also knew I would miss the camaderie with the backstage crew and the few speakers I had gotten to know well. Most of my other work is done in virtual isolation. I do not go to an office where there is a social environment. The SUCCESS tour team, the a/v crew, and the speakers I hung out with in the green rooms would be missed.

I also felt obligation to Peter. We could not find a replacement for me, that would replace the revenue I produced for the company. This had been a great opportunity, Peter had been good to me, and I hated leaving him in any kind of a lurch.

Finally, pragmatically, the business issues. Over half of all my new customers and Inner Circle Members had been acquired through my speaking engagements on this tour. Nothing else I'd ever done before, and nothing else I could imagine doing in the future could provide as steady a stream of new customers, free of cost. Not only would I be walking away from about $500,000.00 a year in income from my info-product sales at these venues, but I would be turning off the flow of more than 3,000 new customers a year. I believed the prominence I had by being on this tour helped with getting books published and promoted.

However, by the time I exited, I was the proverbial bad employee, even though I was not an employee in W-2 terms. I had mentally and emotionally quit two years prior to my physical exit.

Selling my product business was another difficult decision, made difficult by some of the same concerns. To liberate myself and Carla, and to advance toward the semi-retirement lifestyle I visualized, no other alternative seemed viable. Still, letting go of the business built from scratch, through enormous sacrifice and effort, and letting my name and persona be attached to something I no longer controlled was not easy to embrace and sleep comfortably with. It was the right decision. It was a beneficial decision. Later, the subsequent sale of my newsletter business (to Bill Glazer) was an easier decision to make, and has worked out even better than the first.

There are lessons in this I might mention. Entrepreneurs have enormous difficulty saying no to opportunities or exiting profitable situations. One of the biggest reasons is guilt ; the feeling that it is an insult to God to reject opportunity that has been directed to you. I have always viewed my rising good fortunes as contrast to my father's situation, and felt like an ungrateful, lazy wretch when saying no to any good opportunity. The other big reason is fear. vs. certainty of abundance. This keeps entrepreneurs in situations, partnerships, client relationships, even in entire businesses they would prefer exiting.

If I turn off this income, what if I can't replace it? Even though you may intellectually understand that vacuums fill, or philosophically believe in unlimited abundance, it is still difficult to stand facing the pipe pouring money and turn the knob to "off."

There's a joke amongst boat owners: the two best days in a boat owner's life are the day he buys his boat and the day he sells his boat. I have a similar feeling about my tenure on the SUCCESS tour.

Leaving, changing, even accepting change takes courage.

Letting my 22 year marriage end was a very difficult decision. Following Carla's filing for divorce, I was despondent , and when I allowed myself to focus on it, in a very dark place for months. There were several times when I believe, had I made a totally committed, massive effort to reverse the divorce and change her mind, I could have done so. And I was very tempted to do so. However, her actions at the very end of the marriage made doing so, in my mind, impossible; I felt that if I succeeded in stopping the divorce, I'd be married to someone I could not trust. Truth is, I am not a trusting person. In fact, the only person I had ever totally, unwaveringly trusted in my entire adult life was Carla, so deciding that trust was irretrievably and irreparably shattered was a painful and difficult conclusion to reach. (To avoid confusion or speculation or gossip, let me quickly say, this had nothing to do with infidelity.)

This list of difficult decisions is relatively short. I could make a much longer list other decisions that others might have found difficult, that I did not. I am rare indecisive. I believe in "when in doubt, don't" and rarely require more than a fe minutes to, at most, overnight, to decide what not to do or choose from optio of what to do. General Norman Schwarzkopf, who I followed on the SUCCE tour some 40 times, said that you make decisions right more often than yc make right decisions, and my friend Gary Halbert has the axiom: motion bea meditation. There is usually more than one way to get to a satisfactory outcom so getting moving is the most important thing. I see a lot of people chronical suffer from the paralysis of analysis. It's not a pretty sight.

Partial List Of Celebrities, Authors, Business Leaders & Others Dan Kennedy Has Appeared On Programs With As A Speaker

Political & World Leaders
President Gerald Ford*
President Ronald Reagan*
President George Bush*
President Donald Trump
Gen. Norman Schwarzkopf*
Secretary Colin Powell*
Mikail Gorbachev*
Lady Margaret Thatcher*
William Bennett*

Legendary & Celebrity Entrepreneurs

Ben & Jerry* (Ben & Jerry's Ice Cream)
Debbi Fields*
(Mrs. Fields Cookies)
Jim McCann* (1-800-Flowers)
Joe Sugarman* (Blu-Blockers)
Donald Trump
Barbara Corcoran (Shark Tank)
Steve Forbes*
Kathy Ireland
Kevin O'Leary (Shark Tank)
Joan Rivers*
Gene Simmons (Kiss)
Ivanka Trump

Hollywood Personalities & Entertainers
Johnny Cash
Naomi Judd*
Mary Tyler Moore*
Christopher Reeve*
The Smothers Brothers
Willard Scott*
Barbara Walters
Charlton Heston
Mickey Dolenz (The Monkees)
Adam West (TV's Batman)

Broadcasters
Larry King*
Paul Harvey*
Deborah Norville

Authors & Speakers
Zig Ziglar* *(See You At The Top)*
Brian Tracy*
Jim Rohn*
Tom Hopkins*
Mark Victor Hansen*
(Chicken Soup For The Soul)
Tony Robbins* *(Unlimited Power)*
Mike Vance* *(Dean, Disney Univ.;*
Think Outside The Box)
Michael Gerber *(E-Myth)*

Sports Personalities, Athletes & Coaches
Joe Montana*
Troy Aikman*
Peyton Manning*
Mike Singletarry
Coach Tom Landry*
Coach Jimmy Johnson*
Coach Lou Holtz*
George Foreman*
Muhammad Ali*
Mary Lou Retton*

Other Newsmakers
Lt. Col. Oliver North
Gerry Spence*
Alan Dershowitz*

Health
Dr. Ted Broer*
Dr. Jack Groppel*

*Indicates more than one appearance

CHAPTER 49

Who Do I Envy?

Maybe 'envy' is the wrong word. I don't envy anyone anything in the sense of wanting to take what is theirs away from them. A better word might be 'admire.'

I admire the talent and skill of the really great stand-up comedians, like Newhart, Berman, the late Sam Kineson, the early Joan Rivers, the early Roseanne Barr, Emo Phillips. Bill Maher, when he was funny. Jackie Mason. I also envy the people involved with Saturday Night Live in its glory years, the Chevy Chase, John Belushi and Dan Akroyd period. I have comedic ability, both as a writer and performer, but I know very well that there is a gigantic difference between getting laughs from a seminar audience versus getting it done in a comedy club or on a TV show.

I envied and admired Johnny Carson. I don't envy Leno; he has had to so dumb down 'The Tonight Show' that doing the interviews at this level wouldn't be interesting, performing the monologues a grind. But the job as Carson did it was, I think, the best job in show business and, to me, the best job in America period. You can't tell, though, until you have the job. As I noted in the previous Chapter, thousands of speakers would have volunteered a body part to get the spot on the seminar tour that, after seven years, I desperately wanted out of.

I envy Rush Limbaugh his opportunity to voice his opinions, influence millions and be highly paid for doing so, but I do not envy him his work schedule or the degree to which it owns him. I admire him for creating such a marketable personality and for marketing it so effectively. I'd love to have his gig, if you could do it one day a week.

I sometimes envy everybody their personal assistants and secretaries, but I have long been unwilling to pay the price - and incur the risk - of having one myself. I sometimes actually dream of having the "gal Friday" of the old Cary Grant era movies, somebody to pay my bills, file my piles, fetch my dry cleaning, but an employee is just out of the question. If only you could still have an indentured servant. (Before you shed tears for me, my assistant, office manager Vicky Tolleson does a lot. But still, I type most of my own correspondence, write checks, send some of my own FAXes, run errands, grocery shop. So now shed tears.)

I admire Karl Rove, even though I identified a blind spot in his thinking during the George W. re-election campaign. I'm a politics junkie, and have done a little bit of consulting and copywriting work with candidates and 527c's, although I've not pursued any of it.

I envy the really great, prolific novelists' their tremendous talent - and their books brought to life as movies and television shows. I would love to be able to write like Elmore Leonard, Robert Parker, and have their success. Love to see a truly outstanding actor like Pacino or Hackman portray a character I created. Rich Kaarlgaard, an editor at 'Forbes' once favorably compared my writing (in the No B.S. Business Success book)) to novelist Tom Wolfe's. That's enormously flattering, but also, unfortunately, enormously generous. Read Wolfe's 'Bonfire Of The Vanities' or any of his other novels, and you'll see for yourself just how generous the comparison. I have been working on a novel, off and on, for over a decade, and I'm roughly three good pages further along than I was in 1993. Writing business non-fiction is ridiculously easy, writing good fiction is, for me, too difficult to get serious about.

I increasingly envy people who age in good health. Napoleon Hill correctly identified "fear of ill health" as one of the most dangerous, insidious 'ghosts of fear' that steal quality of life far in advance of any realities that eventually occur. My mother spent the final two years of her life confined to bed, fed by tube, unable to speak, able to communicate only by hand squeezes and eye movements. My father believed they could converse this way and I hope he was right. Visiting her was extremely painful for me and I confess, I didn't do it nearly as often as I should have. There were times I walked down that hall, found her sound asleep, quietly hung around for a half hour, but when she did-n't awake, left relieved, counted it as a visit. My father had a number of debilitating health problems including Guyanne-Barre Syndrome. With this as background, my own diabetes - a disease with no cure, and the onset of age related conditions like worsening eyesight and memory, I quite frequently find "fear of ill health" sneaking up on me, attempting to wrest control of my thoughts. I envy people like harness racing driver Joe Adamsky. Joe is the same age as my father would be if he were still alive. They stabled at the same fairgrounds for two winters when I was a kid. Joe jogs a few miles everyday, is thin, fit, apparently in perfect health, able to train and continue to drive in races. At his age, I'd like his health and vitality. Some days, at my age I'd like his health and vitality.

As an aside - a way off subject aside - I think it's important to understand and acknowledge what you fear. Everybody fears a thing or two. You don't want to just deny it. It's easier for it to infiltrate your decision-making, easier for it to influence you if deny. It's better to see it, know it, acknowledge it, and whack it back into its hole whenever it pops up. Not easier, but I believe healthier.

I admire entrepreneurs who've used their ability and time to build the kind of businesses that have widespread public recognition, brand identity, bricks 'n mortar locations. A friend of mine, a speaker and consultant, Nido Qubein and I had a lunch conversation about this. He mourned the invisibility of our successful businesses. Most people cannot even understand what business I'm in or how I make my living, let alone appreciate it. They can't drive down a street or into a shopping center and see a building with my name on it, go to a grocery and see a can or jar of something with my name on it, open the daily newspaper and see my department store advertised. They can't buy stock in it. My grandkids'll have to be young adults before they could possibly grasp what I do - or did. By comparison, every time I go to Disney, I wistfully think: look at all this! Walt drew a mouse, created a vision, and now there's all this bearing his name, known to everybody. Nido went and did something about it, and has become CEO of the Great Harvest Bread Company, a national franchisor of bakeries. Every time I've contemplated involvement in a normal business, I've talked myself out of it. My anathma to having employees, my phobia for commitment and obligation, my love of freedom out-weighs my envy for Trump, with name emblazoned on buildings and planes and casinos.

You should *not* mistake my expressed envy as complaint, dissatisfaction or absence of gratitude. I fully appreciate how incredibly fortunate I am. I have built financial independence engaged in business activities that interest me, working only with people I enjoy working with, on my terms. You can count the time I've spent doing work I've disliked, putting up with people I dislike, in my entire life, in hours rather than weeks, months or years. I'm exceedingly fortunate that there is an audience, still growing rather than shrinking, continuously interested in what I have to say and choose to write about, willing to pay well to hear and read it. I'm fortunate to have attracted and surrounded myself with a small circle of key people who run the businesses that publish my materials, host events where I speak, and provide me with an ample income. These individuals, notably

Bill Glazer and his staff, Pete Lillo and his wife, Donna, Tracy and Vicky Tolleson are extraordinarily competent, dedicated and trustworthy. So I've got nothing whatsoever to complain about.

I would make the point that, while some of this good fortune may be attributed to divine providence, to luck, to coincidence, most of it has been methodically, purposefully and strategically designed and created by me. I have developed and doggedly pursued goals, confronted and conquered demons and adversities, and invested enormous amounts of time and energy and sums of money, in creating my reality. I make this statement not as pat on back, but so no reader misses this point: anyone can, and in fact, everyone does create their own reality. Either deliberately or unwittingly, they design the life they live, the choose the destinations they travel toward and arrive at. We humans were granted self-determination.

There's a great story, you might say parable about this, told well by Earl Nightingale, in which a pastor stops to talk with a farmer tending to a field, his entire farm obviously flourishing. The minister says "God has certainly blessed you with a magnificent farm."

"Yes He has," said the farmer, "but you shoulda seen it when He had it all to Himself."

I do not see any virtue in being falsely humble about your accomplishments. For the most part, others' recognition of your ideas, vision, investment, risk, work, sacrifice, and ultimate triumph will be fleeting, often grudging. The kind of self-esteem required for entrepreneurial achievement must be nourished and nurtured, and I find, you've got to do a lot of that for yourself.

I like to see people rise up to exert far greater control over their lives than they did before my influence. If you are reading this and, for any reason, less than pleased with any aspect of your life, I want to deliver the message that changing it to suit you is well within your control.

And I like to see achievers and builders and innovators celebrated - and celebrate.

It's okay to envy others. I imagine, impossible not to. But reign it in. Don't be the foolish farmer obsessed with others' greener pastures, far greener viewed from a distance.

It's good to admire others. But don't forget to admire yourself, your own accomplishments, your own value.

What to aspire to:

**" I am one of
the lucky people
in the world.
I found something
that I've always
wanted to do
and enjoyed
every single minute
of it."**

Johnny Carson

CHAPTER 50

Six Handles On A Casket

True friends are few. True friends for life, even fewer.

One of my earliest mentors said that there were six handles on a casket, because the most fortunate man would have, at most, six true friends by the end of his life.

When I heard this at age 18, I thought it ridiculous and cynical. At age 50, I find it optimistic.

One friend of mine once served 5 years in the Arizona State Penitentiary. During his life he had positively influenced over 500,000 people, and taught at least 10,000 the attitudes needed to become millionaires and multi-millionaires in many different fields. Countless people owed him enormous debts of gratitude. In those 5 years, I believe only three people, myself included, ever visited him. Fewer than two dozen gave any money to assist him or his family. The late Charlie Givens, famous author of 'Wealth Without Risk' was one of the dozen. I was another.

Former President Richard Nixon once said: do not judge friendships when you are on top of the world. Assess friends when the world is on top of you.

Many people think they have a lot more friends than they have. Actress Hillary Swank, in her 2004 Oscar acceptance speech, acknowledged her "best friend and publicist." Jon Stewart observed that her "best friend" was somebody paid to say good things about her to others! My father tended to project more into casual relationships than they warranted, and count people as friends who weren't. He did have a lot of friends, but still, fewer than he counted.

I think one of the cleverest things I ever heard was the lottery winner who, the night before going public and claiming his millions, called each of his relatives and friends, told each one he had an urgent, desperate need to borrow $5,000.00, and asked for help. As you might imagine, he heard a variety of excuses. No one rushed to his aid. Imagine their surprise when, the next day, he appeared on TV as the Mega Millions winner.

My Christmas card list shrinks as time passes. Shelley Berman used to do this comedy routine that I never found funny. It was poignant. Very well written and done. He portrayed a guy who calls his "best friend" and discovers there was a party to which he had not been invited. Once that's out of the bag, he asks "Who else was there?" And it comes out, one by one, that all his "friends" were there. After some awkward silence, he says to his "friend" -"How come I always call you? How come you never call me?"

Phone lines run in both directions.

I am a man with hundreds of casual friends, most evolved from business. Literally hundreds. We are collegial, some of us close. We've been together for 7, 10, 15, 20 years. I like them and enjoy their company. But I have no idea how many or how few would prove to be true friends. I suspect, few. If I could no longer contribute to them, advise them, assist them, be of benefit to them, or if I suddenly, urgently needed money, or I was disabled, or in trouble of one kind or another -*how many would respond to my call, as a friend in need?*

For that matter, how many would see me answer the clarion call? I think true friendship is important and I've tried to be a good friend. Sometimes it has been costly, sometimes difficult. Mostly, I give myself pretty good marks on this. But not an 'A'.

You have heard the adage "a friend in need is a friend indeed." The more frequent truth voiced behind closed doors is "a friend in need is an ex-friend indeed."

Some country-western personality said if you are arrested for public drunk-ness, a friend will come down to the jail, put up your bail and drive you home. A true friend who can't post bail will come down, drunk, get arrested, and spend the night in the cell with you.

I am absolutely rock solid certain of only five true friends. Lee Milteer, Pete Lillo, Tracy and Vicky Tolleson, and Clair Umholtz. I hope never to need to test them, or to test a number of others on the 'possible list.' I'd rather not know for sure. But with five of the six handles spoken for, not bad.

CHAPTER 51

Days In The Life

A lot of people express a lot of curiosity about my schedule, how I actually live and do business day to day, so I'm including this sampling.

First, some particularly hectic days.

February 7, 2005, Monday, I had a scheduled writing day, then that night I drove in three races, finishing at midnight. Tuesday the 8th was a full day of consulting, with a private client who flew into Cleveland from Las Vegas.

Wednesday the 9th, from 7:00 to 8:00 A.M. I finished checking edit work done for me on the manuscript for the revised edition of 'The Ultimate Sales Letter' and readied it to FedEx to the publisher; from 8:00 to 9:00 AM, I taped a Gold Members' monthly tape interview with Ken Glickman, from 'I-Power' and Boardroom Reports. From 9:00 to 9:30 AM, I did some critiques. From 9:30 to 10:30, I had time blocked to work on a copywriting project for a client. From 10:30 to 11:30, I had some accounting and banking to take care of. From 11:30 to 12:30, two errands, then a lunch meeting at the Hilton from 12:30 to 1:30 to plan the Renegade Millionaire Retreat. I was back home at 2:00, for another two hour block of time assigned to a client's copywriting project. My daily call with Vicky at 4:00. Then a brief rest, and I had to be at the racetrack at 6:00 PM, to drive in the first race.

I want to make the point, which I'll elaborate on later, that everything that Wednesday was pre-scheduled, so nothing "new" was permitted to interrupt or interfere.

Thursday and Friday were my monthly Gold/VIP coaching call days, with each client calling in for their 15 minute private calls, which are set in the same time slots for the entire year. During these days, I take one call right after the other all day long, with only four fifteen minute breaks.

Saturday was a work day, fully pre-committed. As it was the only work day prior to a seven day road trip, there was a long list of small things that had to be done - FAXes to be answered, preparation for the speaking engagement in the coming week. The entire day was blocked out on Wednesday, 15 minutes allocated to one thing, an hour to another, from 7:00 AM to 4:00 PM. Because Saturday was fully blocked on Wednesday, I paid no attention to anything new occurring on Thursday or Friday - that would wait its turn until after the trip.

Sunday the 13th, a travel day, 14 and 15 vacation - during which I do not even check in with the Vicky at the office. On the 16th, I was in San Antonio, Texas on personal business, then an evening flight to Phoenix. On the 17th, I spoke all day at a seminar for Tracy Tolleson's mortgage broker clients. The 18th, I was in the role of client, consulting with Somers White on financial matters, the day interrupted only so I could make an appearance at the lunch at Tracy's seminar.

The 19th, I stayed in Phoenix to sit in the sun and work on editing this book. Unfortunately it poured rain all day, so I spent most of the day in the Barnes & Noble coffee shop. Dinner with Tracy and Vicky. 20th a travel day.

Basically, from the 10th until the 21st, I let inbound telephone messages, FAXes, correspondence, etc. accumulate. Obviously there was no open time to deal with anything or anyone not already scheduled into those days.

This sort of schedule is not unusual for me. I travel only about 15% as much as I did at my peak travel years, so there are two, three, even four week periods where I am home, and those tend to include a lot of pure writing days entirely assigned to clients' projects, my own sales letters, newsletters and books, and on such days that is all I do; I do not have any phone appointments, I do not look at or respond to FAXes, and I work 100% protected from interruption or distraction.

Several times during the month, I set aside from half a day to a full day for scheduled telephone appointments, accommodating clients, new clients, publishers, my agents, the media. People are typically offered a choice of several appointment dates and times when they ask to discuss something with me on the phone. I deal with 90% of my FAXes and mail only once a week, typically running one to two weeks behind. With rare exceptions, I take all such inbounds in order, priority "juggling" given to my private clients who pay very sizeable fees.

February 24th, for example, was given up to the telephone. Vicky scheduled a number of people for phone appointments from 15 to 60 minutes in length all morning, I had a Gold+ group call from 1:00 to 2:30, my monthly phone meeting with Bill Glazer about Glazer/Kennedy Inner Circle business from 2:30 to 3:30, a brief break, then an evening tele-seminar for Steve and Bill Harrison from 7:30 to 8:30. The morning phone appointments were given to people who had requested them from two weeks to a month in advance.

I can only work with people who learn to plan ahead and communicate with me efficiently. Many who find this annoying at first come to appreciate it, as it benefits them almost as much as it does me. There's *never* any "phone tag." The other person knows exactly how much time they have with me, so they can organize their questions, topics to discuss accordingly. Being forced to prepare and be organized winds up saving them time.

In short, **the vast majority pf my days are "scripted" well in advance.**

Many are 100% committed months in advance, and then "closed" to any new or additional scheduling or use. I reserve a small amount of blocked time several times during every month for short-term purposes, to try and accommodate people, tasks, emergencies that cannot be anticipated a month or more in advance, but this flex time is limited and when it's gone, it's gone. To give you an example, I wrote this chapter late in February. At that time, 14 days in May were already 100% scheduled, with absolutely no open or flex time left in them. 11 days in June, closed. 13 in July, closed. As those months draw closer, more and more time will be assigned in advance, so that by the time a week is current, there may very well be no time available for anything new that week or the next.

All this has its rather obvious drawbacks, but compared to every alternative I've lived previously or watch others live, its benefits far, far outweigh its disadvantages.

I find people who have their every day in unpredictable chaos amusing. They engage in constant phone tag, tolerate any number of interruptions, let their priorities be hijacked, and are slaves to cell-phone, e-mail , FAXes. Some years ago, I did a lot of consulting with a well-known time management company you would know by name. They sell a particular name-brand 'system' including calendars and software, and teach seminars inside hundreds of major corporations, for both executives and sales professionals. Their CEO told me of a never published study they conducted, tracking over 500 users of their systems over a 6 month period, monitoring the completion of daily priority lists. In essence, everybody started each day with their list of priorities, ranked A, B,C. Anything not accomplished had to be moved to the next day. He told me if you averaged it all, fewer than 20% of the A items, and fewer than 10% of the B and C items got completed the day intended.

I complete over 80% of my A items (I only have A's day to day), and over 50% of my B and C items by the week. Not because I've got a better day planner. Because I refuse to let my time be hijacked; **in fact, I am forcibly prevented from allowing hijacking** because almost all the time is committed minute by minute. That's a very important point. It's not that I'm such a superbly disciplined individual. I'm not. Left with "loose" time on my hands, I'm prone to waste it. I'm as susceptible as anybody to letting others interfere willy-nilly with my productivity. But my scheduling approach prohibits me from being my own worst enemy.

There are, of course, people I interact with who just cannot or will not "get this." They simply refuse to work and communicate with me in a way compatible with my advance scheduling and honoring of commitments. Some become very annoyed and frustrated. My attitude about that is: sayonara. I need no relationship, no deal, no client, no publisher badly enough to compromise the work plan and work style that makes me at least 10 times more productive than everybody else!

I see a lot of people completely knuckle under to the ever-mounting, relentless pressures of multiplied communication media, the demands of others for easy access and rapid response. I see many of these people gradually rendered impotent and ineffectual. They become completely unable to focus on the important rather than the urgent, on their carefully chosen priorities versus others' far less beneficial priorities. I believe it is more important than ever NOT to let this happen. Even using every militant attitude and every strategy I possess, I still find pressure and stress sneaking up and wrestling control of my own life away from me; then I fight back. You have to fight too. Fight the temptation to give in.

I now find myself at a very interesting and challenging place: the demand for my services, advice and time has never been greater, the sums of money offered and available to me to work have never been larger, yet I am striving to cut back on work, to further reduce access to me, to reduce time made available for work. My deliberate shrinking of supply is at war with the increasing demand. This has produced something of a pressure cooker environment that began boiling over in mid-04 and continued into 05. I am busily, hurriedly rearranging work and altering relationships to relieve that pressure.

There is a fundamental choice to be made: respond to demand at the sacrifice of my peace of mind, preferences and desires, or prioritize, knowing a growing number of people will be frustrated, annoyed, even angered with me, and some will terminate their relationships with me as a result. I choose the latter.

"A person with an hour to kill usually spends it with someone who is trying to beat a deadline."

- Steve Tyra's Little Book Of Weird Stuff, Volume 1

CHAPTER 52

I Have A Lot Of Trouble With Ordinary Life

One of the stoppers for a lot of people is the belief that super-achievers are somehow superhuman, imbued with mental powers far beyond theirs, so they don't even try. They envy super-successful people but think they simply can't match their achievements.

One of the most successful entrepreneurs I ever worked with was so absent-minded he carried no less than eight pair of glasses with him on every trip, because he would lose seven of them. We were once on a bus, on a 'field trip', to Glenn Turner's castle. This multi-millionaire had slipped out of his shoes on the bus. Then forgot them. Got off the bus and waltzed across a rain-soaked lawn, oblivious.

I cannot use coupons. Ever. Never. If I try to use one, I'll have overlooked the type in 2 point invisible, in gray ink on the gray background that says: not good on the third Tuesday of the month. Or: only good on the third Tuesday following a full moon. I actually took a coupon to a neighborhood car wash once and was told "Sorry, we don't redeem those on sunny days." It's like they see me with a coupon and make up the rules.

I have a lot of trouble with ordinary life. Single, I do my own grocery shopping. Nine aisles. Eenie, meeine, miney, moe. Every time, I get behind the woman with three items missing bar codes, and the clerk who doesn't know how to use the p.a. system to call for a price check. And the woman is paying with a check drawn on a bank in Armenia, and her ID doesn't match the name on the check.

I have a lot of trouble with ordinary life. Now that I've moved back to a place where the time changes, my clocks are only right half the year. Every appliance I own battles me. Together they conspire against me. My toaster grips my toast and refuses to let go of it until it is black ash. The telephone suddenly sounds as if I am under water - only in the middle of a tele-seminar I'm conducting for several hundred listeners. The television remote controls, plural, are a mystery to me. Occasionally I tap the wrong button, and my entire cable system disappears into ether. Only ten or fifteen minutes of trial-anderror pushing different combinations of buttons brings it back. Every once in a while, my computer requires an exorcist.

I cannot hang a picture straight, and I have extraordinary difficulty changing batteries in my smoke detectors. I usually just let them beep, even for days, until the handyman can stop by. I am a klutz.

There are all sorts of things many people can do easily that I cannot do at all. Things simple and obvious to others that mystify me.

CHAPTER 53

They Laughed When I Sat Down At The Piano, Until I Started To Play

Most of you will recognize the famous John Caples headline. It is so successful, so timeless, so oft-copied and used because it hits on one of the most commonly shared of all human experiences: being laughed at by others when trying to do something. Being criticized, being told we "can't".

I've been criticized to my face and more behind my back, laughed at, ridiculed, and certainly underestimated many, many times in my life.

When you do well, people seem to somehow get the idea things have come easily to you, or that you've gone from womb to success without a stop sign. This is rarely the reality. Definitely not my reality. My life has frequently featured failure and humiliation. As a kid, stuttering; in high school, poor; in business, bankruptcy; in speaking, criticized by leading National Speakers Association members; in harness racing, struggling. I have actually, rarely been treated with respect by professional peers, unless they were trying to get something from me. Nothing has come easily - except money, in the past ten years. I still earn it, but it is easily attracted. But every thing I've come to do well, I started out doing badly, embarrassingly so.

I have outright failed at first, at just about everything I've wound up doing successfully. In some instances, I've left an endeavor to return years later, and be successful at it. In most cases, I've started over right after a meltdown, the ashes still swirling around me. Generally, my viewpoint is not one of 'success' and 'failure', but rather of 'unfinished business.'

Just as example, the very successful business I ultimately built, centered around my 'No B.S. Marketing Letter', publishing and distributing information on marketing, sales, entrepreneurship and success had a number of very unsuccessful predecessors. One attempt involved the retail success store, 'The Self-Improvement Center', intended for franchising. A bust. Another, acquiring the severely troubled, nearly dead General Cassette Corporation with intent of re-configuring it as a Nightingale-Conant like business. Bankruptcy. Another, a business built around full-page magazine ads selling low-priced books, to fuel subscription of a prior newsletter, 'The Business Secrets Letter.' Lost a ton of money. Another, a magazine, 'Philosophy Of Success.' Failed. Another, a nationally syndicated daily radio program, 'Entrepreneurial Viewpoint.' Got it on hundreds of stations but couldn't make any money from it.

I have amassed considerable, possibly unmatched experience in how NOT to sell "success education."

Ultimately, I developed several business models that worked and that work extremely well. Built a large info-publishing, mail-order company with over 40,000 customers and nearly a hundred products. Built the Inner Circle business, to encompass thousands and thousands of active members. I now edit three different newsletters that, in total, generate millions of dollars a year in revenue and are influential in thousands of peoples' businesses and lives. I've built myself into a recognized brand name. And, through a replicated business approach, consulting and coaching, I've helped nearly 100 different people create large information businesses in a vast variety of industries and professions. Combined, this "network" of consultants and advisors directly bring "success training" to over one million people a year. My work with Guthy-Renker, adding life to their first infomercial, 'Think And Grow Rich', my books, my work with Psycho-Cybernetics, have all made successful contributions to my big goal, too.

I always intended to play the lead role in getting "success training" delivered to millions, to more people than anyone else. I've gotten there only via a circuitous route, a zig-zag path, after many false starts and dead ends and failures - although, again, I never viewed these things as 'failures', but as part of a process.

As a kid, I desperately wanted to be a harness racing driver. I finally got there, but not until age 42.

As a teenager, I first saw Zig Ziglar speak and send a stampede of buyers to the tables. I began developing an interest in speaking, visualizing myself speaking to huge audiences and creating such stampedes. At the time, I still had a significant stuttering problem. There was no reason to think about doing this. Later, when I actually started speaking, I backed into it by accident. In 1978, my first year as a "professional" speaker, attempting to make a living from it, I mostly spoke for free any place I could, in real estate offices and car dealerships, to four salespeople, ten salespeople, at breakfast clubs, civic groups, selling tickets to my own seminars. And frankly, I wasn't very good. A long, long, long way away from standing on stage in front of thousands, then sending them stampeding to buy my materials.

A famous sales speaker I won't name here, because he's since become a friend, was overheard - by me - telling two other speakers that I was one of the worst speakers he had ever seen.

As a writer, well, you should see my box full of rejection slips from book publishers. One English teacher flatly told me I had no talent whatsoever.

I have wound up climbing to the very peak of three different professions or businesses: speaking, consulting, and copywriting.

I believe I now command the highest fee+royalty compensation of any freelance copywriter. My fees are higher than all the freelancers' fees listed in the trade directory, 'Who's Charging What?'. It is common for me to be paid from $30,000.00 to $75,000.00 plus royalties to write copy for a client's complete, multi-step direct-mail campaign. Over 85% of all clients who hire me once do so again. And I am contemplating 'closing the doors' to new clients altogether, and instituting an 'access retainer' that must be paid each year just to be in the group who can hire me for copywriting.

As a consultant, I've been charging over $7,000.00 a day for basic advice-giving for a number of years, raising that fee every year with no drop in demand.

There are at least 6,000 people who make part or all of their living as professional speakers, who are not celebrity speakers. By that I mean, they are 'business' speakers, not Hollywood celebs, athletes, ex-Presidents. About 3,000 or so belong to the National Speakers Association. I'd guess fewer than 10% consistently make over $200,000.00 a year, fewer than 2% make 7-figures from speaking. Very few have career longevity of 20+ years; they come and go. In fact, if you have an NSA Directory, you can look at how few have been members since I have, 1978. And, in the 10 years or so that Peter Lowe's SUCCESS events were THE big show in the entire industry, only three speakers were constants, appearing on every event. Zig, Peter and me. These days, I make more money from less than ten speeches per year than most make from doing fifty to a hundred.

This isn't just a bragging rights resume. I do take pride in being a 'rare bird' and in getting to the top of not just one mountain, but one mountain after another. But I catalog all this to make a couple of points. First, that successful achievement is definitely a process. Going from worst to best is a *process,* a mechanical, methodical process that I understand, and that anyone who takes the trouble, can learn and duplicate. If you are determined to go from worst to best or from zero or even below zero to success, prominence and wealth, you can. If I can, you can. Second, to make the case that sustained success rarely comes easily or directly to anyone. Everybody you see at a mountain top traveled a bumpy, muddy, winding road before finding the elevator.

Incidentally, I took piano lessons for several years. And if I sat down at the piano and started to play, you'd laugh.

CHAPTER 54

Nostalgia

Writing this book has, in part, been an exercise in nostalgia, and nostalgia plays tricks.

In an interview in Vanity Fair (10/04), Barbara Walters was asked when and where she was happiest. This is THE Barbara Walters. The television icon from 20/20, The View, the countless specials with statesmen and celebrities. Arguably, the most respected, most celebrated, most successful woman journalist. When was she happiest? She answered: "In Paris and Italy, *the summer after graduating from college.*"

When I read this, I wondered how many successful people were happiest at other times, in other places, than at the peak of their success, wealth and influence? The memory plays tricks on all of us, and nostalgia is pleasingly inaccurate. Still, I returned to the activity of my youth I was happiest with, harness racing. I feel like I was happier at other, previous times in my life even though saying so makes me sound like an ungrateful wretch. However, I wouldn't want to re-live most of what came before. I'm happy most of the time now. I don't know about Barbara. But most days, most of the time, I feel pretty good.

They also asked Barbara if she was to die and get to come back as a person, who would she choose, and she said she'd want to be herself, to do it all over again - but take more vacations. Sometimes I wish I'd taken more vacations. But I don't mind not taking them either. I used to say, hey, we live in Phoenix. This is where people come to go on vacation. Here we are.

If you really like what you do, like the home you live in, like where you live, why is it such a big deal to get away from it? To me, the big thing is to get up in the morning with purpose, with something to do that interests you, that you are motivated to do. Getting up in the morning at a great resort with the ocean right outside the patio, lying on the beach, that's something. But I don't like it any more than getting up at home, pulling on jeans and a sweatshirt, driving to the track and jogging horses. Or getting up, making a cup of coffee, going to my computer, and writing. I'm about as happy doing any of the three.

It seems to me that the most successful people I know like good vacations, but like not being on vacation too.

They also asked Barbara Walters what qualities she liked most in a man. She said: "A sense of humor and a private plane."

Might be that the second part of that answer's more honest than the first part. Many a truth spoken in jest. As Totie Fields said: I've been rich and I've been poor. Rich is better.

A lot of famous people get asked what they want the epitaph on their tombstones to read. I won't have a tombstone, but I've thought about legacy, like, I imagine, everybody does when they push past 50. I always liked the joke about the guy who wanted to be buried vertically, head down, butt up, so the world could kiss his ass. Mostly I think legacy's exaggerated in importance. Elected leaders worry about it a lot. But after you're gone, what does it matter? As a writer, the written works can live on long after the person. Ayn Rand, Napoleon Hill, Dr. Maxwell Maltz, so many others, influenced me through the works they left behind. Someday, will someone be influenced by my written words long after I'm dust? The thought has some appeal, but it doesn't strike me as much of a reason to write, either. It means somebody will be making money from my words but I won't be getting any royalties, and that has no appeal whatsoever.

CHAPTER 55

Use Of Influence

I n 2003, I decided to help several good friends expand their prosperity by leveraging my brand and influence, as one of my last major endeavors before retirement.

With Pete Lillo, I created two new publications, THE NO B.S. *INFO-MARKETING LETTER* and LOOK OVER MY SHOULDER, and we quickly built it to over $150,000.00 a year in income, and growing - not bad for a little 'side business'. Pete runs the business; I contribute the content for the publications and marketing advice. I also began aggressively promoting Pete's printing services to my lists, and a steady flow of good, new clients have resulted. He has run with that ball, and 2004 was his biggest year in the printing business. (Go take a look at his web site, petetheprinter.com.)

For Lee Milteer, I devised a new type of coaching program "co-op", in which a number of information marketers, consultants, coaches and associations all provide Lee's 'Millionaire Mindset' monthly telecoaching sessions to their members. They each get a valuable service to "bundle" with their other services, as added value for their customers/members, at a fraction of their cost of buying it or creating and delivering it separately. She gets to use her considerable talents in a very efficient way, liberated from the incessant travel required by speaking. Armed with this breakthrough business model, access to my Platinum Members and clients, and my endorsement, she built a large coaching business almost overnight.

At last count, over 8,000 people were getting her monthly tele-seminars. (Her web site is milteer.com.)

For Tracy Tolleson, I devised a plan for "cloning" his very successful and innovative system for securing loan business from Realtors, to one mortgage lender per exclusive area. As of this writing, I assisted with the launch-meeting, attended by six lenders, all six of whom signed up, initially at $19,000.00 each, increasing to $29,000.00 each by the time this book is published. This business will have generated at least two million dollars by the end of 2005, possibly twice that. (His web site is PinnacleClubForRealtors.com.)

Each of these people have been extremely important to me, in my business life, but also in my personal life, as exceptionally good friends.

I mean them no disrespect by writing about this. They were all already quite successful in their own right, and had no *need* for assistance from me. However, I think they will all confirm I've been instrumental in helping them achieve life-improving goals and develop a higher level of financial success and security.

The reason I tell you this, is **to suggest a direction for you.** The more successful you become, especially if successful in ways that give you considerable influence over a particular industry or profession or other group, the easier it is for you to lift others up and open up opportunities for others.

It has been instructive to watch Trump's behavior after the huge success of 'The Apprentice'. One of his executives on the show, Carolyn Kercher, and the winner, Bill Rancic, both got book deals and have had books published. Bill's been speaking. Others who competed on the show have also gotten agents, speaking engagements, other opportunities and publicity. In fact, one of my Platinum Members, Rory Fatt, CEO of Restaurant Marketing Systems, hired Kristi Frank from 'The Apprentice' to speak at his 2005 Restaurant Marketing Boot Camp. To the best that I can observe, Trump has encouraged and supported all of this, been of direct assistance in some cases, and let them all leverage his name and their association with the show to the greatest extent that they can.

Nido Qubein got me thinking seriously about what he called "success vs. significance" about five or six years ago. I began devoting real effort to doing things for reasons other than pure self-interest. Not without self-interest, mind you, but for other reasons in addition to self-interest. Being in a financial and philosophic position to think these kinds of thoughts, and to act on them, is a great privilege. It is a wonderful outcome from a lifetime of ambition and hard work.

I hope you will reach a similar place in your life, if you have not already arrived there, and will seek ways to reward the people in your life who have been most important and helpful and loyal to you, never with a hand out, but with a hand up. By creating opportunity.

Make no mistake: I believe in self-interest as a virtue. I believe the greatest social good comes out of individuals acting on ambition, motivated by unlimited reward, acting honestly in their own self-interest. Immodest as it is to say so, I believe my work has been significant. I know hundreds of people who have found it so, who have risen from debt, turned troubled businesses into winners, ordinary businesses into extraordinary ones, sent their kids to college, supported churches and charities, and otherwise improved their lives, and their families' lives by acting on the principles and strategies I teach, the information I provide. My seminars, coaching groups, and my personal introductions have put countless people together who would otherwise never have met, who have formed alliances, assisted each other, done profitable joint ventures. My books, my recordings, my seminars have been very significant to hundreds I know personally, tens of thousands more I do not know, but who know me. But I have never written or spoken a word only to help others; always to increase my own success. For that, I make no apology. And I encourage you to unashamedly embrace self-interest.

I encourage you to be alert for ways you can align your self-interest with being of service, of help, of inspiration to others. As a successful individual and entrepreneur, you often have opportunity to open a door for another at no cost to yourself, even at profit to yourself. Do not ignore such opportunities. Be particularly alert for the most deserving individuals - those who work hard and display initative, who possibly lack the knowledge you have or some small assist, such as an introduction to someone you know and they do not. Don't hesitate to actually create opportunities for people who appear and impress you with their desire, drive and potential. This is how you can align success and significance.

SECTION FOUR

Marriage, Divorce

"Do you know what it means to come home to a gorgeous lady who gives you a lot of love, affection, tenderness, and is eager to cater to your every sexual desire? It means you're in the wrong apartment."

— *boxer Jake LaMotta*

CHAPTER 56

Men Are From Mars, Relationship Experts Are Full Of Shit

"Well, what do women want, anyway?"
— Sigmund Freud's last deathbed words

Just like Freud, I'm winding up, after 50 years, clueless about what women really want. The only think I am rock solid certain about is - what they want is *not* what they say they want.

By comparison, males are pretty damned simple. Dr. Laura Schlessinger, surprisingly, has suggested: offer him sex. If he's not horny, make him a sandwich. For the record, a large part of the time you women wonder, and too often ask, what we are thinking, we are thinking about nothing. Other times we're thinking about how to avoid having a conversation about what we're thinking. And some times we are thinking about things that, if you could read our minds or pry a straight answer out of us, would send you screaming from the room. It seems to me that women live for invasion of privacy, men desperately try to protect it.

It's odd to me that, in just about every other type of knowledge, I feel smarter now than I was ten or twenty or thirty years ago. I feel like education and experience have led to greater knowledge and greater confidence. Only in this area, about relationships, do I feel like I know less. But I'm not convinced anybody else knows anything either.

Here's a juicy little fact a lot of people don't know: two of the most famous experts and bestselling authors advising us on our relationships and marriages are divorced from each other. Bitterly divorced *from each other.*

I was at an awards banquet of the National Infomercial Marketing Association when one won an award. And I overheard a very, very loud hallway-outside-the-ladies'-room diatribe of hers about her ex. Most of it unprintable.

I share the majority male viewpoint about her ex; that he is a twit. One of my favorite morning radio personalities once broke off an interview with him and asked him if some woman had his balls in a jar back home on the mantle.

My own experience with a marriage counselor was amusing. When Carla and I were separated, then getting back together, we were referred to a therapist and Carla was quite enthusiastic about going - until we went. I knew it was ill-fated as soon as I detected that he, our marriage guru, was sharing a home and office with his significant other; she also a marriage counselor; however they weren't married. Apparently somebody was a little commitment phobic. Next, contrary to Carla's presumption we'd be fixing me, he zeroed in on fixing her. This, I believe, had a great deal to do with his determining who was signing his checks. Ultimately, he was more interested in pumping me for information about becoming a published author and speaker than he was in anything else.

I do have one observation about women, and it's certain to offend most women reading this. I don't think they can dispute it. But they won't like it.

First, an analogy. Cats. There's a reason women like cats. If you watch cats, the one thing they want is to get into the room they're not in. Wherever there's a closed door, they want to be in that room. But as soon as they get into it, if you close the door, they want out, into the other room.

Both of my wives were big on re-arranging furniture. Wife #1 would do it everytime I was out of town. I can't tell you the number of times I came home late at night and walked smack into a piece of furniture in the dark, moved to a new place. Comparing notes with other guys, it seems most women share this insatiable need to re-arrange the furniture. Whatever is where it is, they want it somewhere else.

Most women are very big on travel, too. They love going someplace they haven't been before, and definitely someplace other than where they are. A lot of guys seem to be like me; we wind up with a few places we like returning to again and again. In Vegas, for example, I have a hotel I like and I'm perfectly content staying there every time I go to Vegas. My ex-wife, the woman I'm involved with now both prefer staying in a different hotel every time they visit Vegas. Comparing notes about this with other guys, I hear this same story.

So here's my observation: what women want is - *whatever they haven't got.*

One other thought about women, and relationships. In some movie I can't recall title or plot of, the character played by dour Charles Grodin is arguing with the female lead and, at the height of exasperation, says "Okay, I'm going to sit down and listen and I want you to describe exactly what you want, everything you want from me." He then sits on a couch as she recites a marvelously, unbelievably, incredibly long, long, long list. When she finally runs out of gas, Grodin says: "But I already have a full-time job." Uh-uh.

Several months after my divorce from Carla, I was in the Barnes & Noble store I frequent, looking at business books, and in the same aisle next to me, there was a dynamite blonde. Tall, long blonde hair, good body, pretty face. She noticed me, I noticed her. I was just about ready to initiate a conversation when she turned to face me. Her T-shirt, stretched over an impressive front, was imprinted with a headline: "What I Want In A Man", underneath, items listed, numbered #1 through #22. I said: "Too long a list" and quickly walked away.

Don't misunderstand. I'm not down on women anymore than I'm down on men. I think each side brings its own pile of problems to relationships. Nor am I down on relationships. I'm just not good at them. And I think they are especially difficult when one of the people in the relationship is a hard-driving entrepreneur. My observation is that the other partner likes the increasing success and prosperity but almost at the same rate that increases, dissatisfaction, even disapproval with how that success is created occurs. One client's wife told me that she was thrilled with their three homes, great vacations, financial security and her husband's celebrity, but she wished he'd come home by 6:00 P.M. everyday, not think about work evenings or weekends, and be more available for what she called 'ordinary life.' This is like saying you love the zebra you own if it weren't for those damned stripes. But there it is.

For some people, success actually fosters insecurity. When the husband and wife are starting out together, and there's not much money, everything's fine. As one begins achieving really significant success, the other partner's negative imagination goes to work, worrying that the increasingly successful and celebrated partner will have an increasing array of options, including younger, more attractive partners. Suspicion about money sets in. If one partner has a low prosperity set point, what I described earlier in the book as Success Rejection Syndrome, look out.

"Not good dinner conversation," Hawk said. "But it's on the table. If you love me, you could have me. You love somebody else and insist I be him."

"Oh, shit," Cecile said.

ȷ from 'Cold Service', a Spenser novel by Robert Parker

CHAPTER 57

First Wife, Second Wife

"Why, I wonder from my living room couch in the dark, do I always think the nicest things about my wife when I'm alone?"
— *Robert Huber, writing in 'Esquire'*

J oan Rivers has schtick about first wife, second wife, and it was turned into a little humor book with that title at Price/Stern/Sloan when I was there.

I have been married twice. I did not murder either one, although it did cross my mind more than once with #1.

There's not that much to report about first marriage. I was too young and unprepared. Carolyn was older, divorced, and brought more emotional baggage than I noticed until it was piled high in the closet. We were volatile. The James Tolleson mess made it virtually impossible to overcome the other stuff. I loved her passionately but disappointed her severely, as she did me. We parted on barely amicable terms. She returned to Ohio, I remained in Arizona, and she left behind her cat, possibly out of spite since the thing hated me. We are lucky not to have been Michael Douglas and Kathleen Turner in that movie, *'War Of The Roses.'* Still, I bore her no ill will, and chalk the lion's share of that marriage's demise up to me, not her. Although there are a few things *I'm* owed apologies for, if anybody reading this knows her, please pass along my overdue apologies.

In a funny twist of something other than fate, she introduced me to Wife #2, Carla, before departing.

There's also a "it's a small world" piece of trivia. Working with me, Carolyn had become an extremely smart marketer. She had already been an extremely adept executive assistant. When she returned to Ohio and started looking for a job, she got snapped up by Denis Haslinger, Gary Halbert's ex-partner in the original Halberts business, morphed into a business called Numa, Inc. As soon as Denis discovered she was "Kennedy trained" , he hired her. As a result, Carolyn and I saw each other a couple times post-divorce. But I have not heard from her in more than twenty years. I heard from somebody she'd married again. And again, the last time to a pro golfer. I would imagine that ruined his game.

My second divorce was briefly tense and contentious, but still concluded quickly, efficiently and, ultimately, amicably. To this day, Carla continues to do editing, manuscript preparation and other project work for me, prepare both the Glazer-Kennedy *No B.S. Marketing Letter* and the Kennedy-Lillo *No B.S. Info-Marketing Letter,* and do projects for a number of my clients. Like

Wife#1, she was quite capable when I met her. Now also 'Kennedy trained'. I've often noted that Jimmy Carter's been a pretty good *ex*-President. Carla's been a good ex. I'm genuinely sorry she became unhappy in our marriage, appreciate her assistance post-divorce, and wish her nothing but the best.

I saw a profound "shock" go through the Inner Circle Membership, my clients, as a result of our divorce. Carla had been running the office, at all the seminars, and had a good relationship with many of the Members and clients. Beyond that, ours looked to these people to be a fine marriage. After the divorce, I had client after client confide their own secret concerns about their marriages and more than one said "If you two couldn't make it last for life, what chance do I have?" This again represents, in part, the feeling that I am somehow super-human, and I'm not. It is also the natural by-product of my making "Be Like Dan" part and parcel of my marketing. In that way, Carla and I were both public figures. My divorce emboldened and encouraged clients and coaching members to talk to me about relationship matters they never raised in conversation before. I became aware of how many were frustrated, were wrestling with their own problems.

I do have some things to say, about my divorce, that I know would answer some curiosity questions people have on occasion, expressed, and in the interest of producing as complete a document of my life as possible in this book, I wrote a lengthy Chapter. I am aware that Carla's strong wishes are for me not to deal with this in print, and at last minute, I decided to leave the Chapter out solely for that reason. If there's ever a follow-up to this book, with more years elapsed, it will probably be used.

For the record, the relationship I've had with a woman that lasted longer than both marriages added together has been with my hair stylist all the years I lived in Phoenix, who I also dated between marriages, dropped for Carla (in a way that I'm sure I owe apology for), and am still good friends with today. And it won't be long now before my friendship with Lee Milteer outlasts the marriages. The secret might just be distance.

CHAPTER 58

Married To A Pisces

I walk into the living room. Seems a little cool. Adjust the thermostat. Here's what she's thinking:

" I wonder why he's adjusting the thermostat. If he's cold, why isn't he wearing the sweater I got him for

Christmas? Come to think of it, he hasn't worn that sweater in months. He must really hate it. Unless there's more to it than that. He'd be warmer if he sat next to me on the couch but he sat in the chair by himself. Oh my God! He's having an affair. That explains everything. I'll bet it's that bimbo I saw him getting off the plane with when I picked him up at the airport three weeks ago.

What have I done to deserve this? I'm calling the attorney first thing in the morning."

"The only time Rifkin
and his wife
experienced
simultaneous orgasm
was when
the judge handed them
their divorce decree."

- Line by Woody Allen,
from his movie 'Husbands And Wives.'

SECTION FIVE

Renegade Millionaire Strategies

CHAPTER 59

How Far We Have Come

I was born in 1954. I am writing this book 50 years after my birth, in 2004.

O nly 50 years before I was born, here's what life was like in the United States. The average life expectancy was 47. Only 8% of homes had a telephone. There were only 8,000 cars in the whole country, and only 144 miles of paved roads. The average wage was 22 cents an hour. 90% of all physicians had no college education. 20% of adults could neither read or write.

When I read about, and think about the industrialists and entrepreneurs who created businesses under these conditions, I marvel. It is criminal and dangerous that we are allowing American history to be rewritten, so that today's students are taught that these builders of modern life were evil, greedy bastards, rather than heroic figures.

My friend Joe Sugarman made his first millions in mail-order before the Internet, the FAX machine. He was the first person to offer to accept credit card orders via a toll-free 800-number in mail-order ads. I built my businesses and made my first fortune pre-FAX, pre-voice broadcast, pre-Internet. It is hard for a 30 year old entrepreneur today to even imagine trying to do business without e-mail or cellphones.

In one of my businesses, built from scratch to millions in the early 1980's, to add 150 new clients, we had to do three direct-mail campaigns into five cities, rent hotel meeting rooms in all five cities, put a speaker on the road for the week, have him present a three hour evening seminar each night for five nights. Today, I have a client marketing a very similar service to that same industry. He does what we did with one FAX campaign and a one two-hour teleconference. The other night, I was a guest speaker on a tele-seminar and sold $49,200.00 of my materials in 90 minutes. I was relaxing on my couch, eating a good dinner thirty minutes later. In 1983, to do $49,200.00, I would have traveled to five cities and done five evening seminars, worked in front of audiences for fifteen hours.

What it took me all year to do in adding new Members to the Inner Circle business, through a monstrous amount of travel and speaking, and costly direct-mail, Bill can do in 1/3rd the calendar time, at far less expense, on the internet, via affiliates.

What it took Mary Kay two decades to do, in terms of number of customers for skin care products, and sales volume, Guthy-Renker did for its skin care products in only a handful of years via infomercials. Mary Kay needed a massive salesforce, an army of pink-suited agents and recruiters of agents, infrastructure, meetings, conventions, award programs. Guthy-Renker needed a media buyer. One has to wonder why anybody relies on old-fashioned sales organizations.

It is easier than it has ever been to become a millionaire, a multi-millionaire, from scratch. There has never been a time in America when there were so many different options available to just about anybody, to start from zero and create a prosperous and successful business. If you would like to be rich, there's really no good reason not to be.

CHAPTER 60

Evolution And Revolution

It is a true cliche: the only thing constant is change. Embrace it or be run over by it.

I 'll give you examples from my own businesses. Evolution takes place gradually, slowly. My business evolved over years, almost ponderously, from a disjointed collection of activities -- speaking, selling product, a catalog of products, consulting and copywriting -- to a synergistically organized business, with speaking and product sales putting customers into the top of a funnel which led to "membership", with consulting and copywriting as a back-end. "Membership" became the focal part of the business. The ascension model evolved too, from Silver and Gold, to Silver, Gold, Gold+. The decision to reduce speaking was impetus for addition of coaching. Coaching evolved over five years from a simple start with one-on-one tele-coaching and a Platinum group to a more sophisticated layering of Gold/VIP on top of the ascension model. The five-years-to-retirement plan led to the sale of one part of the business in 1999, another in 2003. Emerging, evolving from that, the center-of-theuniverse plan, where I have a number of 'satellites' paying me for providing content and use of my name, "brands", likeness, endorsement.

All of this is 'evolution', occurring naturally, as a progressive result of changing circumstances, new knowledge, necessity.

Revolution occurs suddenly, disruptively, and is more challenging to cope with - but often, the greatest opportunities are revolutionary rather than evolutionary. Often they are sparked by adverse events, like 9-11, or a media taken away as illegal, like broadcast FAX. Sometimes they are related to new media becoming useful, like the internet, or a true breakthrough technique, like 'forced continuity.' A revolution changes everything. Speaking on the 'Success' events sparked revolutionary change in my business. 'Forced continuity', revolutionary change in my business and my clients' businesses. The "swipe" of Bill Phillips' car contest by Joe Polish and I, moved to sale of premium priced coaching inside information businesses, revolutionary.

Every entrepreneur faces and must make choices about and manage both kinds of change.

My father's original business went from prosperity to extinction almost overnight almost entirely thanks to a single decision he made about evolving technological changes. I might very well have made the same decision. I inherited his stubbornness. But observing it taught me an important lesson, and I've been more aware of my tendency to resist unpleasant changes. In fact, one of the main reasons I decided to sell the Inner Circle business when I did rather than continuing to run it myself for several more years was my belief that the internet had finally evolved to real importance, value and pervasive use, and presented real opportunity. I wanted nothing to do with it personally, but to continue refusing to focus on it carried risk of reversing the growth and prosperity of the business. So it needed to be in the hands of somebody willing and able to embrace the change. Bill, with Yanik's help, has, in fact, created revolutionary improvement and expansion by focusing on what I would not.

If you pay attention to business success stories, you'll find both evolution and revolution. Listen to Richard Thalheimer's audio program about the development of his 'Sharper Image' business and you'll hear about a lot of evolutionary changes. But you'll hear about one revolutionary change: his decision to refocus the business on products they invented from scratch and had manufactured only for them as exclusive, proprietary products. These same story lines exist in almost every successful business.

The people I work with, as private clients, or in coaching, work with me to understand and effectively manage the evolution of their businesses, but also to find ways to spark revolutionary changes. In the past two years, I have created revolutionary breakthroughs for people like Darin Garman, Scott Tucker, Dr. Ben Altadonna, Bill and Steve Harrison, Corey Rudl, and the list goes on and on. A *different* revolution in each business.

Our theme for my Platinum group in 2005 is 'revolution.'

Maybe it should be your theme, too.

CHAPTER 61

Business Secrets I Wish I'd Discovered Twenty Years Sooner

There are so many! Too soon old, too late smart.

I do my best to start using them as soon as I discover them, and to pass them along through my speaking and writing. There's no way to summarize them in brief here. They are dealt with in detail and depth in places like the recordings from my *'Lifetime Of Secrets / Ultimate Marketing And Entrepreneurship Boot Camp'* and my *'Renegade Millionaire System.'* However, three of the many are, I think, bigger, more universally applicable than the rest, so here they are:

First, price elasticity. I don't think I've yet fully grasped or capitalized on just how elastic 'price' can be. I have, however, come a long way and brought a lot of other people forward, in understanding that there is no restriction on what people will pay; there is only self-imposed limits, both psychological and practical in nature. It is absolute truth that we set our own prices, and more often than not, set them lower than necessary. Most people under-value themselves, their services, their products, poorly package and present those things, and under-estimate what the market will pay.

It is vital to grasp that we set our own price. As Foster Hibbard taught, teaspoon, pail or tanker truck, the ocean doesn't care. You choose.

I will also admit, I have to keep re-learning these lessons. Even I tend to under-price, or fail to use the best, most creative means of packaging for maximum price. Just as I was polishing this chapter, I spent a day as a client, consulted to by Somers White. He challenged me on a particular pricing intent I had. He added a zero. So I'm perfectly capable of using the teaspoon when I could use the tanker truck.

Second, the secret of transaction size. Simply put, it requires fewer $5,000.00 sales than $500.00 sales or $50.00 sales to get to each million dollar benchmark. But it is not proportionately difficult to create and sell a $5,000.00 thing than to create and sell a $50.00 thing. However, even in relatively mundane businesses, innovative entrepreneurs find ways to dramatically boost average transaction size, and astute corporate management looks for ways to boost transaction size. That's the thinking that brought "Super-Sizing" to the fast food industry, the thinking that replaces the coffee shop with Starbucks.

Three, the power of continuity. Think Max Sackheim's remarkable invention, Book Of The Month Club. It turns out that I'd be several million dollars richer had I built my newsletter/Inner Circle business on continuity rather than renewal from the very beginning. And I would be at least ten million dollars richer had I tied forced continuity membership to every *'Magnetic Marketing System'* sold. I miss those millions. Everybody ought to strive and fight and work to find ways to create continuity income streams in their business, and if they can't, to get involved in a business where they can.

I would encourage you to make these three secrets of wealth creation the focus of your research, investigation, study, to learn as much about them as quickly as possible. To keep studying them. To very carefully consider them every time you launch new product or service. To get a second opinion or several opinions from people who "get it", who might see a way to price higher that you overlooked.

I also have a comment about the emotional and ethical and even spiritual aspects of this, that might trouble some: there is no virtue in settling for less than you are worth, less than you deserve, less than the market will cheerfully pay. I refuse to believe you get a chair closer to the air conditioner in hell by virtue of accepting less than your customers would gladly give you for whatever you provide.

RESOURCE!

If you are reading this book but do not own my Renegade Millionaire resources, I urge you to look into them – to learn a lot more about these three secrets, but beyond that, my entire approach to business success. There are multi-media Original Renegade Millionaire System, Renegade Millionaire Retreat and Renegade Millionaire Marketing kits available, via NoBSInnerCircle.com.

" He who knows best knows how little he knows. "

- Thomas Jefferson

CHAPTER 62

Me & Employees

One Sunday morning I took a call from a distraught, close friend. She went to her office to find something, used her employee's computer instead of hers, and wandered into a rat's nest. The trusted employee of 8 years, recently given a raise to $15 an hour, and recently increased from three to four days a week in response to insistence there was too much work to do in three, was running not one, but two businesses of her own out of my friend's office. All twenty of the most recently visited web sites had nothing to do with my friend's business. Entire brochures for the other businesses had been built and stored in the computer, printed out in who-knows-what-quantity on the color printer. E-mail campaigns sent. Even banking done on line. Apparently the employer was getting the 4th day each week - the other three going to the employee.

This is *not* an unusual story. I hear variations all the time. And it's going on in a lot of businesses unknown to the owners. In fact - in most the employees are, in one way or another, or in many, stealing. No business owner ever wants to believe such a thing can be going on under his nose, nor that *his* loyal bunch would engage in such behavior.

Here's the reality: the employer-employee relationship is essentially, inherently and unavoidably adversarial.

The happy-face, new agey, warm 'n fuzzy we're-all-on-the-same-team, ownership-mentality stuff sold by business gurus who don't have employees or are being victimized by them - is all 1000% bullshit.

Nothing can alter the core essence of this relationship. From the employees' viewpoint: the owner is dumber than they are, getting rich on their hard labor, lucky, and undeserving. You won't change this with pizza parties, employee of the month merit badges, or even with cash.

Personally, I would rather have multiple root canals without even topical numbing than again have employees. For many reasons. But I have had as many as 47, for a number of years 5 to 8, and, of course, I work with businesses of all sizes who have from several to several thousand. And I do know THE secret to getting productive behavior out of them, and to protecting yourself from much damage from them.

That secret is:

Realism.

I remind, as I so often do, that one of the seventeen principles enumerated by Napoleon Hill was: accurate thinking.

So here, I'm going to give you my smart uncle's lecture about employees.

Let's begin with thievery.

There are many kinds of theft. Outright theft of money, merchandise or supplies is one definition. But like Bill Clinton's semantically tortured definition of "sex", there are many other ways to define theft. Direct, deliberate disregard for a rule, procedure, process or script, for the way you want your business conducted is theft, because the employee is paid by you to do what you want done the way you want it done, and presumably their refusal to do so interferes with optimum sales or profits or customer retention or referrals. Deliberate refusal to follow your procedures is theft just the same as taking cash out of the register.

The reality of employee theft is as follows: 95% steal. Some more than others, some more frequently than others, some more blatantly than others. But 95% steal some. In the security courses my client taught, research was quoted indicating that 5% of the population is hard-wired for total honesty, 5% hard-wired for total dishonesty. In between, the rest of us practice what I call 'situational ethics.' Mostly, we try to do the right thing, but the line between right and wrong moves around a little. We are constantly making assessments and decisions about each situation presented to us.

I saw some very recent research in a report on CNN, stating that one in twenty-five adults are true sociopaths. They have zero conscience. You have a one in twenty-five chance of employing one, doing business with one, having one next door to you. Fortunately, they don't all become serial killers.

Anyway, 95% of all people WILL steal, if three conditions exist: need or perception of need, ability to rationalize the theft, and belief they will go undetected. You cannot control the first two. As employer, you can only control the third. **Until and unless you fully accept and embrace the fact of the 95% and act to control the only thing you can control in response, you leave yourself vulnerable to abuse, and you will be abused.**

This brings us to the **three-sided triangle** you must operate if you have employees, whether one or one thousand: **Leadership, Management, Supervision.**

Leadership means laying out the course for the trip. The vision. The philosophy. It also refers to the example you set. If your own behavior is out of whack with what you're expecting from the troops, you're doomed. Leaders need Moral Authority.

Management means converting the big vision to practical day to day operations. This is all about the operations manual, the rules, the procedures, the scripts, the way things are supposed to be done. As a manager, you set the processes up, you teach, you train, you coach, you motivate, you dispense recognition and reward.

Supervision means enforcement. Police work. Checking, investigating, spying, tracking, reviewing stats, making mystery shopper calls, spot checking quality control, surprise role-playing of sales scripts. Taking no shit. When you find unsatisfactory behavior, I suggest Chuck Sekeres' 3-strikes-and-you're-out. Fire fast (hire slow).

Another three sided triangle is: productivity, profit, protection. Little point in mastering the first two without taking care of the third.

So, you have to "count the cookies". The story: Mom and little Johnny are at home, no one else there. Mom bakes a dozen chocolate chip cookies, which fill the kitchen with the warm, aphrodiasic, seductive scent of fresh baked goods. Mom is going to walk out to the mailbox, get the mail and come back. If she wants to avoid leaving Johnny open to extreme temptation, if she wants twelve cookies left after her walk, she must call Johnny into the kitchen, show him the cookies, count the cookies, then say: "There are twelve. Only you and I are here. No one else. No dog. I am going out for five minutes to get the mail. The minute I return, before I do anything else, I'm going to count the cookies. If I don't count twelve, I'm going to whip your ass." Then when she comes back, she damn well better count those cookies, because Johnny'll be watching, and storing what he sees in his memory, to decide how he'll behave the next time Mom tries this trick. That's *protection.*

In the *Renegade Millionaire System,* I talk about the worst number in business being one. Only one of anything. Protection means two or more. Ignore this at your peril. I can tell you three different horror stories from three Gold/VIP Members in 2004 alone.

Well, what about trust? What about it? It's a nice concept. But statistically, as a practical matter, it's silly. I quote Reagan: trust but verify. In a poker game, trust but cut the cards. Listen very, very, very carefully: there's no bonus added to your bank deposits for being a trusting person. There's zero upside. Lots and lots of downside risk. Zero upside.

I would suggest that you look at ways to reduce the number of employees. Most of - not all, but most of my Renegade Millionaire clients and friends operate with no more than a few, to one, to none. Many like me have tried the other way and given it up.

Let's look at a client of mine, in a business similar to mine. In 2003, he had 14 employees, I had 1. He did about 5 million in business, I did 2 million. But if he pays each employee as little as $35,000.00 including wages, taxes, benefits and bonuses, that's $490,000.00. At a 50% operating margin, he must get $980,000.00 in revenue to pay them before there's the first dollar for him. Then there's his time, playing parent. Mental distraction. Police work. When it's all said and done, he might have put no more than a million more in the bank than I did, net, net, net. But I had a lot less grief.

He also has a personal assistant coming into his home office twice a week, when only he is present. I'll wager sometime within a 5 year term, she threatens a sexual harassment lawsuit and nails him for a $50,000.00 to $100,000.00 settlement. Without being sexually harassed, I might add. Two clients I know of have had this happy experience in the past three years. One has a wife who believes him, one has a wife who didn't. $2.6 mill gone in that divorce.

"Wait a damn minute. Surely there are some really good employees."

Yes there are. For some period of time. And if you are going to have them, then you have to use the triangle AND you have to invest time, energy and money in sifting and sorting good from bad, building the morale and skills of the good, keeping the good. I recommend my friend Lee Milteer's materials and coaching in this area - visit www.milteer.com.

I have had some very, very good employees. Two of them wives. But, in addition, Vicky, Lucinda. Albert and Christina Hernandez, once I was able to create an environment for them that left their work hours up to them and didn't require them to be on time. My very first employee, incidentally, a high school student, Holly, who died of Hodgins Disease at age 17. It was heart-breaking. My offices were on the second floor, up a steep staircase. She wanted to be there, to be productive, even as she got so weak she couldn't navigate the stairs, so either Dad or I carried her up and down the steps. My second employee, Stacy, was hired as a secretary as much for comic relief as skill. I had her re-file everything by alphabet - she set up an entire wall of file drawers: Misc. A, Misc. B, Misc. C. She actually tried cleaning a typewriter roller by rolling flypaper into it. My Dad was, 90%

of the time, a good employee. But I've had plenty who weren't very good or who went sour.

My racetrack saying, about our racehorses applies: THEY ALL GO LAME. It is not a question of 'if', only of 'when.' Today's apparently good, productive, loyal, happy employee is a ticking time bomb.

CHAPTER 63

Why I Admire And Have Closely Studied Donald Trump

I began paying close attention to Donald Trump long before his reinvention as television star and media entrepreneur. People who prosper, then crash, and are criticized and made fun of, then rebound bigger and better and more celebrated than ever fascinate me.

Now let me tell you some of the things that Trump has revealed about himself, in his books and interviews, that he and I are in total, absolute agreement about...

Never Delegate Your Checkbook

For one thing, he signs his own checks. "For me," Trump says, "there's nothing worse than a computer signing checks. When you sign a check yourself, you're seeing what's really going on inside your business, and if people see your signature at the bottom of the check, they know you're watching them, and they screw you less because they have proof you care about the details." With the exception of a few years when Carla issued a lot of the checks using my signature stamp, I have always signed all my checks, and for the most part, handled the invoices and written them out myself. As Trump says, by doing so, I've always had a firm sense of everything going on inside my businesses. I have, on occasion, caught vendors double-billing and overbilling, and other problems. I have given this advice to my clients - most of whom ignore it. Including the one ripped off for nearly $600,000.00 by his trusted office manager who he handed his checkbook, another swindled out of $350,000.00 by his book-keeper, yet another out $200,000.00 to "phantom vendors" set up by his accountant.

Don't Let Yourself Be Seduced By Technology

Another area Trump and I agree is technology. He flatly advises: "Don't depend on technology." He adds, "A lot of it is unnecessary and expensive." I use a computer and a laptop, but that's about it. No cell phone, no e-mail, no Internet, no Palm Pilot, no other gadgetry. And I often find entrepreneurs and small business owners imprisoned by their own technology; it's common to hear "our computers won't let us do that." I am firmly convinced that you shouldn't attempt doing anything with computers you can't do manually. Relying on your computer to do what you can't means you don't understand it.

So far, no one with a PDA has been able to find a person's phone number faster than I can in my little spiral-bound directory. And my legal pad has yet to crash and lose all my notes.

Who Needs Vacations?

Here's an interesting one: Trump says: "Don't take vacations." He insists you should be enjoying your work so much you don't want to be separated from it by vacations, and says that he "never quits working." Well, I enjoy an occasional vacation, with all work turned off. But I admit my mind never quits working. And I do agree with Trump that the person who needs or wants frequent vacations, who looks forward to weekends away from their work, cannot be trusted when they also claim they love their work and are pursuing their passions.

Let 'Em Underestimate You

One of Trump's most interesting pieces of advice is, quote, "it's often to your advantage to be underestimated." I have a pet theory about The Donald's famously weird hair. Clearly, Trump is too well-known to sneak up on anybody in a negotiation or business deal. I think he uses his hair deliberately as a distraction. While the other person is wondering why on earth such a rich sonofagun doesn't do something about that hair, maybe even thinking Trump has to be a little off to keep that oddly contrived, coiffed style, he picks their pockets.

I have frequently been underestimated, often, as Trump says, to my advantage.

A lot of people let their egos rule their lives to such an extent, they're so busy trying to show off how much they know, who they know, how much money they have, they set themselves up to be taken advantage of by quieter, smarter, more discreet, more pragmatic people.

Be A 'Curious George'

Another piece of Trump's 'Think Like A Billionaire' advice is: be curious. I'll always remember the ill-advised 'field trip' to the strip club with a group of guys from a seminar, and finding George Douglas, a brilliant entrepreneur, back in the dancers' dressing room, oblivious to the fact that he was seated between and facing nearly naked, large breasted women as he quizzed them about their business. He was far more captivated by their techniques for building up 'transaction size' and working their customers than he was by their physical attributes. Now that's entrepreneurial curiosity!

I'm insatiably curious. Especially about businesses of every kind. I read, I observe, I eavesdrop, I question. And I am very often surprised at how un-curious a lot of entrepreneurs are. One very successful client told me he would never have watched 'The Apprentice' if I hadn't made such a big deal about it. I can't imagine how an entrepreneur would resist tuning in.

Let Yourself Work The Way That Works For You

Here's another one. In 'Think Like A Billionaire', Trump wrote: "I do not keep a particularly neat office, because I have so many things going on at once. I have an enormous desk and a big round table, and both are usually covered with current projects that need my attention."

Like Trump, I have a lot of things going on simultaneously --- at this moment, this book, two other books, eight clients' copywriting projects, getting financial information ready to send to my CPA, two newsletters, this week's FAXes and correspondence, a research project, and a seminar to prepare for. I've given up filing. I need to see it to do it. I have a large desk, credenza, a large set of shelves for projects in a file room, a story-board on the wall. I put some client and project piles in gigantic zip-lock bags, to keep everything together.

I'm all for organization - in fact, I'm constantly striving to be better at it. But I've also learned to let myself work in ways that work for me. I long ago stopped trying to make my work and work area conform to someone else's ideas of what an office ought to look like or how it should be organized.

The Cardinal Rule For Traveling Like A Pro

I traveled a lot. It seemed like constantly. I consider myself a real pro at travel. And I checked luggage less than once a year. Amateurs check luggage. A pro learns to pack what he can carry on, and carry on what he packs. I hate, really hate traveling with anybody who has to check luggage, or has to schlep more than they can handle. If I have to take that much, I use FedEx to send it ahead, and send it back. Trump says: "Never check luggage. That's a cardinal rule. Checked luggage is lost luggage." And all it takes is one time, when you are in a hurry or going to an important meeting.

The Cardinal Rule For Great Success

Study and emulate people who are great successes. That's why I've studied Trump. Of course it pleases me that he and I agree on so much! But a very good reason to study successful people is for verification and validation. That's almost as useful as discovery of a new or better way of doing something. I've figured out a lot of what I do on my own, so I value hearing that my deductions and decisions are right, from somebody who's opinions I can value.

UPDATE!

Well, it's now *President* Donald Trump. At least for a while, given that the possibility of impeachment and/or forced resignation looms, as I write this immediately after the 2018 mid-terms. Given his temperament, it's extremely unlikely he'd leave voluntarily, but one can never know. Unlike any other President, he has been exposing the ugly underbelly of government to such an extent and so indiscriminately, he has *no* allies. Despite the unrelenting maelstrom of concerted opposition, he has also gotten more done than any other President in 2 years. I won't list the proof here, but it is fact, and I can prove it if challenged on it, with a wager of sufficient size to make it interesting.

Prior to this, I had hired Donald Trump as a speaker for a client's big real estate investor conference where I also spoke, been on two programs with him, hung out back stage with him, hired and been on programs with his long-time deal-making right-hand man George Ross, and hired and been on one program with Ivanka. Also several Apprentice contestants, including the country/western singer and entrepreneur John Rich. And Joan Rivers, who won a year's *Celebrity Apprentice*, was a client and friend of mine. I have also witnessed Trump's management in action. And had in-depth conversations with several of his executives. In short, I have a fair amount of "close in" observation informing my opinions about and explanations of Mr. Trump.

One savvy author about entrepreneurship, a Carter Henderson, described it as the confrontation of one problem after another after another, some requiring near super-human perseverance to solve. I would say that is Trump, and it has been very visible for those who care to look, in his presidency. As example, with tax cuts; with Justice Kavanaugh (who would have been abandoned by any other President). If you take nothing else from observing Trump, I'd suggest mentally banking this: getting big and difficult things done often takes an enormous amount of immunity to skepticism and criticism and resistance as well as finding ways to *compel* cooperation rather than create voluntary collaboration or consensus. This is more applicable to business from whence Trump came than in government, but it is nonetheless the reality.

"If You Don't Set Your Own Agenda, Others Will Set It For You."

President George W. Bush

CHAPTER 64

What's Your Schtick?

All the greatest comedians were famous for their own, individual schtick.

Schtick is based on a character that people identify with.

Dangerfield's hangdog persona, the man who got no respect.

Bob Newhart's mild-mannered, put upon, befuddled every man. In his driving instructor routine. In the first Newhart show, as psychologist. In the second Newhart show, as bed 'n breakfast proprietor.

Sam Kineson's party animal. Screaming mysonginist.

Lewis Black's last angry man.

I have schtick.

There's my no b.s., professor of harsh reality, schtick.

There's my tough, crusty curmudgeon schtick.

There's my independent, live-life-entirely-on-my-terms, inaccessible schtick.

For those who get closer, who are private clients, or in the higher levels of Membership, there's the stern-but-loving parent character, developed based on an idea I got from Dr. Kirby Landis.

In advertising language, this is 'positioning.' But it is more complex than that. I have deliberately created a character, in whose voice my sales letters and my books and newsletters are written. He is me, but sharpened, exaggerated, enhanced, dramatized. Over the years, this character has evolved and gotten more nuanced and more interesting, much the same as a mystery novelist's hero becomes a deeper, fuller personality over years, from his first appearance in the first book to his twentieth appearance in the twentieth book. If you read and compare the first Nero Wolfe novel with the twentieth, or the first Spenser novel with the twentieth, and focus on the main character, you'll see what I mean. Or, compare my newsletters from the first year to the current year. There are plot lines of my life, too, handed over to this character, also embellished and sharpened and dramatized. I talked about this in some depth for the first time in the Sales Letter Writing Workshop that I conducted in 2005, for a group of ten very serious direct-response marketers. I believe any savvy marketer does this same thing, whether marketing his restaurant locally, or himself as an industry guru globally.

Another kind of schtick is the stock material, the stories, the parables you use, use repeatedly, polish to perfection. These stories have to be synergistic with and appropriate for your character. People like self-deprecating stories, rags to riches stories, overcoming adversity stories, inspirational stories, and, of course, humorous stories. I've included a small collection of my most popular stories later in this book.

Some of my clients and Members, my Renegade Millionaire associates, have done this too, whether consciously and strategically, or more as a response to discovery of what works. Dr. Nielsen, for example, has developed a character, the doctor constantly putting something over on his staff, or having something put over on him by his staff. He has turned the famous "s. mouse" letters into continuing schtick. Platinum Member

Ron LeGrand, who teaches thousands to start from zero and get rich in real estate, has fabulous true-life schtick, as the ordinary-Joe car mechanic who went to a real estate seminar advertised in the newspaper - and the rest is history.

You can give yourself a tremendous advantage in marketing whatever product, service or business you're involved with by developing a strong character and story lines for yourself, as well as a collection of personal stories that work for you in selling situations.

CHAPTER 65

Lessons From Sinatra

I have always been a big fan of Sinatra, and have made a point of reading much of what has been written about him, watching TV biographies and so forth. There are three things about Sinatra that stick in my mind and that have affected the way I've chosen to live my life.

Sinatra once said anyone who needs anything more than a microphone and a spotlight is a punk, or something to that effect. And certainly in his heyday, Sinatra needed little else to hold an audience in the palm of his hand, to move them through an entire range of emotions. Few of today's singers can say the same. They require computer-produced enhancements, laser light shows, costume changes, etc. to put on a show. I doubt any will enjoy the enduring popularity Frank - or for that matter, Tony Bennett and Dean Martin has.

This idea has played itself out a number of different ways for me.

In advertising, as a copywriter, and in producing my own ads, direct-mail pieces, even my products and newsletter, I've pretty much ignored aesthetics, graphic enhancements, even photographs, and let the message itself carry the water, and I've been very successful with my, let's say "minimalist approach" for three decades. Time after time after time, I've beaten direct-mail controls, replacing full-color, glitzy brochures with plain-jane, black on white 8, 12, 16 and 24 page sales letters. I often observe very weak ad and sales messages presented with enormous, enormously expensive fanfare and wonder why, instead of attempting to wrap nothing with glitz they don't work harder at creating something that does not need glitz. If you've been a client or just a student of my copywriting, advertising, direct-mail or information product work and wondered about the plain, at times ugly appearance, now you know its source of inspiration.

As a professional speaker for more than 29 years, I have stubbornly refused to move into 'power points presentations', computer graphics and other audiovisual techno gimmickry. I have several reasons for this. One is that the herd eagerly adopts each new techno tool, and that alone tells me to do the opposite. Another is that I am certain it adversely affects platform selling. But a broader, more philosophical objection is the Sinatra position. If you need all that crap to deliver your message and hold an audience's interest, there's something lacking in your performance, your message or your selection of audience. I have a lot of disdain for so-called professional speakers getting paid to deliver a great performance, who lazily rely on PowerPoints to do their work for them. Virtually none of the 'greats' in the world of speaking rely on this stuff. Zig doesn't. Tom Hopkins doesn't. Jim Rohn doesn't. I have always used an overhead projector, but frankly more as a tool for keeping myself organized than for the audience's benefit. And I am quite capable of keeping an audience involved for an hour, a day or a week with nothing but me, a microphone and a stool to sit on. I've done all three, the hour, the day, the week.

Finally there's the matter of celebrity vs. privacy and private life. Elvis became a prisoner and victim of his own fame, as many celebrities do. Sinatra refused to let that happen and often made the point that he owed his audiences and fans only the best possible performance on stage, but nothing off stage. He went with friends to bars, restaurants, theater without being badgered by the public. I determined early that I was not going to sacrifice privacy or private life for any of my careers, author, speaker or consultant. Throughout my speaking years, I have steadfastly refused to go to cocktail parties or dinners the evenings before I speak, rarely went to luncheons before or after speaking, and did not mingle with audiences before or after. With my multi-day seminars and my Inner Circle Members, I've been a bit more accessible, but still I go to my hotel room for breaks and brook no interruption. I have, in my writings and seminars, used my personal life experiences as content, so my personal life has mostly been an open book, however I have and stick to clear limits. I autograph books and have photographs taken sometimes after a speech or at a seminar, but I never hesitate to refuse, if being interrupted while eating or in a private conversation with someone. And I have very firmly roped off my offthe-clock time and space; I rarely take unscheduled business calls at home only from a very few, very close clients. I have rarely been in my office, so drop-in visitors have been extremely rare, and usually disappointed.

I see many people, including many in my businesses, who are accessible 24-7-365, with cell phones, beepers, constant checking of e-mail, permitting their public to invade their lives, time and space with impunity at almost any whim, and feeling compelled to not only welcome the invasion but to be instantly responsive. This is to their detriment in every way imaginable. It is to the detriment of their health, peace of mind, relationships, overall quality of life, and it is actually detrimental to making money as well.

I have chosen not to surround myself with things to impress others with, either. Things like Tony' Robbins' castle and helicopter, or a Rolls-Royce, or a gigantic, ornate home, or the insecure celebrity's entourage, these sorts of props haven't been of interest to me or used by me since I was about 22 or 23. Frankly I'd rather have the money and use it for the lifestyle that suits me, not a lifestyle designed to impress others. My early mentor, James Tolleson, said that it was easy to impress people but more difficult and more worthy to inspire them. I've let my messages, my know-how, my work stand on its own, and avoided doing things to impress. This is not to say that I don't shamelessly promote and use self-aggrandizement for profit; I have, I do. But I focus attention on the successful results I create, not trappings.

I constantly tell such people that of all his books, Napoleon Hill's most important was not his most famous; not *'Think And Grow Rich'*; instead *'Grow Rich With Peace Of Mind'* - and I urge them, and you, to read it and give it serious thought.

When I first read this book, I was in my 20's, and it made little sense to me. Now that I am 50, I completely, totally, thoroughly understand it. I have few things I long for, lust for. But I often find myself longing for peace of mind. And I am striving to arrange my life so that I will have it.

What do ALL Renegade Millionaires have in common with Sinatra and with me? They have some clear, strong ideas about how they want to live their lives. Most people do not. Most people actually give this very little thought. Sinatra was the center of his universe, with everyone and everything else in it revolving around him. Occasionally someone has said to me - do you think the whole world's supposed to revolve around you and what you want? And I confound them by answering: yes. I have a magnet on my refrigerator that says: I want it all, and I want it delivered. Hey, why not? I have even developed and implemented a business strategy for these last few active years of my career I call the Center Of The Universe Plan.

A lot of entrepreneurs feel uncomfortable with this. Most of their discomfort comes from childhood conditioning, societal programming, peers' criticism, fear of what others will think of them, not from practical considerations. From a purely practical viewpoint, asking for what you want, setting out to get what you want, endeavoring to arrange your life to suit yourself, and getting the world around you to cooperate makes perfect sense. Insisting on peace of mind makes perfect sense. It really is a matter of personal esteem and self-respect, and of belief that all things are possible. Taking control of the relationships and circumstances that make up your world and molding it all, like a ball of Play-Dough, to suit you is a statement of deserving, and a statement of optimism. If you find it troubling to do so, you ought to ask yourself why!

As Sinatra said...."my way."

" *I'd like to be remembered as a man*
who was as honest as he knew how to be
in his life and in his work.
Also, a man who gave
as much energy in what he did everyday
as anybody else ever did.
I'd like to be remembered as a decent father,
as a fair husband, and a good friend. "

FRANK SINATRA

CHAPTER 66

Whose Opinion Matters?

Three days before finishing this Chapter, I stepped to the stage, spoke for 90 minutes and sold $91,000.00 of my books and audio programs - $1,000.00 per minute. My net, after product cost, and 50% split with the event host, $40,000.00.

If I'm not mistaken, that's more money than any of my high school teachers made or would make even today, in a year. Including the one who gave me a B- in 'Speech.'

I could do that just about as often as I like, by the way. I'm just no longer motivated to do it very often. However, at, say, once a month, it'd be more money made in a year speaking than most if not all of the anointed ones in the National Speakers Association, those who hand out the awards, those who teach the other members, might make in 2, 3 or 5 years.

There are also, not infrequently, people from audiences who accost me after a presentation, eager to give me advice. The dumbest yet was at a major seminar about information marketing, where I spoke for two hours, then sent a stampede of people to the back of the room to buy my materials. One nitwit avoided the stampede and headed toward me, notes in hand. Uh-oh. He had actually sat there and stick-counted the number of times I'd said "uh" and the number of times I'd put my hand in my pocket. I told him, since he had traveled across country and paid a $3,000.00 fee to be in the room, he might have been better served by being a student instead of a critic, and I suggested he go stick count the number of buyers at the back of the room.

When I was speaking 25 to 27 times a year on the Success Tour, averaging about $25,000.00 per speech in net income, and appearing with a veritable who's who of the business world and celebrities, I had offers of voice coaching, storytelling coaching, and "help" to slow my pace, change my body language, even "punch up" my speech - all from people not making $25,000.00 a day. Or week. Or month.

I have had twelve books published by major publishers, translated into 8 or 9 languages, published in, I think, 17 countries, on bestseller lists.. To the best of my knowledge the total number of published books authored by all the English teachers I ever had added together is - zero. Same thing for the four different editors who've worked for my publishers and fought me over the content of the books. If they're such geniuses, how come they're editing my books for wages?

I don't mean to pick on teachers. But. Just for the record: the math teacher who said I had no math aptitude whatsoever - hey, I've been able to count money. Oh yeah, I would have flunked geography were it not for a teacher just giving me a pass. I remember my parents going out and buying me a globe right after a parent-teacher conference. I still can't name all 50 states, most state capitols or tell you what country borders Argentina. But I have discovered something useful. Airline pilots seem to know how to get just about everywhere. So I've been able to get around to all 50 states to pick up money without much confusion.

I really had no athletic prowess as a kid. But I was tall, and no matter how clumsy, I could do three things on the basketball court. I consistently, routinely made 90% of my foul shots starting about age 13. I hit over 60%

long shots. And I could get in a guy's way pretty good. Unfortunately, the 7th grade gym teacher and coach insisted on fixing my shooting style. I shot one-handed. He browbeat and threatened me into switching to the 'classic' two handed, knees bent, push off shot. After I mastered it, I dropped to 50% from the line, 0% from outside.

I once sat in a bank president's office, when taking over a severely troubled company in hock to his bank for about $400,000.00, and had him glare at me and say: "I don't think you're qualified to run this company."

I said: "I'm not dumb enough to have loaned these clowns $400,000.00."

About once every month or so, I get the unsolicited critique of my newsletter from some grammarian or graphic artist, along with an offer to fix it for me. Their pity is palpable. They criticize the grammar, the mix of type fonts, the layout, you name it and they don't like it. For a number of years, it has been the most successful newsletter about marketing for all businesses. Its subscriber count has grown every year. In the business built around it, and sustained by it, the annual value of each subscriber far, far exceeds that of any other newsletter businesses' subscribers.

I once got a letter from an 'Internet guru" very popular with the NSA crowd, criticizing my web site and offering to fix it, for a fee. I agreed to hire him if he would simply provide his credit card merchant account records and tax returns to show his own web sites were making more money than mine. Never heard from him again.

A few years ago, I sat in a big corporation's big, fancy boardroom and watched and listened as their big, expensive ad agency's team of big shots presented the new TV commercials the client was to spend over a million dollars airing. These things were so dumb, so awful they actually gave off a stench. To my horror, he approved them. Afterwards I asked him what he was thinking. He said: "Well, they're the experts."

Pfui.

An expert is too often the consultant who knows 52 different sexual positions but can't get a date on *any* Friday night.

This is not to say I'm perfect at anything I do or can't improve in any area. I can. And I do spend good money each and every year on information and advice, from experts I do my best to carefully pick.

Nor is this to say that money ought to be the only measurement of the validity of someone's opinions. It is a measurement worth considering. You have to ask yourself why all the psychics live and office in ratty, rundown buildings. But not the only measurement.

It is to say that you have to be very, very, very cautious about letting others' opinions interfere with what you want to do or the way you want to do it. Especially the opinions offered gratis, unsolicited. Far too often, these come from people making themselves feel good about the absence of accomplishment in their lives by criticizing or deterring you. You have to consider the source and the motive.

Glenn Turner frequently used the quote: Many statues have been erected to the criticized. None honoring critics.

I have ignored criticism my entire life. I plan on continuing to do so.

"Lose the puppets.
They're going nowhere."

— Advice to Jim Henson, creator of The Muppets, by his boss.

CHAPTER 67

A Defiant Contrarian, An Equal Opportunity Annoyer

I have openly, visibly defied 'the rules' in just about every environment I've ever entered. In doing so, I've often annoyed, angered and inspired the ire of industry leaders, peers and the 'rule makers.' Some of this is testament only to my own obnoxious personality. But more of it is linked to good sense, to common sense, to a strategic and deliberate approach to business success.

A big part of the Renegade Millionaire philosophy is questioning and often defying industry norms - often to the profound disapproval of the industry.

I'll tell you where I first heard anything like this enunciated, although it was in broader, more general terms. The very first success educator I ever listened to on audio cassette tapes was Earl Nightingale. You've probably heard Earl's recordings too, and if you haven't you should. One of the things that leapt out at me from the hours of Earl's messages I listened to repeatedly was his statement that, if you did not have a successful model to follow, you could just observe what everybody else was doing and do the opposite. Earl asserted that the majority was wrong about money and success and happiness, proof being that the majority lacked all three.

With each successive exposure to an industry or business, or a group of people in a business, I became more and more convinced that Earl had hit it right on the mark. You could go to work just about anywhere, in any business, with no training, carefully observe what the majority of people were doing, do the opposite, and get ahead.

There have been many demonstrations of this principle in action in my life. Here are a few that have always stuck out in my mind:

In my first and only job, I was hired as a territory sales rep for a book publishing company. Only weeks after being hired, with no training, and believe me, very wet behind the ears, I joined the company's other reps from all over the country to work the big booth at the giant Chicago Gift Show. I'd never worked a trade show before and knew nothing about doing such a thing. The 'old dog' reps quickly encircled me and explained the facts of trade show life to me; you can't actually open any accounts or write orders there, you pass out catalogs, press flesh. Mostly it's a big waste of time. The store owners putting their business cards in the drawing box were all mooches. Etc. I decided to ignore them and, in essence, do the opposite. I approached people, pitched them, asked for orders and got them. I opened over a hundred new accounts in three days to management's astonishment and to the utter dismay of the other reps.

When I became a speaker and became a member of the National Speakers Association, I quickly encountered the 'old dogs' and the ingrained industry norms. For example, at the time, everybody invoiced clients for fees and expenses after they spoke. I started from day-one getting 50% as a nonrefundable deposit the day a speech was booked. Most believed and insisted you had to "ask for permission" to sell from the platform, and acquiesce to any client who balked. From day-one, I made the sale of appropriate educational materials normal, customary and mandatory. My bank account benefited enormously from ignoring industry norms.

In most businesses, industries, professions and groups there is a lot of the *"alright now, new boy, here's what you do - you take it real slow, grovel, pay your dues and maybe, years from now, you can be like us."* This is utter bullshit in 99% of the cases. For the most part, there is no real ladder and we Renegade Millionaires know it; we are **leapers, not ladder-climbers.**

Anytime somebody's showing you a ladder, there'll be a lot of rungs between where you're standing and where they're sitting. They want it to take a long time for you to climb those rungs. Be suspicious. Be very suspicious.

CHAPTER 68

Sooner or Later, You Sleep In Your Own Bed. Might As Well Please Yourself.

Please - get rich. Really rich. It is noble: the rich support the lower 2/3rds of the American economic pyramid. It's upside down and it's going to stay that way. All universities, libraries, art museums, medical research, troubled communities' redevelopment, etc. is principally funded and made possible by the rich. It's damned near necessary. It's easily doable. It's liberating. It can give you the time and power to get something worthwhile done, or to support someone doing something worthwhile. Give you the time to write a great novel or paint a great picture or be with your kids. By all means, go ahead and get rich.

But get rid of the idea of having to pay a horribly huge price for the privilege. Of having to sell your soul to the devil. Turn over your life to your clients. Trade away control of your time and life and sanity.

A big part of Renegade Millionaireship is doing business on your terms. In fact, I'm able to judge most peoples' true levels of success and expertise by this acid test: *are they conducting business on their terms or as others dictate?*

Renegade Millionaireship is about how you make money, not just about making money. Actually just making a great deal of money is easy, if you are willing to make whatever trade-offs present themselves along the way.

I've refused to make some trade-offs and am pleased with my decisions. But I've also made some that, as I get older, I question. I've had to do battle with the demon of "excess work ethic." I've had to struggle to break the work-money link imbedded in my subconscious. I've gradually discovered that the link is easily broken, that money can be attracted rather than manufactured. It hasn't been an easy understanding for me to embrace and live. It's only been in the last ten years that I've really "got it."

All of life, everyone's life, is endless trade-offs.

You trade away freedom, sexual promiscuity, leaving dirty socks and pizza boxes lying around in favor of a meaningful, cohabitative relationship with one partner. You trade away even more freedom to be a parent. You trade off doughnuts and pizza for weight loss. You trade off, constantly. The list of trade-offs we make is endless.

Being a Renegade Millionaire is not an escape from trade-offs. Instead, it is its own framework for trade-offs and, admittedly it's not for everybody. But the trade-off you definitely need not make is servitude and slavery for money. After all, that's the trade poorly paid people make - what's the point of suffering the exact same enslavement just for bigger zeroes on a bank book, if that's all that's gained?

Most people are servants to their businesses. I have long insisted my businesses be servants to me.

For that to occur, customers or clients must be rigidly controlled. Expectations carefully managed. And you must have a willingness to repel or cut loose clients who cannot be satisfied, employees who can't be managed, vendors who can't be patronized without compromising your lifestyle preferences. This is all about clarity, decision and determination. And about brass balls.

Some years ago, I was on the verge of signing a very lucrative deal with a new copywriting client. This company is in a field where I'm very familiar and adept, and knew I would be extremely effective and successful. They mailed millions of pieces of direct-,mail a year and creating winning campaigns for them could provide me with hundreds of thousands of dollars a year in royalties. And we had agreed to a six figure retainer. The only stumbling block was the entrepreneur-CEO's unwillingness to assign projects on a schedule, communicate with me mostly by Fax and, when phone conversation was needed, by pre-scheduled calls. He insisted he had to be able to pick up the phone and get me when he felt the need. He begged me to carry a secret cell phone no one would know about but me. With a sigh, I turned him away.

In case you are not familiar with how I work, let me take you through it. It is instructive. First you need to know that I did business pretty much the same way long before I could afford to do so. I do not own a cell phone or beeper, nor do I personally use e-mail. Nor do I intend to. I am not easily accessible at all. Most communication at the present is by FAX. Only a small cadre of key clients and friends have any kind of direct access to me. Almost all my inbound FAXes, phone messages and mail accumulates all week, is sorted and packaged for me, and sent to me in a weekly box. I begin addressing it the following week. It is normal for there to be two to three week delay in my response to phone messages, FAXes or correspondence if important, twice that if unimportant. I am never stampeded. People requiring my attention are taken in turn. There's a waiting line.

New clients are usually asked to prepare and submit a one to two page memo describing their businesses, interests, needs, or if involving my speaking for them, the details of the event and audience. Only after I've seen such information will I ask Vicky to arrange a telephone appointment if warranted.

I "clump" my telephone appointments, so there are often only two or three days during any given month when I've set time aside for this purpose. Appointments are pre-determined in length, and booked back to back, so I finish one and immediately take the next. If someone is late calling, tough. The 30 minutes that had been allocated to them becomes 12, because someone else is scheduled for the 31st minute.

I schedule only a small block of time into each week for the unexpected. I'm fond of Henry Kissinger's statement: 'There can be no other crisises this week. I am already fully booked."

I *detest* having my time disrespected or wasted. That's the surest way to wind up on my shit list. I have terminated working relationships with clients, even refunding as much as $70,000.00 to one to get rid of him, because of sloppy, irresponsible, disrespectful treatment of my time --- missing scheduled calls, for example.

I never invoice clients for fees. There's a contract covering every project or relationship that spells out agreed on payments and the schedule for those payments, and I expect the client to honor it, keeping track however he must: Post-It Notes on his mirror, an alarm bell set off by his Palm Pilot. But if I have to ask for money, I won't ask much; I'll just replace the client.

I pretty much avoid doing business with big, dumb companies, committees, or the woefully ignorant.

In 29 years of speaking, I only got one speaking engagement from a bureau. I am what is called "bureau unfriendly." That's because I can't be reached by phone, I never return calls quickly, I'm picky about who I speak for and where I go, and refused to speak without both fee and selling appropriate resources from the platform. None of this proved much of a handicap, even though every 'authority' said it would.

I have written about the time management aspects of all this extensively in my book *No B.S. Time Management For Entrepreneurs.*

Many reading this will be tempted to simply label me a 'freak', and they will instantly rattle off a laundry list of reasons why they could never exercise such firm and complete control over their business life. Their customers would never tolerate it. If they're inaccessible, clients will go elsewhere. Their field is different. Yada yada. But the list of people who have altered their business practices and modeled their approach to time and access management after mine, and successfully trained their clientele to accept it, is long, from a very diverse variety of businesses and professions. Darin Garman, a commercial real estate broker; Tracy Tolleson, a mortgage broker; Michael Jans, who runs several businesses; Jerry Jones, who provides direct-mail services to dentists; Jeff Parrack, an accountant who works with people with IRS problems, come immediately to mind. Most have found their incomes have increased, not suffered.

And now I will tell you the most important and chilling truth about you and your business: if you still insist you cannot create such control and independence for yourself, you are admitting the fact that your clientele views you as a common, interchangeable commodity. There is no worse position. If commoditized, you are at the mercy of competitors who will cut prices to a point of losses or who will give in to customers' every demand no matter how intolerable. Your customers will make choices based on price or convenience. Commoditization is prelude to extinction.

I remember speaking for the second year in a row at the Advertising Specialty Institute National Convention, an industry immersed in commoditization, in part thanks to the internet. If you are going to buy imprinted cups or golf balls or pens, it's easy to shop by price online. I started my speech by saying "If you are in a commodity business, get out." A woman attending misunderstood, stormed out and later sent a nasty letter. Here, I say it again. If you are in a business where you are being commoditized, get out. I mean, re-invent your business. And at the same time, you might as well re-invent the way you *do* business. To please yourself.

CHAPTER 69

"I Planned To Change The World But I Couldn't Get A Babysitter"

For a while, I was a partner in a cosmetics company, with retail salons, where skin care product 'systems' were sold by bringing women in for free makeovers. In Arizona, we did not need licensed cosmetologists as long as the salesperson did not apply any product. The customer applied everything as instructed by the salesperson. So we hired people and instantly trained them and put them chairside, selling. A lot of these "counselors" were young women, fresh out of high school, with, let's say, undeveloped work skills. They were famously unreliable. But incredibly creative at coming up with excuses for being late or missing days of work. They reported to our sales manager, a coarse, tough 'street guy' named Shelby . Shelby developed a large wall sign with a huge list of these excuses, numbered for everyone's convenience. From across the hall, you could sometimes hear Shelby yelling: "Just tell me the number."

Saved a lot of time.

In my years, I've heard thousands of excuses for not getting started, not doing well, not being able to utilize good marketing, not following through, not getting things done, from employees, associates, vendors and clients. If there's one talent possessed by all, it seems to be excuse-making. I can't recall ever taking a class on this, but somehow everybody learns to do it.

I have a good one I never utilized for anything, but could have. One morning my car wouldn't start. Investigation by my father determined that a body part of a cat had gotten wedged into in the fan blade and stopped it from turning. Apparently, the poor, stray cat had crawled up in there after I'd parked the car for warmth. I'd re-started the car to pull it forward to the garage unaware of the cat. In the course of this investigation, my father noticed an odd odor emitting from *inside* my car. Our further investigation uncovered a meat loaf wrapped in aluminum foil my mother had given me to drop off at a neighbor's house two weeks earlier, that I'd forgotten about, that got covered with newspapers and trash on the floor in the backseat. Disturbing this smoldering, toxic mess made me violently ill. I had to vomit, then lie down. Now this would have been a nifty excuse for being late to some appointed place, wouldn't it?

It pales in comparison to the convoluted complexity of many I've heard.

There are lots of irritating ones, that should be embarrassing to say. Business owners actually say "my employees won't let me". Incredible.

Other excuses are elegant in their simplicity. Like the ever-popular: my alarm clock didn't go off. I overslept. I was up all night with a sick child/ spouse/friend/pet/plant.

When I was broke, I had a lot of excuses for being broke - as everybody who's broke does. When I was boozing, I had a lot of excuses for boozing - as every drunk does. When I was lugging around 248 pounds, I had a lot of excuses for being so overweight - as every fat person does. Gotta a news flash: you can't lose weight until you lose the excuses. You can't quit drinking until you quit making excuses. You can't fill your bank account until you empty your mind and mouth of excuses for being broke.

Here's the thing: excuse-making is a destructive cancer that destroys your reputation with others as well as your own self-respect and self-esteem. Excuse-making is a sickness, a type of mental illness, a delusional distancing from rational thought and reality. Excuse-making robs you of opportunity, squanders talent and ability. Excuse-making is a sad statement of lack of character and integrity, a warning to others that you are not to be trusted.

Renegade Millionaires are extremely intolerant of excuse-making, from others, and from themselves.

If you aspire to great success, you must stop the habit of making excuses yourself and stop accepting them from others. Whenever you catch yourself making an excuse, you must stop yourself, take yourself into a corner, and demand that you be honest with yourself and with others. Hold yourself to a higher standard. If you raise your standards, you automatically raise others' respect for you, automatically raise your income. **People and opportunities are magnetically attracted to the individual who makes no excuses.**

It is interesting that one of the most important things to do when selling to others is to tell them "it's not your fault." In selling, we want to let people off the hook. To let them be excuse-makers. We say to them, you have lots of good excuses for your situation. You bear no blame or shame for where you are. Now, finally, we have arrived with the "secrets" that have been kept from you, by the world conspiracy that exists to keep you broke or fat or unhappy.

But when managing ourselves for maximum achievement, we must tell ourselves: it's my fault. My responsibility. The fewer excuses I make, the more opportunity I have, the more able I am to exert control.

Frankly, we sell by pandering to most peoples' love of excuse-making. But we achieve by disavowing excuse-making. For high achievers, there's no such thing as 'a good excuse'.

CHAPTER 70

It's Still Early And You Can't Judge How The Day Was Until You See The Sunset

In my *'Wealth Attraction For Entrepreneurs Seminar'* (available on CD), I talk about this principle: "all news is good news." It is an extraordinarily difficult principle to truly, completely accept, internalize and live by. There are incidents that occur that seem to defy the principle. However, I have come to believe in it, I try to trust in it. It is a mandatory precursor to using Napoleon Hill's admonition: in every adversity lies the seed of equal or greater opportunity. Nothing is ever as good or as bad as it first appears.

From my life, a few of many examples:

Had I been able to go to college, I would possibly be a veterinarian, more probably have wound up with a journalism degree, and could be covering flower shows and funerals for the Tuscaloosa News Journal, making $42,600.00 a year.

Had Environmental Structures, Inc. not had its deal-with-the-devil, forcing its use of flawed coverings, thus erecting buildings certain to self-destruct, I might have been a corporate marketing director with a desk job. Gray suit, gray tie, gray hair, gray inner being.

Had I been of the temperament to work for someone else, and held onto my sales rep job with Price/Stern/Sloan, I'd probably still be a territory sales rep in the publishing industry, schlepping sample case, driving endlessly, on the road five days a week.

Had it not been for the worst winter in Cleveland's recorded history, I might never have moved to Phoenix, never have started speaking. Not met Carla. Not, in any way, had the life I've had.

Had I not "burnt out" on the SUCCESS tour, I would still be flying to two cities every week in the post 9-11 world, quite literally spending my entire life standing in security lines, hanging out in airports, arriving bleary-eyed at hotels late in the evening, going through the motions doing something that long ago ceased interesting me.

The National Speakers Association has been a mixed bag for me in many interesting ways. But one thing, if my entire NSA experience had been horrid, one thing that came out of it would have made it all worthwhile: my friendship with Lee Milteer. Lee is my truest and greatest friend and I actually cannot imagine life without her in it.

I'll bet you can create a similar list from your own life experiences. If you stop and look back reflectively, you can re-trace the road map of your life as a series of detours that looked bad at first but turned out well. It's useful to keep this mind in the present, as you are zipping along at 70 MPH on a straight, paved road, on a bright, sunny day when suddenly, out of nowhere, a giant tree crashes down across the highway, you yank the wheel and go careening off to the left, through a ditch, onto a winding dirt road.

Which, incidentally, is gonna happen.

SECTION SIX

Political

Commentary

CHAPTER 71

If I Ran For President

A t one time, I was very seriously interested in running for political office, and had the governor's office in Arizona in my sights. Couple small problems. Carla was adamantly, vocally, rigidly against my pursuing political ambitions. And, doing the disclosure on all my relatives' arrest records and other exploitable problems would have required hours.

I include political commentary in most of my writing and speeches, because I don't see how you can separate your political views and your success philosophy. As a result, I have been asked more often than you might think: what would your platform be, if you ran for President? Here are a few planks, in no particular order.

Illegal Immigration

I'd tell Mexico's government: you've got six months to stop the flow of illegal immigrants and of illegal drugs flowing across our border or you become Cuba to us. We build a 50 foot high wall and close the border to all traffic. Complete embargo. No import or export, no tourists allowed to go there, no nothing. I'd go on national TV and tell the American public why nothing less makes any sense, and tell them to call their Congressmen and demand they support my policy.

I fully support *legal* immigration.

However, I also advocate 'English required.' To be an American citizen, you should have to learn, read, write and speak our language. We do nobody any favors by letting them attempt assimilation and success in our society without the first prerequisite for doing so. Nor is it fair to ask taxpayers to incur the very substantial, rarely discussed costs of operating a tri-language government.

Taxation

Our income tax system is an indefensible mess. A criminal mess. Kept in place by politicians who use it for social engineering, idiots, tax lawyers and the IRS. If it were replaced with something that makes sense, a whole lot of these people would be out looking for honest work. Either a flat tax or a national sales tax, accompanied by a constitutional amendment requiring a 75% majority vote of both houses of Congress to raise taxes or enact any new taxes of any kind - that's what I would push for.

Capital gains tax and estate tax should be eliminated altogether. The money was already taxed once. Once is enough.

States should be forced to keep their income, sales and property taxes within a sane range or be denied federal aid.

No one should pay combined taxes taking away more than 30% of what they earn.

You might ask how the nation could possibly afford such a radical change and reduction in taxes. Easily, that's how. First of all, Presidents John Kennedy, Ronald Reagan and George W. Bush ably demonstrated that income tax bracket reductions increase tax revenues. Second, the productivity and investment boom that would occur thanks to truly comprehensive tax simplification and relief would more than compensate. Third, I would put heavy surcharge taxes on vices. Fourth, I would take an axe to foreign aid and government waste. A big axe.

Legalized Vices And The Underground Economy

You pay at least 400% more in taxes than you should, so everybody in the underground economy can enjoy tax-free income. You pay excessive taxes so pimps and prostitutes, bookies, drug dealers, dealers in stolen merchandise, and layers and layers of organized crime and gang leaders can pay zero taxes. If you approve of that plan, you need to see a mental health professional. I actually think it could and arguably should be the other way around: you and I should pay zero income tax, and tax on those in vice businesses should support us. Essentially, Nevada operates that way. Zero income tax for its citizens. Taxes on the casino industry more than take care of the whole tab.

Prohibition is a failure. The only segment of society that benefits in any way, shape or form from gambling, prostitution and marijuana being illegal is organized crime. It is asinine to continue these completely unsuccessful prohibitions, that suck up monstrous quantities of economic, law enforcement, judicial and penal resources. The entire mess is a gigantic cost to you and me, a gigantic opportunity for criminals. There has to be a better way, and we ought to find it.

Why I Object So Strenuously To Paying Taxes

I know, I know, taxes are the price we pay for living in such a sophisticated society, with so many government services. And that would be fine if it weren't for the rampant waste and criminal graft that permeates every government agency, every bureaucracy, that inflates the costs of every government service.

President Reagan had the industrialist W. R. Grace conduct The Grace Commission and document literally thousands of very specific examples of waste and graft and theft that could be corrected. Not a single recommendation of that extensive report was ever implemented. President Clinton stuck Al Gore with a similar futile assignment.

I will give you one outrageous example, from a February 18, 2005 news article in *The New York Times*. Reported, that the Department of Homeland Security has allocated hundreds of millions of dollars to protect our seaports post 9-11, but less than 1/4th of the $517-million dispensed between June of 02 to December 03 had even been put to use by 2005. Worse, the money has been moved around in some very questionable ways. For example, Wyoming received four times as much anti-terrorism funding per capita than has New York. I basically flunked high school geography, but I think Wyoming is short on seaports. And probably less likely to be attacked by terrorists than New York. 80% of all inbound freight comes through only 10 ports, but those ports didn't even get 20% of the money. If you can read a news report like that and feel good about paying your taxes, I don't get it.

Hunting Season

I would make a big dent in the federal deficit with this plan. Twice a year, for a two week period each time, for $5,000.00 you could buy a hunting permit and legally shoot anyone talking on a cellphone in a public place. And get their heads mounted, cellphones stuffed in their mouths, to hang on your wall. And the hunter who bagged the most would win $100,000.00.

Who Could Oppose Aid To Tsunami Victims?

I can. As I was finishing this Chapter, the tsunami aid hysteria was in full swing, and, under public and global pressure, Bush had quickly upped an initial aid commitment of, I think, 35-million dollars to 350-million to 600-million. And we had military on the ground in huge numbers. Incredibly, the government of Indonesia made it known it didn't like us sending military to deliver our aid and protect non-military workers, doctors, etc.

I do not believe our tax dollars should be doled out to victims of disasters and tragedies in foreign lands unless we are sitting on nice surpluses. When we have a massively overdrawn federal checkbook, it should stay closed. This does not mean I lack concern, compassion or desire to help in such circumstances, it just means I believe the help should come from citizens, charities and companies voluntarily, of their own iniative. Not from the money forcibly extracted from us as taxes. Tax dollars should be used domestically. Were I elected, I would institutionalize the involvement of former U.S. Presidents and others in fundraising as needed to deliver aid to victims of tidal waves, floods, fires, volcanic eruptions, starvation, etc. outside our borders, but I would eliminate the use of tax dollars for such purposes, and set caps on how much military support can be provided per disaster and relief incident.

Here's something I found very interesting about the tsunami. It galvanized all sorts of people demanding that our government do more and leaping into the fray with telethons, benefit concerts and web sites. Well, where was all that earnest concern, compassion and iniative the week before the tsunami? Plenty of starvation, children going without health care, disease, crumbling, rat-infested inner city tenements right here at home the week before. Plenty of disease, pestilence, even genocide overseas before. Apparently a lot of people are eager to be charitable with my tax dollars and their own only when there's a dramatic, *popular* disaster in an exotic location. Pfui.

Education

I would privatize education, with federal government and local school board oversight. Here's a simple, astounding fact: top quality private schools deliver education for less money per student than do the worst public schools. Yet they pay their teachers better. And provide better education.

I would also make two courses mandatory in high school, one on the free enterprise system, the other on 'fundamentals of personal success' - from how your paycheck works, how credit card interest works, to setting goals. Both would be taught by local businesspeople who volunteered, not the regular (liberal) teachers.

Federal Government Reform

With professional politicians for life, we've replaced the British royalty with royalty of our own. I would switch Congress to part-time, convened only two weeks every other month. Members of Congress would be housed in nice barracks, work every day, sleep in the barracks at night, do the public's business, then return home and work or run a business in the real world. To help reduce their workload, a limit on the number of new laws and bills that can be passed each year. Six seems about right to me. That way all the voters could pay attention and know what's going on, and the government would be forced to focus on really important things. Term limits: absolutely, and we need to make approving them a litmus test to get on the Supreme Court. As long as income tax exists, every elected official should be audited every year, and be required to fill out all his own tax forms. With term limits, part-time legislature and a limit on new laws, lobbyists will diminish in number and influence. Finally, lawyers ought to be prohibited from serving in Congress. We have a judicial branch. We are not supposed to have two judicial branches.

Gee, whatdya think the chances are of me getting elected?

CHAPTER 72

Darwinism - And The Secret To My Success

During my drinking years, I frequently drove home from bars drunk as a skunk. I'm not proud of it. I have a couple very funny stories about it that are funny only because they involve no tragedy - but they could have. The spiritual interpretation of this might be that angels watched out for me, that I had some important things to do with my life so that I was protected from my own idiocy by the grace of God. Given that, I should probably be more compassionate and sensitive about my next thoughts. Nevertheless....

Every year in Phoenix, on New Years Eve and on the 4th of July, there are news reports of imbeciles shooting guns aimed straight up into the sky, then being killed by the bullet coming back down to earth, stopping short of terra firma, path interrupted by the idiots' heads. Recently, I read a news report of a woman driving home from the store, who decided to take a shortcut: driving on railroad tracks. She drove head-on into a train. Another news item told the tale of two thugs who stuck up an isolated convenience store in the north-woods, led police on a dangerous chase through curvy mountain roads at speeds up to 90 miles an hour, eventually gave the cops the slip only to realize they were completely lost. Fortunately they came to a small convenience store and, unlike most men, stopped for directions. At the same store they had robbed an hour before. Its owner watched them get out of the car and, as they walked in, he shot them both dead with his double-barreled shotgun.

Darwinism, survival of the fittest, implicitly says some are not fit to survive. Some people are too dumb to live. I'm a big fan of herd thinning via self-selection. Not genocide, not societal neglect. Self-selection. Death by stupidity.

I also believe we need a Prison For The Criminally Stupid. The woman who went up to Mike Tyson's hotel room late at night and was then surprised to be sexually assaulted by a rabid brute, and Mike Tyson for taking a young woman up to his hotel room late at night and assaulting her - they should be in adjoining cells. Kobe Bryant, I doubt is guilty as accused; I doubt his accuser as innocent as she insisted. So were I on a jury considering that matter, I'd never send him to prison for rape. But I'd give him five years in The Prison For The Criminally Stupid. Sending Martha Stewart to jail for lying about a non-crime, for which she was not and could not be prosecuted, is outrageous. But I'd give her 36 months at the Prison For The Criminally Stupid, for endangering her multi-million dollar personal fortune and all of her trusting stockholders' investments in an attempt to pocket a measly $40,000.00 on a side deal.

Most observers think that I have spent my life helping people get smart and become successful, many fabulously successful. I have not. I have been busy helping smart people get smarter, successful people become more successful. It is more than a semantic distinction.

I have no illusions about what I've been up to. It is my belief that just about every person who gives me some credit, to a lot of credit for their success would ultimately have become just as successful even if they'd never encountered me, even if the angels had let me drunkenly drive my car off the side of a cliff, which I made a pretty good attempt at doing, twice. These people are winners. Winners are winners are winners. They somehow emerge. If I didn't exist, they'd have found someone else to point them in productive directions. If I wasn't there to reveal certain strategies, they'd have uncovered them elsewhere or figured them out for themselves. Maybe at a slower pace. Maybe with more struggle. Maybe not. But winners become winners.

I do not believe this is as simple as genetics or destiny. But I believe a person collects certain fundamental traits and drives early on, maybe from family, maybe from environment, maybe from terrible dissatisfaction, from observation, from multiple sources and influences. They become a determined, ambitious winner. Then they figure out how to win. Conversely, others are losers. Ignorant, lazy, unambitious, unmotivated, immature into adulthood. You can train them, coach them, motivate them, finance them, put them in good environments, introduce them to opportunities and they will still figure out how to lose. They will fire guns up into the air and stand there waiting for the bullet. One way or another. Do I think people change? No. I believe a person *can* change if that person determines he will change. But I do not believe anybody changes without personally determining to change. Losers lose. Winners win.

For nine consecutive years, I appeared on more than 25 events each year with Zig Ziglar. Even though he and I have not always seen eye to eye and never become buddies, I have great respect for Zig and I have reason to believe he has respect for me. This does not dissuade me from cautioning you against accepting one of his most famous quotes at face value. Zig says: if you help enough other people get what they want, you will get everything you want.

Like most profundities, it is truth only as far as it goes.

But the truer truth is that you might not live long enough to get everything you want by *indiscriminately* attempting to help other people get what they want.

I consider myself very, very fortunate to have learned early the futility of trying to turn losers into winners. It may be an admirable, heroic, spiritual endeavor. But it's definitely not the way to get everything you want, unless you are feline and plan on stringing nine lifetimes together, or are satisfied with the promise of rewards in heaven instead of on earth.

Three pieces of advice on this that I have paid heed to:

One, from James Tolleson: "Only when a person needs, wants, accepts, values and appreciates your help can you help that person."

Two, from Joel Weldon, a speaker, and early in his career, a Nightingale-Conant and General Cassette distributor, selling audio cassette programs business to business, door to door, person to person. Joel told me to decide how much time to invest in a prospect based on the books and audio cassette programs visible in his office. If he had few or none, drop a catalog and get out. If he had shelves full and not an inch to spare or opening to fill, stay as long as you could. Because a buyer is a buyer is a buyer. A non-buyer is a non-buyer. A winner a winner, a loser a loser.

Three, from Paul J. Meyer, founder of Success Motivation Institute. A 'secret' sign concealed in his office. "You can't make chicken salad out of chicken shit."

I have gotten just about everything I want in life. I have few regrets. I have some unfulfilled desires, some things I still want to get done, some marks I'd like to hit. But I lack for nothing. I have gotten just about everything I want.

I have done so by designing my businesses and directing my energies and efforts to helping winners win bigger, win more, win more often.

I *have* discriminated. I have done all I can to attract to me winners, to repel from me losers. I make no bones about it. I offer no apologies. In fact, I suggest it as strategy for you. Take great pains to surround yourself with winners. To attract winners. To be of great service to winners. To conduct your business with winners. Because my experience is, if you help enough winners get what they want in life, you will get everything you want in life.

CHAPTER 73

Who Should Vote?

Immediately following the 2004 Presidential election, a number of liberal pundits and Hollywood loudmouths began telling anyone who'd listen that the "red states" got more from the federal government than they paid for, and were, in fact, "welfare states" supported by the "blue states" - and that it was fundamentally wrong for the people in the states like New York, Connecticut and California paying all the bills not to call the shots in government policy.

I agree with these sore losers. In fact, this position totally supports one I've long advocated: **only taxpayers should be permitted to vote.** The liberals upset with the Bush re-election and I appear to be in complete philosophical agreement on this idea: it is fundamentally unfair for anyone not kicking in to the grocery budget to have a voice in meal selections. But my proposal is more sensible than theirs. Fairer. More just. No geographic discrimination. Only a simple, nationwide standard: only those putting money into the kitty get a vote on how the money is spent. How can you argue with the justice in that?

So, to vote, you must have paid income taxes the prior year. If you got back more than you paid via the 'earned income credit' or you are on welfare or retired and paying no income taxes or, for whatever other reason, you didn't pay federal income taxes, you shut up, stay in the stands and be a spectator.

This, incidentally, is reasonably representative of the founding fathers' original wisdom. They knew that the single most destructive force to attack a democracy would be voters only taking from government, not contributing to it. Their attempt to safeguard against such a thing was permitting only landowners to vote. Today, that standard would obviously be unreasonable; we live in a renters' world. Lots of renters do pay taxes and are entitled to an opinion about who gets put in charge of the pot. But the modern day justice would be to simply substitute "taxpayer" for "land-owner."

Where is the justice in my paying $300,000.00 in income taxes and having my vote cancelled out by a third generation welfare recipient or 18 year old kid taking a year off after college at his parents' expense?

My proposal is simple and undeniably just.

If there are six people living in a house but only five kick-in for rent, food and supplies, the sixth, with roof and meals provided only due to the generosity of the other five, better not complain about his mattress, view from his room, or meal set before him. Beggars, as the saying goes, can't be choosers. People not paying taxes should never be choosers.

CHAPTER 74

The Book Chapter That Wasn't

I n the spring of 2004, I had delivered the three manuscripts for my NO B.S. books to my publisher (Entrepreneur Press), one of which included a chapter titled *"Michael Moore, You Are A Big, Fat, <u>Anti-American Idiot"</u>* which the chief editor had seen and approved months before, and which supported a publicity strategy we had all discussed aimed at conservative talk radio and television media. But very late in the final editing, the chapter suddenly became "unacceptable." At first, they said it was a legal issue; then they said it wasn't, instead that they only objected to the vitriolic tone. Hours were invested in negotiating a new solution, splitting the chapter into an 'open letter to Michael Moore' and a somewhat neutered chapter about free enterprise. We agreed to the 'open letter' being separate, in the front of the book; the chapter last. And I believed we had agreement.

But only two weeks or so before Book Expo, when a race to get galleys printed was on, I discovered, literally by accident, they had renigged on the deal, were only putting the chapter in, omitting the open letter, but intending to print the letter separately only to use for publicity purposes. Not only did this alter the book, make the last chapter unwarranted, but it hung me out 100% liable for the letter. They would get all the publicity benefit, none of the risk. I objected, let's say, strenuously. And the book was published absent both chapter and open letter.

At the time and right through to November, Michael Moore was ever-present in the news. His anti-Bush film, *Fahrenheit 911,* that Disney refused to release, was released by Miramax, won an award from France (naturally), and was heavily promoted. Moore was once again the talk show gadfly. I couldn't have timed the situation better. My book was promoted at Book Expo in May, nearly simultaneous to Moore's film, and put on book-shelves in August, at the height of Moore's self-promotion. I believe, had the chapter stayed in my book, you'd have seen me on O'Reilly, Hannity & Colmes and Crossfire, and heard me on the radio on Glenn Beck, O'Reilly, Limbaugh. *No B.S. Business Success* would have enjoyed weeks on the New York Times bestseller lists.

It's been my experience that publishers are generally dim-witted and clue-less about marketing. In this case, this publisher's people understood - to some degree - the marketing opportunity. They were just gutless.

I hope they were not driven by a concealed, top down liberal leaning, by secret agreement with Moore on the issues I raised. After all, they publish Entrepreneur Magazine. Not 'You Can't Get Ahead In America Maga-zine.' So I presume only gutless.

I am not.

And I see no legitimate legal issue. We have a constitution. It protects free speech. Moore is a public figure who has no legal recourse against criti-cism. Unless libeled. Which I did not do. Presumably if Al Franken can title a book 'Rush Limbaugh Is A Big, Fat Idiot', I have the right to com-parable opinion about Mr. Moore. The entire chapter is my opinion and makes no assertion otherwise, except to quote Mr. Moore's own words.

I bear Moore no ill will personally. I think he is a destructive force and a hypocrite, but he has every right to be those things and to express his opin-ions. On a very few things I actually agree with him. I use him as he uses himself; as a lightning rod. For me, he is a convenient representation of a widespread, insidious force in American society. He is a means of putting a face on a collection of voices, voices that tell people the American dream is a lie, that discourage iniative, responsibility and achievement.

I believed and continue to believe this chapter makes an important statement. It is now somewhat dated in some of its references, but still very relevant. So, here, I publish the book chapter that wasn't.

(It is a slightly altered version of the first version and the negotiated-with-publisher second version.) If you wish to reprint it, feel free; just please also credit me and www.renegademillionaire.com. If you would like a copy of the chapter by itself for reprint purposes, furnished on a CD, simply send a request to me at my Phoenix office.

CHAPTER 75

Michael Moore Is A Big, Fat Anti-American

To succeed as an entrepreneur, you need total confidence in our free enterprise system, the unlimited opportunities it provides, and in the unlimited power of the individuals. You have to be an avowed capitalist, passionate in your admiration and appreciation of capitalism.

One of the currently popular voices of anti-capitalism is Michael Moore. Chapter #7 in his book *'Dude, Where's My Country?'* is so offensive, and so false, I have written this Chapter in response.

Here, in part, is what Mr. Moore wrote:

"We're addicted to this happy rags-to-riches myth in this country. People elsewhere in other industrialized democracies are content to make a good enough living to pay their bills and raise their families. Few have the cutthroat desire to strike it rich....most people outside the U.S. don't live their lives based on fairy tales. They live in reality, where there are only going to be a few rich people, and you are not going to be one of them. So get used to it. ...... we bought the Kool-Aid. We bought into that lie that we, too, could someday be rich."

Mr. Moore says the very idea that you, an ordinary American, can get rich is a cruel lie. I say he is either a fool or a liar. Let's look at the facts. It's important to do so because Mr. Moore represents a lot of voices, all telling you "you can't do it", urging you to cool your jets, accept your lot in life. These voices are dangerous. You - and everyone who hears them - need to know just how wrong they are.

Michael Moore, Meet The Forbes 400, The Richest People In America

Maybe Michael Moore doesn't read *Forbes*. Each year, *Forbes* publishes an issue featuring brief profiles of the 400 richest people in America. Multi-millionaires and billionaires - what he says you can't be and shouldn't bother trying to become. The *2003 Forbes* list, the truth, destroys Moore's fiction.

Certainly, a number are on the list due to inheritance - although the original source of the inherited wealth is still instructive. But let's look at some of the people who got there doing what Moore says you can't.

First, the top ten richest. Bill Gates. He started his business in a garage, only 30 years ago. Four of the top 10 are Sam Walton heirs. Sam opened his first little store in 1962. Now, as we go deeper in the list, we get a much clearer picture of just how wrong Moore is.

Richard Egan. A Marine **helicopter pilot** in the Korean War. In 1979, Egan launched a small **storage company** with six employees. He took the company, EMC, public in 1986. He's worth **$1.3-Billion.**

Harold Simmons. **A school teacher's son,** once employed as a bank examiner. In 1961, Simmons put together just $5,000.00 and bought a small

drugstore. Just 12 years later, he sold the chain of stores he built, Eckerds, for **$50million.**

Wayne Huizenga. **A college drop-out** who started his **garbage collection business** with one used truck. He built that business (Waste Management) and sold it, then bought a small chain of 19 video stores, and built that into the Blockbuster chain, sold just seven years later to Viacom for **$8.4-Billion.**

Leslie Wexner. This Ohio State **law school drop-out** started with **one womens clothing store** in Columbus, Ohio, in 1963. He methodically built a chain of more than 4,000 stores. Seven different brands, including The Limited and Victoria's Secret. Worth **$2.7-Billion.**

Kenny Troutt. This 55 year old **bartender's son** grew up in a housing project, held jobs in construction, selling insurance. In 1988, he started his own network marketing company, Excel Communications, **selling discount long-distance.** He built it to $1.4-billion in sales, sold it in 1998 for **$3.5-billion.** He owns the stud farm where the 2003 Kentucky Derby winner, Funny Cide, was born.

James Jannard. A **college drop-out** who started a small business in 1975, making motorcycle grips. Expanded to sunglasses and apparel. Built his brands by giving free samples to celebrities. Worth **$1.1-Billion.**

Margaret Whitman. **Harvard MBA,** worked at Proctor & Gamble and Hasbro, before taking something of a career gamble, taking the top job at an unproven new company: eBay. Worth **$1.1-Billion.**

Gary Comer. Turned his hobby into a business, beginning with a small mail-order operation, **selling hardware to boat owners.** Added clothing. Turned the catalog into Land's End. Sold to Sears for **$1-Billion.**

Oprah Winfrey. You know her. Came from a **very troubled background.** Started working in local TV. Turned nationally syndicated show into multi-media empire. Her motto: "Own it." Worth over **$1-Billion.**

John Menard Jr. Opened a little **hardware store**, after building barns to pay his way through college. Has 184 stores. Worth **$3.5-Billion.**

David Green. Opened a small store to sell his **handmade picture frames.** Today, 307 craft stores in 27 states. Worth **$1.1-Billion.**

Sydell Miller. From my hometown, Cleveland, Ohio. She started an eyelash make-up company in 1971, built it up from scratch, sold it in 1984 for a paltry $3-million. Started again, **mixing batches of hair care products in the basement of a hair salon.** Turned that company into Matrix, sold to Bristol-Myers Squibb. Worth **$595-Million.**

Let's review. We have highly educated; we have college drop-outs. Men and women. People in mundane businesses like hardware stores and garbage collection.

Who will be on this list five, ten, fifteen years from now? A whole bunch of people Michael Moore insists can't possibly get there. Why not you?

Michael Moore, Meet The News

Maybe Michael Moore doesn't read newspapers. It's hard to find a daily newspaper anywhere in America that, in any given week, doesn't run at least one story that proves what a fool or liar Mr. Moore is. The news is chock full of accounts of very ordinary people achieving extraordinary success and wealth. As just one example, here's a piece of news from *The Cleveland Plain Dealer*, October 28, 2003. It concerns a rust-belt manufacturing company and a janitor.

"**A former janitor** for Tinnerman Palnut Engineered Products has formed a group of investors to buy Tinnerman's retaining ring unit. Anthony Lee, who rose from janitor to product manager, said he will be vice-president of the new company, Ring Lasters LLC."

Mr. Moore frequently wails about the sad plight of the working folk in America, losing jobs as their employers consolidate or outsource. Looks like Anthony Lee did something other than complaining and woe-is-me'ing. But had Anthony Lee heard from Michael Moore early enough in his career, surely he'd have accepted "janitor" as his permanent and appropriate lot in life. Had Anthony Lee read Mr. Moore's book, he would have been educated about the utter futility of a former janitor trying to assemble investment capital and buy a company.

I dare you: pick any city, take a full week of its daily newspaper, read them cover to cover, and NOT find at least one story comparable to this one about this former janitor. A janitor fortunate to have escaped Mr. Moore's advice.

Michael Moore, Meet My 'Students'

I have more than 100 millionaire, multi-millionaires and men and women earning over a million dollars a year in my Inner Circle groups. Most have gotten there by starting diverse businesses from scratch, in as few as 3 to no more than 15 years. Are they somehow so genetically superior or 'weird' that ordinary people cannot do what they've done? Not at all. Let me introduce a fair sampling.

Louise Nielsen. At age 38, deeply in debt, considering bankruptcy. Her work experience: housewife and mother. She started a very un-glamorous business — **cleaning houses.** With a bucket, mop and business card. Grew the business to employ 200 people. Sold the business for a very nice sum. Wrote a book about how she did it, which has sold tens of thousands of copies, self-published. **If she can start like this and get rich, Mr. Moore, why can't anyone else?**

Jeff Paul attended my seminar, desperate, living with his wife and kids in his sister-in-law's basement, more than $100,000.00 in debt on credit cards, struggling to get a mail-order business going. Within months of that seminar, he had his first $100,000.00 income month. He has since developed multiple businesses, sold more than 150,000 of one of his products on QVC, and become a much sought after marketing consultant. You might have seen his TV infomercial.

Joe Polish, a once dead-broke **carpet cleaner.** He searched for and found ways to succeed in that business and has since provided his 'system' to more than 5,000 carpet cleaners worldwide. In his 'Better Your Best Contest', he awards top carpet cleaners new Hummers and Corvettes. Joe is now a published author. Owns his own building. Has a 7-figure income.

Darin Garman is a former Iowa prison guard who bumbled onto Napoleon Hill's book 'Think And Grow Rich', gathering dust on the warden's bookshelf. **That book told Darin what Mr. Moore says is impossible: you, an ordinary guy in a dead-end job, can get rich.** Darin taught himself the business of buying and selling apartment buildings. Today, his brokerage controls over 60% of all such transactions in his local markets, he advertises nationally in Forbes and Investors Business Daily, and investors come from all over America to do business with him. I own properties with him myself.

Chet Rowland has gotten rich in another dull, mundane business: **pest control.** He comes from a disadvantaged background. Started from scratch, with a spray canister. Built the largest pest control company in central Florida, with thousands of customers. Has become a consultant to other pest control operators. Chet has also prudently managed his money, and actively invests in high-rise condominium developments.

Ron LeGrand was an **auto mechanic** working for a paycheck when he saw a newspaper ad Michael Moore would make fun of, claiming anyone could learn to get rich in real estate --- even with no money to invest and no credit. Ron went to the advertised seminar. He had to borrow the $450.00 to go through the course sold at the seminar. Within a few months, he had acquired more than 70 properties. He has since bought and sold thousands of houses. He has taught his "we buy houses for cash" and "quick-turn" strategies to over 100,000 people, too. **The annual reunion of his students has been attended by as many as 7,000, a goodly number of them from-scratch millionaires. A lot of them, the kind of people Michael Moore says can't get rich and shouldn't bother trying.**

I could share hundreds more stories like these. These stories are the real American story, the real story of life in America.

Michael Moore, Meet Me

I did not attend college. My parents were in deep financial trouble throughout my years in high school so I began with no family financial resources. Before age 50, solely via my own, started-from-scratch businesses, I amassed a fortune large enough that, if I so chose, I need never work another day in my life. Every marketable skill I possess was self-taught, diligently acquired in ways anyone, absolutely anyone could emulate.

Like Mr. Moore, I am a published author. A dozen books, published in more than a dozen countries, translated and published in Chinese, Japanese and Russian. Two of my books have been on bookstore shelves continuously for 12 years. One is 'the bible' of its industry. One was recently on the *Business Week* bestseller list. Unlike Mr. Moore's books, mine glorify America and encourage and inspire people to do more, aspire to more.

I also became one of the most popular business speakers in America, addressing audiences of 10,000 to 30,000, and repeatedly appearing with former U.S. Presidents and world leaders, other famous authors and legendary entrepreneurs --- although I stuttered uncontrollably as a child.

Like Mr. Moore, I am an entrepreneur, although he tries his best not to have that noticed. Like Mr. Moore, I have much to thank capitalism and the American free enterprise system for, although he tends not to express such gratitude.

Michael Moore, Meet Thomas Stanley

Thomas Stanley, Ph.D., is the author of the bestselling book *'The Millionaire Next Door',* which summarizes results of an exhaustive 20 year research study examining who actually gets rich in America and how they do it. Maybe Mr. Moore missed this book.

To quote Stanley: "How do you become wealthy? It is seldom luck or inheritance or advanced degrees or even intelligence that enables people to amass fortunes. Wealth is more often the result of a lifestyle of hard work, perseverance, planning and, most of all, self-discipline. Who becomes wealthy? Usually the wealthy individual is a businessman who has lived in the same small town his entire life. This person owns a small factory, chain of stores or service company. He is a saver and investor. And he has made his money on his own. 80% of America's millionaires are first-generation rich."

Michael Moore, Meet The Man In The Mirror

Everybody I've presented in this Chapter contributes something meaningful to America. They build or have built viable companies, providing jobs, career opportunities, prosperity to communities, inventions, innovations, and positive inspiration to others. Combined, their efforts have provided opportunity for millions. What has Mr. Moore done that might be comparably honorable? Nothing. He has written and promoted only critical, venomous books and films that glorify nothing, help or encourage no one. He has wasted real talent as a writer, film-maker and promoter, delivering nothing that might improve any-one's life. He is what Ayn Rand called a 'destroyer.' The people I've described here, who so ably prove his thesis wrong, are 'builders.'

The Tortured, Twisted Logic Michael Moore Uses To Discount The Great American Millionaire Explosion

Even Mr. Moore acknowledges the existence of a recent 'millionaire explosion.' But he views it as a conspiracy! From his book:

"The American carrot is dangled in front of us and we believe we are almost within reach of making it. It's so believable because we have seen it come true. A person who comes from nothing goes on to strike it rich. There are more millionaires now than ever before. This increase in the number of millionaires has served a very useful function for the rich because it means in every community there's at least one person prancing around as a rags-to-riches poster child...."

Mr. Moore has a 'conspiracy theory' that America's super-rich use the 'lie' that you can get rich to control you, to keep you from taxing them more, or, presumably, boiling and eating them. If Mr. Moore's theory wasn't so destructive it would be laughable.

Facts *are* facts, whether Mr. Moore likes them or not. There *are* more millionaires than ever before and that proves it is more possible, more realistic than ever before for you or any other American to set out consciously and deliberately to get rich. And, incidentally, there are more tools readily available to everyone, to use to get rich, than ever before. I built my earliest businesses *before* the internet, *before* e-mail, *before* the FAX machine.

Mr. Moore is also fond of the term 'strike it rich.' This is strategic, said this way to diminish the act, the process, the feasibility of getting rich, to suggest it is freak accident or stroke of luck. The fact is, the majority of the rich don't 'strike it rich' at all - they earn it. Just as Thomas Stanley documented.

Why I Think Mr. Moore Is Anti-American

There is nothing less American in my mind than stealing peoples' dreams, dowsing their ambitions and extinguishing their iniative. There is nothing less patriotic than lying about the greatness of America and the opportunities our capitalist system affords each and every citizen. Radio commentator Glenn Beck, a rags-to-riches example himself, called Mr. Moore's messages "poisonous." He is right on target. There's no good in it, for any individual or for America.

I might add, what could be more reprehensible than getting rich yourself by telling everyone else they cannot?

While disguising himself in scruffy clothes and posing as the working-man's friend, Mr. Moore is actually an elitist. He apparently believes that the success, celebrity and wealth he has created and enjoys is beyond the capabilities of most Americans. Why he would think himself so gifted and special, beyond me.

To justify his elitist beliefs, his silly conspiracy theory, his insistence that the average American cannot get rich and shouldn't try, he points to the majority who do not create wealth for themselves. But this is an empty argument, a red herring. It erroneously confuses "don't" and "won't" with "can't." Mr. Moore says because many won't, you can't.

I say, if someone does, if some do, so can you.

If you choose to follow Mr. Moore's doctrine, you get excuses as your reward, and a diminished, depressing view of America and American life as your philosophy.

If you opt for my doctrine, you get unlimited opportunity.

You choose.

CHAPTER 76

America, The Amazing

Has it ever occurred to you to ponder that countries decades and decades older than ours, with a massive head start, and with far more natural resources, remain comparatively in the stone ages?

When we "invaded" Afghanistan, most places still had no running water. They go to wells in the center of their cities and towns to fill buckets, to slog home. Only a few paved roads in the whole country. In much of the world, farming is still done with oxen or horses. Africa is overrun with unchecked disease. China continues to enslave child labor in aborrhent working conditions, a situation we outgrew and abandoned a century ago. Most nations have no labor laws, no pollution control and environmental protections. What was the Soviet Union still has most of its population living in abject poverty.

Even in England, central heat in homes remains a luxury.

America has only 6% of the world's land area, a comparable fraction of the population, yet we put out close to 1/3rd of the world's gross domestic product.

Only four centuries ago, America was untamed wilderness and frontier.

Why have we come so far so fast, leaving the rest of the world so far behind?

One of the books about this that I recommend reading, and that everyone in government should be required to read at gunpoint, is 'An Empire Of Wealth' by John Steele Gordon, a regular contributor to *American Heritage Magazine.* I also urge reading biographies and, more importantly, autobiographies of Andrew Carnegie, J.P. Morgan and other great industrialists and financiers who forged the American economy and led the industrial revolution, as well as great entrepreneurs from Conrad Hilton to W. Clement Stone.

There *is* an answer to the question I posed above. There is a relatively simple, certain foundation, a collection of operating principles unique to this nation and foreign to or sharply criticized by the rest of the world, that produced the prosperity we all enjoy today. Deviation from these principles threatens this nation far more than any external enemy, and collection of terrorists. As Pogo said, "We have met the enemy and they is us." The liberals' determination to rewrite American history, to deny and disavow these principles, may yet make Kruschev's predictions correct. No bombs will be necessary. America will destroy itself from within.

If you like horror movies, enjoy being scared and terrified as entertaiment, I have a better suggestion for you than pulling out the Hitchcock DVD's. Gather together a half dozen college students, grads, young MBA's, and ask them to tell you what they can about Andrew Carnegie, about how the free enterprise system works, about where wealth comes from. I promise, you'll lie awake all the rest of the night,. Staring at the ceiling in stark terror.

This has been an amazing country.

Now it is under attack, from within as well as from without.

Our enemies as well as our "allies" in the world grow increasingly resentful of our success, prosperity and power. Globalization is not in our best interest. We desperately need a new wave of accurate thinking about our relationship with the rest of the world and its relationship to us.

We have become a nation that penalizes the spirit, investment and entrepreneurial, industrialist and investor behavior that built it. Too many in our population mimic our global enemies and 'allies': they deeply resent the success they do not achieve. Today, Carnegie, J.P. Morgan and their ilk would be under constant attack, mired in outrageously expensive litigation, reviled by the media, hampered and opposed and punished at every turn. With the arguable exception of Bill Gates, we have gone a decade and more without any group of empire-builders to compare to those who built our economy. As the "builders" disappear and the "destroyers" proliferate, America will implode. Read 'Atlas Shrugged'.

The accident of birth that put you and I here, in America, The Amazing, at the time we arrived, was a very, very happy accident. Whether it will be that for the next generation or the generation after that is actually open to question.

SECTION SEVEN

A Few Favorite Stories

I think stories are extremely important. Jesus used parables. President Ronald Reagan was a marvelous storyteller. Every really persuasive, influential speaker I've ever been around has been a masterful storyteller. I've worked very hard at learning how to take a basic, simple event and build it into a useful, detail-rich, entertaining story, and at getting good at telling them.

Most speakers start out using borrowed jokes and stories, and I did too. At Cavett Robert's urging, I used the "must be a pony in here somewhere" story. I used Jarvis' bird story. I pulled old material from Bob Hope, Bob Newhart, Shelley Berman, Bill Gove, polished it. Gradually, you graduate from lifted, stock, simple jokes to original material, to new parables built from actual life experiences. Almost all the lifted jokes and stories I used in my first few years' speaking have long since been retired.

I have a bank of nearly 100 stories, some rather simple jokes, others extremely complex. But there are a handful of these stories I've used most frequently, that I've made a good living with for decades. Most readers of this book will be familiar with some or all of them. But people are always asking me to tell them again, and asking me questions about them, so here they are, with additional comments - kind of like the director's cut DVD.

Hope you enjoy,.........

Annoying Pest, Welcome Guest

This is a story I told some 30 to 50 times a year for nearly 15 years - over 500 times. People have often asked me if it's true. The answer is: sort of. The incident did actually occur at the first of my two homes in Phoenix. The details are slightly embellished. Poetic license.

It was a fiery hot day in July, in Phoenix. On a day like this, you actually can go out and fry an egg on the sidewalk before noon. Every summer, a shocking number of fools leave kids and pets locked in cars with windows rolled up tight and come out after a few hours to find them cooked. It's hot. That's important to this story.

On this weekday, I was home alone. I traveled a great deal, and even though I had an office, when I was home I tended to stay home. I found my going to the office disturbed the staff. So I was home alone, sitting at the kitchen counter, a pitcher of iced tea, and on the speaker phone, a client. I was intensely involved in my conversation about this client's business problems, which was infinitely more interesting than dealing with any of my own problems. Anyway, I'm in this conversation when somebody, uninvited, unexpected, begins knocking, banging, hammering away at my front doors.

You probably work for a living and aren't home during the day, but if you stop to think about it, the options of who can be banging on your front door are pretty limited. In bad economic times, the Jehovah's Witnesses and Avon ladies car pool. Anyway, it was a good bet whoever was at the door was an unwelcome pest. So I ignored it, confident that if ignored, it would go away. It was loud and surprisingly persistent and I had to raise my voice to continue my conversation. A contest of wills. I finally won. Ever so briefly.

The pest left the front door but, incredibly, went all the way around to the rear of my property, climbed over an 8 foot high block wall - with shards of glass imbedded on top to discourage this method of entry! Past the cactuses, orange trees, the pool, the spa, up onto the deck, then banging on the patio doors with earthquake intensity. I had my back to these doors. The pest could see me standing there. By any measure, this was the most annoying, aggressive pest ever. But I'm the most stubborn guy ever. I raised my voice louder, continued my conversation, continued ignoring the pest. Finally though I couldn't hold out. I turned around to confront the pest - and found my entire backyard in flames! Flames literally licking the wood across the patio roof. And this determined good Samaritan who thinks I'm an idiot, which is arguable, was there trying to save my life and my house.

I imagine some fool driving through the neighborhood flicked a cigarette into orbit and it chose my yard to land in. We'd had ten straight 110-degree days, so everything was a little dry and brittle.

Instantly, the most annoying pest became the most welcome guest ever to visit the Kennedy household! Because he was there at just the right moment in time with just the right message, in this case "Call 911 stupid while I work the hose."

Most people do the opposite with their marketing. Wrong message, wrong time. If you can fix this, if you can arrive as welcome guest instead of annoying pest, everything changes. This is the first square on the marketing game board. And that's what I do. I help business owners and sales professionals use Welcome Guest Marketing.

Okay, that's the story. Now to sate your curiosity, I'll separate fact from embellishment. Here's what's untampered-with-truth. I was home alone. There was a fire, although actually only in a few bushes in front of the house. He rang the front door bell and I came to the door. And we put out the fire with the garden hose. Had he come around to the rear of the house, he'd have climbed over only a six foot wall, no shards of glass. He'd have come past a spa but no pool. I developed the story over a dozen or so tellings and retellings until it got to its full version. When you develop a story like this for use in selling or speaking, drama's important, little details are important, a laugh now and then important. I think the most useful stories for speaking purposes are self-deprecating and humanizing. Everybody's had the experience of looking foolish as a result of being stubborn, so they can identify with me in this story.

I'll tell you something funny about this story. There's a little throwaway line stuck into it about the Jehovah Witnesses and Avon ladies car-pooling. I swiped it from a humorous speaker, Dr. Charlie Jarvis. I was amused by it. Audiences almost always chuckled and laughed at it. I tried switching the order to Avon ladies first, by the way, and it doesn't work that way. No laughs. Anyway, I always figured there'd be a day when I'd get some complaints from an offended Jehovah's Witness. That never happened. But finally it did offend somebody. An Avon sales manager, at a Success event with a troop of her saleswomen, was mightily offended, horrified and convinced I'd destroyed the morale and productivity of her entire salesforce with my insensitive remark. She wrote a four page complaint letter. I personally refunded their entire ticket purchase and indicated my sorrow over their being offended. I did not apologize nor did I take out the joke.

Al The Plumber

People love this story and I'm often asked to tell it. It was the signature story near the end of my main *'Magnetic Marketing'* speech, and I did create it as 100% original material, from scratch. I'm not exactly sure why this story stays in peoples' minds, but I have people come up to me all the time who heard me tell it two, three, five years ago, and ask me to tell it again. It does actually teach something - a very specific marketing strategy, preceding a sequence of sales letters with what I call an Endorsed Mailing. If you pay close attention, from this story alone, you could extract and use the entire strategy.

Like all the other stories I've developed, there is a foundation of fact. A small foundation, I confess.

It begins as a routine, mundane incident, the arrival of a piece of mail.

In the mail one day arrived an envelope, individually addressed to me, by name, with a live stamp not a meter imprint, and in the return address corner, the name of someone I knew. Not a friend, not a neighbor, a peer, another professional speaker who also lived in Phoenix. It does not matter the relationship, the important thing, I recognized the name of the person who sent me the envelope. So I opened it.

That's important. America sorts its mail over a wastebasket. You have to make the cut or nothing else matters. So I opened the envelope. The letter I took out was headlined: *'I Suppose You're Wondering Why I'm Writing To You About A Plumber.'* I thought to myself: yep, I do wonder why he's writing to me about a plumber. Heck, I don't even get a Christmas card from this guy. We're just in the same kind of business and live in the same town. So, why is he writing to me about a plumber? So I read the letter to find out. And that's important. First you have to get your letter opened and you cannot just assume that's going to happen. Then you have to get your letter read and you cannot just assume that's going to happen either. Curiosity used here, not often the best strategy but it is a strategy.

The letter told a story of this peer having a party at his home on a Saturday night to which I had not been invited, when a pipe under the bar in the den started leaking, a mess ensued, and he needed a plumber. He called ad after ad in the Yellow Pages with no luck but finally got a guy who rushed out, gooped the pipe, didn't have to sell him any parts, cleaned up the mess and charged a fair price, at 9:00 on a Saturday night. So, my peer had written this letter to me - and all his other speaking colleagues in Phoenix - to let us know about this terrific plumber, so if we ever needed a plumber in an emergency, we'd know: Al The Plumber's the guy to call.

This didn't happen by accident. This is called an Endorsed Mailing to a champion's circle of influence. Every happy customer has some circle of influence, some list where his name has influence, so he can be made into a champion.

So I got the letter, opened the envelope, read the letter, and Al The Plumber sounded like a good guy, but I still didn't call him. Why not? Sure - I didn't need a plumber. So all that's wasted, right? Wrong. That's why, about 3 days later, I got a letter from Al The Plumber. *Hi, I'm Al The Plumber. You remember me. I'm the guy who rushed out to your colleague's house, to fix the leak, the night of his party you weren't invited to. He sent you a letter introducing me. I wanted to follow up and tell you, we have this special thing we do, free, just for people referred by our clients. That thing is a free home plumbing problem prevention audit. There are 102 possible plumbing problems that can occur in your home without warning, just like the leaky pipe that was ruining your colleague's party. We come out and check all 102 for free, to make sure you won't have any unpleasant surprises.*

I still didn't call Al The Plumber. I was hearing drips in the night, but I didn't call.

That's why about 10 days later, I got Letter#2 from Al The Plumber. *Hi, I'm Al The Plumber. You remember me. Your friend, the party, the leak. I wrote and offered you a free home plumbing problem prevention audit, I haven't heard from you, and now I'M VERY CONCERNED! As you can see in the enclosed newspaper article, even small plumbing problems can become b-i-g plumbing problems.*

The article reprint is about an older couple going away for the weekend to visit the grandkids. Little drip under the sink, so they stick a Tupperware tub under there and go on their way. There's a photo of the house floating in a pond. Another photo, the family dog clinging to a piece of wood, waiting to be rescued.

As you can see, little plumbing problems can become big plumbing problems.

I still don't call. I'm now looking at pipes, banging pipes. Look okay to me, but what do I know. I'm hearing louder drips at night. But I don't call.

That's why about 10 days later, I got Letter #3 from Al The Plumber. *FINAL NOTICE. I've twice offered you a free home plumbing problem prevention audit, haven't heard from you, and if I don't hear from you in the next 10 days, I'll have to withdraw the offer and extend the invitation to someone else. Enclosed you'll find a sample list of some of the 102 potential plumbing problems, the approximate cost of repair when they occur.*

I call Al The Plumber.

I'll tell the rest of the story, just for fun. But first a quick review of what our genius direct marketer Al The Plumber has done. He got a good, target list, from his champion. He went to the list first with the Endorsed Mailing. He followed up with a sequence of letters, each one a bit stronger than the one before. He created an offer that transcends timing, so you could say yes even if you had no need for a plumber. He did a lot of brilliant things. And I'd say to you, if a plumber can do this, why not you?

Now, for fun, the rest of the story.

Al arrives at my house. No resemblance to a plumber. He's carrying an attache case, not a toolbox. Wearing a tan suit, white shirt, brown and white polka dot tie, little gold tie clip shaped like a wrench. Only resemblance between him and a plumber, a little cloth patch sewn on the breast pocket of his suitcoat that says: Al.

In the house, he opens the eelskin attache case, takes out a matching clipboard, says "Mr. Kennedy, I'm going to use this checklist to investigate the 102 possible plumbing problems. Take me about 20 minutes. While I do that, do you have a video player?"

He gives me a video tape to watch. It educates me about one of the greatest health dangers in America today. I had no idea. It seems people are slipping and falling in their bathtubs in record numbers. Breaking hips, getting pneumonia, dying. Thankfully, they've got this invisible glop, replaces dangerous bathmats, safe, guaranteed you'll never slip and fall in your tub.

The video shuts off at 19 minutes. Al is standing there.

I say to myself: he's done this before.

"Mr. Kennedy, I have good news. You do not have 97 of the 102 most common plumbing problems" ---- 102 minus 97, 5 ---- "and I have everything I need with me to take care of them. I just have to go out to my truck and get my tools. Before I do that, did you watch the video tape? I see you have four bathrooms - do you want to protect just the one in the master suite or do you want to protect all four?"

How do you pick?

$318.00 later, Al The Plumber gets in his tan Mercedes and putt-putts down the driveway.

The Irresistible Offer

The girl I was in a relationship with was away at college, at Murray State University, in Kentucky. I was running my little ad agency in Akron, Ohio. I was supposed to drive down to Murray and pick her up on a Friday, and bring her home for a long weekend. Thursday night, mother Nature, that pixie with the marvelous sense of humor, unleashed the blizzard of the century on Ohio. That's not hyperbole either; it was the blizzard of the century. Actually, one of the four worst winter storms of recorded history. By 8:00 A.M. on Friday, schools, government offices and businesses were closed, roads were buried in snow, highways sheets of ice. The Ohio State Highway Patrol asked everyone who could to avoid using the Turnpike or the major interstates. Another foot of snow and an ice storm were forecast. Attempting to drive from Akron south all the way through the state of Ohio was a suicide mission.

At 8:30 A.M., I got Nancy on the phone to give her the bad news.

Oh, I should tell you, I had a 1974 American Motors Javelin, red with white racing stripes, white top, white leather upholstery, only a few months old. I'd bought her brand new. It was a sporty car, not to be confused with sports car. Very light in weight, small hind end, tiny trunk, no weight over the wheels. If you can't recall this car, it was cleverly, uniquely shaped like a curvy woman's body. If you stood facing it, or looked down on it, you saw the Playboy centerfold shape.

By the time I arrived in Murray late that Friday night, the curves were flat. I smashed every single one of them flat, spinning around in circles on interstate highway bridges, stopping against them.

In that little phone call, Nancy said fewer than 25 words. They cannot be repeated here. They constituted an irresistible offer.

And that is your challenge as a marketer or salesperson or copywriter, to craft an offer so irresistible that your prospect would bundle up, schelp out into a blinding snowstorm, a dangerous blizzard, and risk life and limb driving on icy roads, to get to the post office, to drop order form and check in the mail before the deadline.

Nancy was going to college to become a dietician. As far as I know, she had no experience in sales or marketing. But she she sure knew how to make an irresistible offer!

That particular story has not been embellished. It's all true.

The Cat Who Licked Stamps

When my first wife divorced me and left, she took the better of our two cars, and left me my Lincoln, one plate, one cup, one saucer, one fork, one knife, one spoon, and *her* cat -- who hated me, spat at me, scratched me and glared at me waiting for her next opportunity to scratch me.

After a few days of sulking and hissing and snarling, the cat came to the realization that Carolyn was gone and I was in charge of the food. The cat was a pragmatist. Overnight, my best friend. She became such a possessive ally that when I did become involved with another woman, the cat literally attacked her. Terrorized her. In my absence, I asked the woman to feed the cat and I was told the cat wouldn't let her into the apartment!

Anyway, I was starting over, and I had my little mail-order operation going at a very primitive level. In the evening, I stuffed and labeled envelopes and affixed stamps to them, to mail the next day. Got orders in the mail, walked to the bank to deposit the money, less a little cash to eat on, walked to the copy shop to make the products to fill the orders, and went home to do it again. My most valuable business asset was the cat, because the cat licked stamps.

I would sit on the couch facing the TV, my mailing project laid out on the coffee table in front of me. The cat sat in the middle of the coffee table facing me. I would stretch out a strip of stamps and he'd lick 'em, left to right, *ttthhhllllllppppp. Ttthhhlllllppppp.* Every once in a while he'd get a little water out of a little bowl, then good to go. *Tttthhhhhhllllllppppp.*

I imagine all that glue shortened the cat's life by a few years, but what the hell, they've got nine of them. And I was in no position to feed anybody who couldn't hold up his share of the work.

So I owe my success in direct-mail to the cat who licked stamps.

I usually tell this story to novices and beginners in direct marketing. People getting started in direct marketing, especially in the information products arena, often feel intimidated and overwhelmed by everything they think they need and everything they hear about software, database management, personalized mailings, the internet, and all the rest. But I'm proof positive you start with none of those things, with no assets, no computer, with nearly nothing. Proof you can start in a primitive and simple way. All you need is a sales letter and likely prospects to send it to. A roll of postage stamps. Cat, optional. You can use a little sponge.

Amnesia

My very first professional speech, where I had a great opportunity to sell a lot of my cassette programs, was for a large direct sales group. I flew across country to get there on my own dime, no fee.

This was a great audience. Laughing, clapping, stomping. I was stunningly brilliant. Witty, funny, quick. It was a lovefest. I was a star. I ate up the response, ended with an emotional story, basked in the standing ovation. Even signed autographs.

I was on the plane, a Scotch in hand, celebrating my success - before it dawned on me that I had forgotten to sell anything. Cartons of my cassette programs were still unopened, under draped tables in that convention hall. I'd gotten so caught up in my own performance, I'd forgotten why I was there.

I've never made that mistake again.

Whether you are speaking, meeting personally with somebody, writing an advertisement, producing an infomercial, or doing anything else, it's really important to remember why you're there.

SECTION EIGHT

And Now the End is Near

CHAPTER 77

Why I Have Nearly Quit Speaking

I have spent well over 900 hours in airport restrooms. That's 112-1/2 eight hour days. With waiting time, time to clear security, walking time, delayed flights, the total airport time climbs to about 1,126 days. That's just in the past twenty years. I'm not complaining. And anytime I feel like complaining, I remind myself: I could have been working for a living. Still, enough's enough.

Regarding the speaking itself, well, three decades is long enough to continue doing anything. Speaking to sell, which is what I've been doing all that time, no longer interests or challenges me. Doing the same presentation or even the same bits of material again and again began to feel like glorified factory work several years ago. I'm now to the point that I catch myself doing things on stage for my own amusement, at the expense of optimum sales, and that isn't fair to clients or even to the audiences. I now enjoy speaking without having to sell, and what little I'm doing, I'm increasingly making that - like my Renegade Millionaire Retreat, or the special workshops, like my 3-day Sales Letter Writing Workshop.

For many years, I averaged between 60 and 70 compensated speaking engagements every year. Then about 35 for several more years, Last couple years, about a dozen. For 2005, I'm holding it below ten. In 06, I'm trying for a half-dozen. By 08, I intend to wean myself away from it altogether.

It's hard to walk away when there's still a spotlight shining on you. Few actors, few athletes, few public people are able to do it voluntarily. Even those that try. Many keep coming back, until they are sad shadows and weak imitations of their former selves. I feel like I'm at the peak of my powers as a speaker right now, and would prefer to exit while that is the case.

So, I have nearly stopped accepting 'outside' speaking engagements, only one here or there, otherwise restricting myself to Glazer-Kennedy Inner Circle or Kennedy-Lillo events. A few years ago, I did a series of 'Last Ever' boot camps on different, specific topics. It kind of became a joke, and Halbert suggested I not quit until I had so run out of topics that I held *The Last-Ever Marketing Boot Camp For Typewriter Repairpersons.'* But I was serious. I will not re-visit those topics. So, let's discuss my Last-Ever, Last-Ever Seminar. I have a plan.

Earlier in my adult life, for some years, it was any excuse for a drink. Lately, for my clients, it's been any excuse for a seminar. I urged Yanik Silver to do his 30th birthday bash as a seminar and I pushed Corey Rudl into turning his wedding reception into a seminar. Both were wildly successful and very profitable. But I can top these. I have given Bill Glazer exclusive marketing rights to The Dan Kennedy Funeral Seminar. To conduct a 'Member appreciation seminar' at my funeral. This last-ever Dan event will hopefully occur quite a few years from now, bringing me out of retirement, sort of, to be present. It will also hopefully occur on very short notice, so make sure you keep your current e-mail address on file at Bill's office in Baltimore.

No, I'm not kidding.

I have asked that every single speaker at my Funeral Seminar sell something. No one allowed to speak who doesn't. If there's a eulogy, it must end with a sales pitch and a stampede to the back of the room. No speaker is permitted to use Power Points, or anything else involving a computer. Anyone whose cellphone goes off has to pay $1,000.00 fine and have the phone shoved up their butt by an enforcer like Jack 'Quick Kill' Williams or Matt Furey. Sinatra music on the breaks. Oh, and I wouldn't mind having a young, beautiful, naked woman jump out of a cake either. I know that's completely inappropriate, but I've never had it happen at any other time or place, so why not here?

"You've got to know when to get the hell off the stage."

- Johnny Carson

CHAPTER 78

Why I'm Quitting Business Altogether

Ever since I started discussing my plans for semi-retirement, and for complete retirement, I've realized many people are mystified. Some ask each other if I'm serious, what they know about, what I'm up to. Some suspect a scam, like Cher's 108th farewell tour. Some think I'm incapable. Any such thoughts are wrong. I'm quite capable. I've had to revise the schedule once, thanks to divorce and the related need to replace a whole lot of money, but I quickly got back on schedule and am very methodically hitting my targets.

At age 43, I started gearing up to gear down. That year I licensed out all the rights to my products, sold my mail-order business, and closed down two corporations. At the time, I said I would cut my speaking and travel by half by 2001, and I did. After the above-mentioned brief bump in the road, I sold the Inner Circle business in 2003. Along the way, I virtually ceased traveling to clients for consulting, which I used to do a lot. In 2006, I'm cutting the number of coaching groups back. By 2007, I will be officially semi-retired, working only with a 'closed door practice' of a very small number of consulting/copywriting clients, at most one coaching group, and writing, including providing content to newsletters. I will work only 2 to 3 days a week, and take several extended vacations. And believe me, for me, a 3 day workweek will seem like retirement. By 2009, I will officially, totally retire. I will be 55.

The questions many ask are: *why, at such a young age? And: what the devil will you do with yourself?*

First of all, it doesn't seem that young to me. I've been at this for three decades. I've been working constantly, long hours, often under extreme stress, of late still, always under pressure of multiple deadlines. In fact, I really cannot remember what it is like to wake up in the morning and not be chasing tight deadlines, not having the day fully committed and scripted. It may have been summer vacation, as a kid. I haven't laid on a couch and watched a football game without simultaneously writing with my laptop, paying bills, or doing other work but twice in ten years. For more than 15 years, I also traveled incessantly, and that takes a lot out of you - that folks who don't travel professionally can't possibly appreciate how physically and emotionally debilitating it is. My 50 is many peoples' 90. Compared to a guy who's 50, who works just five day weeks, gets to the office at 9:00 in the morning, takes a lunch break everyday, leaves at 5:00, putzes around the house on the weekend, I'm 280 years old. Overdue for retirement by anybody's standards. In short, I am tired.

The second part of the answer to "why?" is identical to that of a really terrible joke: why do dogs lick their privates? The punch line is - because they can. I actually set this goal when my Dad was 44. I set a goal to be financially independent and able to retire if I wanted to by the time I was his age, and to retire no more than ten years later. I wrote that down as a kid. I am very fortunate. As best as I can calculate, barring a really epic disaster I haven't considered (and I've considered plenty) or an extended period, years of double-digit hyper-inflation, I have more than enough money to stop earning any more, and to live as I wish to live for the rest of my life. I have no need to make another dollar. That doesn't mean, incidentally, that I'm not *interested* in making more, but it does mean the list of what I am willing to do and exchange for more dollars gets shorter and shorter and shorter with passing days.

The third part of the answer to "why?" is simply to do other things: finally finish my novel whether it ever gets published or not, play with my race-horses and spend most mornings at the track as well as the evenings, vacation, sit in the sun and read, heck even do normal stuff like going to the Price Club or getting my car washed.

But there is a fourth answer, and it may have some significance to you. It includes advice. It is my firm opinion that the unmanageable risks and unavoidable burdens of entrepreneurship have multiplied mightily in recent years. For example, I've long kept employees to the barest of minimums, but I've never been able to run my businesses completely without them. Now the government interference in the employer-employee relationship is at an all time high water mark. The *majority* of businesses with 25 or more employees are sued at least once a year by a present or terminated employee. The employer must now police everything from the telling of an off-color joke by one employee to another to how much each person imbibes at the holiday party. The employer must become involved in each employee's pregnancy and child-rearing responsibilities.

The total and diverse and wholly unreasonable liability now attached to being an employer is, to my mind, untenable. One mistake, even one frivolous lawsuit could wipe out everything a person has worked his whole life to organize. The governments and the tax system are profoundly anti-small business.

I deeply resent every single government form that comes my way. My blood pressure rises as soon as I see that "official" envelope. I have a profound physiological reaction to anything involving the government or taxes. I'm fatigued by straightening out their errors, corresponding with people you cannot talk to, being threatened and intimidated, dealing with incomprehensible rules and regulations.

The multiple taxes on entrepreneurial rewards are so onerous to me that they have "de-motivated" me. The business owner uniquely pays corporate income taxes on all the income plus personal income taxes on whatever portion of what's left he pays himself as earnings plus capital gains taxes on whatever might be left as profit, capital gains taxes yet again on what is invested, plus sales taxes, hidden taxes, property taxes, inventory taxes, a special self-employment penalty tax, and he must worry about a government bureaucrat determining that his salary is unreasonable, or dividends unreasonable, and reclassifying monies taken from the business so as to collect a higher tax. With the inverted economic pyramid worsening (fewer and fewer producers supporting ever greater numbers of non-producers), this cannot get better; it must get worse; the entrepreneur must become more and more of a target, of a victim.

When Roosevelt created Social Security it started paying at age 65. The average life expectancy was 67. It was called the Social Security SUPPLEMENT, because it was not intended to fund anyone's complete retirement. It dealt only with retirement, and did not include all he disability and medical benefits that have since been added. There were 43 workers paying in for every retiree taking out. It was still a Ponzi scheme that, if mounted by private enterprise, would land its operators in prison. But it was a Ponzi scheme capable of continuing forever. Except that life expectancy has risen to 77 years. That tilts everything. Most of all, it tilts the ratio. By 2010, it's projected that there will be only 3 workers paying in for every retiree taking out. President Bush's ambitious, partial privatization might very well be part of the cure for those in their twenties. But it will require about a trillion dollars from somewhere other than currently scheduled payments in by workers for the transition. Whether that happens or the Ponzi scheme's collapse begins in earnest or both, where do you think they are going to steal money in order to prop up this foolish scheme? I will tell you: first, from business. In part because the jackasses running government actually think you can tax business. Second, from those who earn high income or have worked and built wealth through business. You and me.

Then there is the regulatory activity targeting certain industries, supported by very frightening Gestapo-type enforcement that ignores constitutional rights. There is the litigation oriented society, with far too many hungry lawyers desperately inventing new kinds of lawsuits. Finally there is the awesome, amazing, mind-boggling levels of incompetence pervasive in employees, vendors of every stripe. All of that combined has created a noxious climate I no longer wish to live in, regardless of potential rewards, anymore than I would live in an ultra-congested, crime infested mega-city like New York or LA for any imaginable salary, or anymore than I would deliberately inhale toxic gasses in order to win a bet.

A sample of what turns me beet red. This is a handful of years ago. On December 23rd, two days before Christmas , the mail brought a perfunctory notice from the Arizona Department of Employment announcing their intended arrival on my office door step at 9:00 A.M. on January 6th to conduct an audit of employment records, long list included. My office was already officially closed for a holiday break extending beyond the 6th, and if Carla hadn't dropped in just to check FAXes, we wouldn't have even seen this notice until after the 6th. But regardless, to me the arrogance and disrespect of delivering such a notice two days before Christmas is intolerable. Dictating when the audit is to occur - rather than asking politely to have someone call and arrange an appointment not disruptive to the business, also intolerable. (Incidentally, we had two employees. Me and her.)

This is the sort of thing that makes my blood boil. I'm pissed off all over again just writing it down.

It will be my great pleasure to employ no one, pay no health care for anybody but me, no business taxes, file no forms except my personal return, contribute to as few government jobs as humanly possible.

My private advice to friends and key clients of late has been: get your money together, establish a lifestyle easily supported only by dividends from safely invested assets, and be able and prepared to opt out at a moment's notice. The race is on to get out of the game before the rules become so unfair that you cannot possibly win. This may surprise many people reading this book. But privately, I have been telling my clients that the race is on, that we are stumbling toward a "dark period" in America when it will be better to have enough marbles to sit out the game. Have the home you live in paid off. Have enough cash to last your lifetime if all you do is eat principal, so there's no income to be taxed at all. And by the way, the purpose of that business you own is not to employ people or support the community. Its purpose is to make you rich. And, a business is something to extract wealth from -- not to put money in, not to accumulate trapped money in. That's a mistake I've made to some extent, ignoring my own convictions. Don't make it.

I am, frankly, pessimistic about the near-future American business environment. I view President Bush's re-election as a brief, limited respite, a delay in the inevitable. Demographic, societal and political factors seem to me to guarantee a gradual, to many imperceptible crawl into socialism and a money grab from the "producers" that will make Canada's tax system appear reasonable.

Of course I recognize this is a terribly bleak and negative view. Still it seems to me that we have perverted our free enterprise system to such a degree that any significant success is not only penalized but places the individual at peril of complete destruction from so many different fronts that defense is virtually impossible. The best defense appears now to be practical invisibility. And I have determined that I can live an interesting life without striving to build a company or amass more wealth or advance a cause.

I don't want to be misunderstood. Let me say, again, as I said earlier in this book that it is easier now than ever to get rich in America, to do so quickly, and to do so in a wide, vast, diverse variety of ways. If you limit the discussion to "ease of creating" businesses, flow of money to you, it's never been easier, there's never been a better time than now. But this is a description of the short-term, of a brief snapshot in time. It is not at all in conflict with my view of the bigger picture, the longer-term, of ever-increasing confiscation and interference. I am *not* contradicting myself.

So I am doing my best to extricate myself from all involvements and activities that make me vulnerable or that subject me to inordinate frustration. As I told my agent recently about a publisher: if I wake up three mornings in a row with sleep disturbed, thinking about the same person, and it's not a woman having sex with me, that person's gotta go.

For the first time in my life, I want peace of mind more than I want opportunity. It is easier to enunciate that, though, than it is to get my own behavior congruent with it. I am compulsive in my response to opportunity. Compulsions are not easily, radically altered.

But, if you think I'm doing a lot, you would be amazed at everything I've said and say "no" to. I have had many opportunities to build or expand businesses that would have employed hundreds, maybe even thousands of individuals and contributed substantially to the economy, but I have talked myself out of doing so every time. I could easily generate several times the income that I currently earn were I to accept every engagement and assignment offered me, but the thought of giving roughly 50% of every one of those dollars earned to governments, to pay for sports stadiums, politicians' mistresses, and assorted fraud, excess and waste stops me in my tracks. I was very recently offered a seat on the Board of Directors of a new bank, an opportunity that was both potentially very lucrative and interesting to me, but I talked myself out of it. It took herculean effort to "talk myself down." Two of the main reasons I finally vetoed it: potential liabilities, and the need to get on an airplane and go to meetings three times a year. That is but one example of a dozen or so significant business opportunities, including ones where equity was on the table for zero cash outlay on my part, that I've held myself back from in the past few years.

A whole lot of people can count themselves lucky that I am not Bill Gates. Facing the relentless litigation and government attacks and interference aimed at his company, I think I would have shut the whole thing down, burnt all the technology in a bonfire, sent everybody home, bolted the doors, taken my personal pile of marbles and walked away.

Of course, nothing that blatant or reactionary is happening. Yet. But I am not alone; a lot of people who could be fueling economic prosperity have gotten out of the game. Early. Others are hurrying to do so. And in business, unspoken, unenunciated negative reactions to the toxic climate abound. You can't even imagine how many small business owners simply do not hire women as a means of minimizing their risk of sexual harassment litigation.

They discriminate. Big companies, like a huge banking chain, replace full-time jobs (paying good salaries and providing benefits) with part-time jobs (paying less and providing no benefits) in order to escape the Family Leave Law. Industrial companies transfer their entire manufacturing operations to foreign countries to escape unions, OSHA, etc. Industries like fast food race to automate as much as possible, to employ as few people as possible, thus eliminating the starting rung on the ladder, in response to minimum wage increases, family leave, lawsuit risks, and so on.

I am a big fan of Ayn Rand. I believe her book 'Atlas Shrugged' was ahead of its time, is metaphor for our time and is quite possibly, eerily accurate in predicting a future we may yet suffer in my time; if not, in my step-daughter's lifetime.

I deeply resent the economic ignoramuses running government, resent the confiscation of my just rewards by them, and even more deeply resent and fear those Rand called "destroyers."

To avoid, ending this book with a Chapter like this, on something of a 'down' note, let me at least say this: I am very, very, very grateful for all the opportunities I've benefited from, and for the support I've received from my readers, subscribers, customers and clients. And I am also enormously proud of the clients, coaching clients I work with, the Inner Circle Members I watch building businesses, inventing, innovating, creating and making a real difference in their industries and communities. When I turn off the news, when I ignore Washington D.C, and focus only on them - on you! - I feel optimistic and hopeful and invigorated.

I believe you can be optimistic and enthusiastic but, at the same time, prudent and protective. To a great degree, you can create your own reality and enjoy your entrepreneurial adventures irrespective of whatever crumbling of the national or global infrastructure is occurring around you. But there's no reason you can't enjoy today's thriving economy and abundant opportunities while simultaneously making sure you have enough nuts secreted away to last through the longest of winters.

Essentially, my ambition has been, and my advice is, to get into a position where whatever business you do you do totally by choice not necessity, that you do only what interests and entertains and psychically rewards you and nothing else or more, and that you can stop at any moment for sabbatical or permanently without worry or sacrifice.

Happy Trails
To You,
until
We Meet
Again

OTHER BOOKS BY DAN S. KENNEDY

Speak to Sell (Advantage)

Make 'Em Laugh & Take Their Money (GKIC/Morgan-James)

The Ultimate Sales Letter – 4th Edition/20th Anniversary Edition

(Adams Media)

The Ultimate Marketing Plan – 4th Edition/20th Anniversary Edition

(Adams Media)

Making Them Believe: 21 Lost Secrets of Dr. Brinkley Marketing with

Chip Kessler (GKIC/Morgan-James)

Magnetic Marketing: How to Attract a Flood of New Customers that Pay,

Stay, and Refer (ForbesBooks)

The NEW Psycho-Cybernetics with Maxwell Maltz, M.D., F.I.C.S.

(Prentice-Hall)

In the No B.S. series, published by Entrepreneur Press:

No B.S. Guide to Maximum Referrals & Customer Retention with

Shaun Buck

No B.S. Guide to Direct-Response Social Media Marketing with Kim

Walsh Phillips

No. B.S. Guide to Brand-Building by Direct Response

No. B.S. Guide to Trust-Based Marketing with Matt Zagula

No. B.S. Guide to Marketing to Boomers & Seniors with Chip Kessler

No. B.S. Price Strategy with Jason Marrs

No. B.S. Ruthless Management of People & Profits, 2nd Edition

No B.S. Grassroots Marketing with Jeff Slutsky

No. B.S. Business Success in the New Economy

No. B.S. Sales Success in the New Economy

No. B.S. Wealth Attraction in the New Economy

No. B.S. Time Management for Entrepreneurs, 3rd Edition

No. B.S. Guide to Powerful Presentations with Dustin Mathews

EPILOGUE & PROLOGUE CIRCA 2019

This book was written in 2004, published in 2005. There are a few things requiring factual up-dating, a few new things worthy of mention. That would be epilogue. There are also a few forward looking items. That would be prologue. The obvious problem with writing a memoir while still alive is that things change. In a span of just a few years, a lot happens in my life.

I'll start with the most important. I am married for the third time to my second wife, Carla. I'm delighted to report that I have finally married into money.

Marrying the same woman for a second time has its pros and cons as does marriage period, and pretty much everything else. In fact, if you ever discover *anything* that has only pros and no cons, please let me know about it. I promise a handsome reward. I now have two wedding anniversaries, but she wisely decided to put them both on the same day. Without turning this into soap opera, it was a long road back and then forward to a better, stronger relationship, so I can *honestly* say I am *happily* married. Most of the time. Which I'd wager is better than a very high percentage of married people can say. Everybody should be so fortunate as to find a mate and partner like Carla. But being fortunate is rarely by accident or gift. Fortunate-ism in any aspect of life is almost always the result of often unseen, extraordinary effort.

Carla also came with her dog, acquired during the gap, who I've dubbed The Million Dollar Dog, because she is *that* spoiled. I always had dogs as a kid, but never as an adult, and I was missing a lot. She has now been the 3rd side of our triangle since puppy to 14 years, and, as Ron White, says is a future tragedy, as is every pet. I fear and dread the day. And, on my list of mistakes I think God made, that I intend taking up with Him, I've moved making dogs' lives too short to the #1 position.

About this book: the response has been and continues to be interesting, rewarding and appreciated. I get letters constantly from people about all sorts of things, outside of business matters. Poignant, when some story of my life has reminded them of going with their grandfather to a county fair and watching harness racing, or brought up other nostalgic memories. Triumphant, like escaping alcoholism or overcoming a speech impediment or coping with a disease or rebounding from bankruptcy or turning some other adversity into success. Inspired, as I hear from quite a few people more than once, about something in the book that has encouraged them to try something, move somewhere, create, invent, repair, etc. When you birth a book like this, you hope for these kinds of reports. I have not been disappointed.

I suppose the most common feedback has been surprise about how open I was, how far I went in exposing myself in this book. Maybe there are a few things that might better have been kept to myself, but I've long had a certain philosophy about my distance relationship with those who look to me for advice, ideas and information: they have a right to know as much as possible about the person behind those ideas --- including my flaws, foibles and failures as well as my success methods and accomplishments. By the way, just like President Bush #1, who I got to know a bit via multiple backstage conversations, I'm not a fan of broccoli. I sleep without pajamas even in winter. I have gone mostly bald up top as did my father. A hair cut is now, nearly a *hair* cut. Not happy about it but not vain enough to use Rogaine®

every day or go get plugs inserted. I generally prefer horses to people, something probably unwise to confess when in 'the people business'. What else would you like to know? Just ask. I'll probably tell you.

On My Deathbed, You Just Might Hear Me Wish I'd Spent More Time At 'The Office'

About the only thing I've failed at repeatedly is retirement. But, as Winston Churchill said, success often comes only to the person who can move from failure to failure without losing his enthusiasm. So, as I write this, I am beginning a 3 year plan, to get to near/semi/quasi retirement. In the interim, while I am slow-walking, I still take on new clients occasionally, still carry a good-sized workload with long standing clients, still accept speaking engagements --- although I'm loathe to travel and only fly by private jet, so most events I speak at are now brought to one of my two home cities. In short , my business life consists of the same activities it always has: speaking (a lot less than prior decades), consulting/coaching, copywriting, and writing. I still get up every morning and make my 3-minute commute to my big basement office and get to work, albeit at a slowing, less frenetic pace.

The somewhat-weird business I created, built up around me, now, again "NO B.S. INNER CIRCLE", has gone through about a decade as Glazer-Kennedy Inner Circle, helmed ably by Bill Glazer, then sold by him* to a private equity group and about a half-decade of painful confusion and handing from one CEO to another, then sold by the second group of investor-owners to Adam Witty, becoming one of the Advantage companies, where it lives as of now. (*I have not had owner-ship or managerial control since my sale to Bill, but have remained the entity's constant in multiple roles, as a contract player, and with what I call 'equity without equity'. It remains as of now my main "home", where I write for its newsletters and other media, speak at its conference, run mastermind groups, otherwise interact with its Members --- many of whom are my "Lifers", with me for 10, 20, even 30+ years, and consult with its leadership team.)

Going through successive corporate ownerships and CEO's and new and varied ideas of what the business is or should be has been an "interesting" experience. It has revealed that I built a ship even drunk captains could not sink. I have customers with whom the relationship is: 'til death do us part, no matter what.

When I characterize it as a "weird" business, I refer to the fact that it integrates a lot of moving parts. It is a publishing and media company. It is a membership association. It is a training company, including seminars, conferences and workshops, "hard goods" and digital learning tools, coaching and mentoring programs. It has even been, deliberately, an incubator for hundreds and hundreds of businesses built on its architecture and model. All told, it is certainly the largest, most expansive, most enduring, and most complex (sophisticated) business of its kind. The sun never sets on the empire, as there are Members, licensees, and affiliates in more than two dozen countries as well as the U.S. It is literally, factually and frequently a "maker of millionaires and multi-millionaires." It has long, routinely been referred to by its Members as "PLANET DAN", and I appreciate the compliment.

Now, for the first time in its 25+ year life, it is moving from being (fiercely) independent to being one of a "family" of publishing and marketing companies under the Advantage corporate umbrella; part of something bigger than itself; a cog in a bigger machine. And we shall see what we will see.

You can look in on it all, and if you like, participate, at **NoBSInner-Circle.com**

Beyond Business...

Outside of business, I continue with harness racing, own a large stable – fluctuating from 15 to 25 horses, and keep a few that I race myself, driving professionally about 100 times a year, year-round, at Northfield Park in Ohio.

For the record, I'm 6'2", down from 6'4" with age, just below 200 pounds, down from a high of 245, but I'm *not a jockey*. This is Standardbred, not Thoroughbred racing. We are in sulkies, not perched on the horse's back. We have a rolling start behind a starting car, not a standing start out of a gate. Thus, while height, and more, weight of the driver does matter, within a range it is not critical. The sport is also more tolerant of age. While success probably favors younger, more agile guys, there are a lot of us in our 60's and 70's competing just fine, and age and treachery can compensate for youth and physicality. Our racing involves strategy, not just speed.

As a driver, I'd say that it satisfies the competitive spirit without requiring one to be a true athlete, somewhat like golf but with the added attractions of rain mud, sleet, snow, ice, wind, eight competitors in tight quarters, real danger to limb and life. It is the best 2 minutes in sport. It has interesting parallels to direct marketing, which I won't bore you with. And the horses are, mostly, noble beasts, extremely knowledgeable about their jobs; equine athletes. Each with his or her distinct personality. Somewhere around 20% to 25% of the success depends on *the horse's* psychology: mental attitude, will to win, resilience vs. adversity, mood of the moment, etc.

Eye on the Prize

If I have succeeded at representing anything to my readers, fans, the Members, clients, and do represent anything, it is: "eye on the prize", meaning being true to enlightened *self*-interest.

My entire life and my business and personal relationships are and have long been arranged to facilitate and support my preferred life-style --- ranging from being able to work in isolation, distraction and interruption free, with iron-fisted control of my time and access to me (described in my book *No B.S. Time Management for Entrepreneurs, 2nd Edition*) to being at home and able to race all nights there is racing. I make no apologies for *my* prize above all prizes being: autonomy. You may or may not have that as your prize. If not, it may be because you doubt the possibility, and of that, I'd love the opportunity to change your mind. If there's a different reason for a different top prize govern-ing your life, that's just fine as long as you are conscious, honest and deliberate about it. As long as it is yours.

I show off my racehorses and racing as well as my entire work-style and lifestyle as demonstrations and symbolism of The Possible. This is the business-of-businesses I'm in; making people aware and confident of their Possible. While I don't imagine you are eager to own racehorses or go through the difficulty and years of getting licensed to climb into a sulky, there is undoubtedly some "comparable" about which you are passionately interested and—if you hit the Mega-Millions lottery tonight—would hurry to make your top activity and priority. What I would tell you is that you are *not* going to hit the lottery, and even less likely to return for another try at life, so you'd best figure out a more practical way to get the life you really want, and sooner not later. Which is the point of everything I teach, all the business strategies I share, all the advice I sell: how to organize everything and everybody to facilitate what *you* really want.

I sincerely want that for you, even if we have not yet even met.

To Connect:

If you want to directly engage with me for any reason, know that I am not on or accessible by social media, do not receive or use email, and can be reached only by fax @ 602-269-3113 (preferred) or mail, c/o Kennedy Inner Circle Inc., 15433 N. Tatum Blvd. #103, Phoenix, Az. 85032 – for business matters, or if you prefer, for other matters, at 154 E. Aurora Rd., PMB # 353, Northfield, Ohio 44067. Any online stuff you see is licensed use of me, not me.

I am told there is a pretty good quantity of me accessible on YouTube. In the neighborhood of 100 hours. Golly. All my books are available at Amazon. You can "come to the track" online, at NorthfieldPark.com.

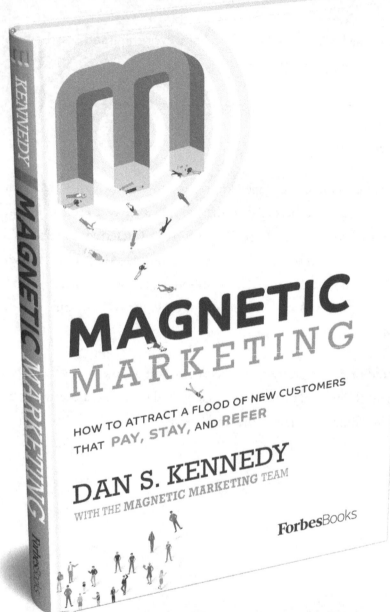

Grow your business with

MAGNETIC
MARKETING

Discover How To Magnetically Attract
A Flood of Customers, Clients,
or Patients To Your Business

...

MAGNETIC MARKETING™ reveals a proven, more productive approach to growing any business by applying the secrets of attraction rather than pursuit. It lays out exactly how to create focused, targeted marketing that delivers the exact customers you want through a carefully engineered lead generation, conversion, and retention system.

Claim Your FREE Copy of Dan Kennedy's Latest Release
MAGNETIC MARKETING™
All we ask is that you pay the shipping!

Order Your Copy at
www.MagneticMarketingBook.com

Printed in the USA
CPSIA information can be obtained
at www.ICGtesting.com
JSHW012018140824
68134JS00033B/2759

9 781599 321097